# IF WAR
# SHOULD COME

# IF WAR SHOULD COME

## DEFENCE PREPARATIONS ON THE SOUTH COAST 1935-1939

### PHILIP MacDOUGALL

SPELLMOUNT

*To my mum who, as a civilian wartime worker, sparked my interest
in twentieth-century social history*

*Cover illustrations. Front, top*: Spitfires take to the skies as a loudspeaker
sounds the alarm (iStockphoto). *Back*: volunteer fire fighters of the
Chatham AFS engage in a practice exercise immediately before the
outbreak of war (KM Group, publishers of the *Medway Messenger*)

First published by Spellmount, an imprint of The History Press, 2011

The History Press
The Mill, Brimscombe Port
Stroud, Gloucestershire, GL5 2QG
www.thehistorypress.co.uk

British Library Cataloguing in Publication Data.
A catalogue record for this book is available from the British Library.

ISBN 978 0 7524 5073 5

Typesetting and origination by The History Press
Printed in the EU for The History Press .

# Contents

# Preface

In wars that involve the British Isles, the south coast invariably takes on an important front-line role. In earlier centuries this was automatically assured, given that any clash was likely to involve the nearby states of mainland Europe, with Kent, Hampshire and Sussex conveniently placed both to provide a springboard for offence and to be a key area in the defence of the island. The Romans, Saxons and Normans all used this geographical area to establish an initial presence, while the Spanish, French and Germans also planned similar footfalls. Such experiences are the foundations upon which this book is set. It is not, primarily, an examination of this area of coastline during such periods of hostility, although this cannot be ignored, but looks at how those who lived in and administered these counties prepared for actual war or, more precisely, one particular war.

It is a book that looks at preparations made in the years immediately preceding the outbreak of hostilities in September 1939. Unlike most wars, this particular conflict had been expected, with its likely date of commencement, give or take a year, accurately predicted. That there is a concentration on the period from 1935 is easily explained. While predictions of war did precede 1935, there are events that occurred in 1935 that are of particular significance. On 1 March Hermann Goering officially announced to the world that the Luftwaffe not only existed, but was a fully fledged organisation, with twenty land and seaplane squadrons. In other words, Germany, through the Luftwaffe, now had the clear ability to inflict great pain upon those who lived on the south coast of England. A second event in that year was when the government established the bones of a Civil Defence scheme by announcing to local authorities that defence of the population against air attack was to be one of their primary responsibilities.

The opening chapter will view the earlier experiences and resulting perceptions of war. Such experiences heavily influenced the ideas and plans that were to be implemented in the months and years leading up to the declaration of a second major war with Germany on 3 September 1939. To this extent, concentration is upon both actual conflicts as well as times in which war was seriously seen as threatening. Here, historical precedent begins with the French Revolutionary and Napoleonic Wars (1793–1815); this was a global conflict that saw an isolated Britain very much threatened by a south coast invasion. Indeed, it was this war that set the yardstick for home defence, with income tax, beachhead defences, a nascent home guard and plans for mass evacuation all generated at this time. Plans created for that war were seemingly dusted down and reintroduced during the opening months of the First World War (1914–18) and also seriously re-examined during the years preceding the Second World War. However, the effect of other wars and threats of war are also examined. Less, of course, will be said of the Crimean (1854–56) and Boer (1899–1902) Wars, as they were fought at a much greater distance from the south coast area. But three specific invasion scares cannot be so easily ignored, all caused by imagined expansionist threats made by the French during the middle years of the nineteenth century. Occurring in 1847, 1851–52 and 1859, they resulted in a searching examination of the nation's preparedness, with particular attention once again directed to the south coast, where any invasion or incursion was thought most likely to occur.

Primarily, this is a book about the Second World War. It is about how the south coast counties – the area over which much of the Battle of Britain was subsequently fought, and where many of the resources for D-Day were secretly prepared – were readied for that future conflict. It is not about the entirety of those counties that border the south coast, but of those areas most directly connected with the coastline, including significant parts of its adjoining hinterland. An area, in itself, without strict definition, I have picked out the part of the coastline that was most exposed to hostile attack from a European enemy. It is also this area of the coast that, over a long period of time, has seen extremely high levels of expenditure on its defence, resulting in many permanently positioned military structures. Geographically, and for these reasons, my defined area encompasses the entire coastline of Kent and Sussex, together with a short stretch of Hampshire that incorporates both Portsmouth and Southampton. The latter will be referred to as the east Hampshire littoral. In addition, and administered as a county separate to Hampshire from 1890 onwards, I have included the Isle of Wight.

Purists might contend that the area of coastline chosen does not technically represent the entirety of the south coast (and might even be seen as taking in parts of the country that are not normally viewed as lying on the south coast), but then most other users of the term can find themselves similarly criticised. It is, however, an easy shorthand expression that encapsulates an area of the British coastline that is most frequently in danger during times of European conflict. More debateable is how far inland this coastal area should be seen to stretch. Here, I have been directed by the relative importance of the coastline to any particular area. Much more of Kent is included, being surrounded on three sides by water, while Sussex (both East and West) and the included area of Hampshire are seen as having a coastal hinterland which is appreciably less affected by occurrences in and along the Channel. As for the inclusion of the Isle of Wight, this seems beyond contention, considering its past importance to the defence of the south coast and its value in the hands of either an invader or forces opposing a potential invader.

A point of significance is this: most books devoted to Britain's involvement in the Second World War begin with, or have at an early stage, the words 'and consequently this country is at war with Germany'. This book does not. Indeed, while these words appear – or rather reappear – they are reserved for pages much nearer to the end of the book. For, once war broke out, the south coast was no longer preparing for war; hostilities, albeit in the form of the 'phoney war', had become a reality. Admittedly, there is some delving into actual wartime events, but this is for the purpose of analysis and allows for the answering of one simple question: were preparations made during the late 1930s truly fit for their purpose?

# Abbreviations

| | | | |
|---|---|---|---|
| AFS | Auxiliary Fire Service | PPU | Peace Pledge Union |
| ARP | Air Raid Precautions | RAF | Royal Air Force |
| CD | Civil Defence | RAMC | Royal Army Medical Corps |
| CID | Committee of Imperial Defence | RDF | Radio Direction Finding |
| | | ROC | Royal Observer Corps (formerly Observer Corps) |
| CH | Chain Home | | |
| CHL | Chain Home Low | TNA | The National Archives (Kew) |
| CPRE | Campaign to Protect Rural England | VTC | Voluntary Training Corps |
| | | WAEC | War Agricultural Executive Committee |
| ESRO | East Sussex Records Office | | |
| FANY | First Aid Nursing Yeomanry | WAAC | Women's Auxiliary Army Corps |
| HO | Home Office | | |
| IFF | Identification Friend or Foe | WEE | Wireless Experimental Establishment |
| IWM | Imperial War Museum | | |
| KAO | Kent Archives Office | WLA | Women's Land Army |
| LDV | Local Defence Volunteers | WO | War Office |
| LNU | League of Nations Union | WRAF | Women's Royal Air Force |
| NAAFI | Navy, Army, Air Force Institutes | WRNS | Women's Royal Naval Service |
| NFS | National Fire Service | WSRO | West Sussex Records Office |
| OC | Observer Corps | WVS | Women's Voluntary Service |

# Part One
## Historical Experience

# Introduction

The war that broke out in September 1939 had been long feared and expected. Those with a reasonable level of prescience could well have predicted, even as early as the signing of the Treaty of Versailles in June 1919, that a future European war was inevitable. Germany, on being forced to lose all of her imperial colonies, together with substantial amounts of European land, and required to pay £6.6 billion in reparations while forfeiting the right to possess all but the smallest of military forces, was bound to react. Furthermore, even those not gifted with such prescience would be aware of the likely consequences of a future war; a conflict that would be fought with weapons so devastating that Prime Minister Stanley Baldwin, in November 1932, felt able to claim that it would wipe out 'European civilisation'.[1]

It was this clear forewarning of a major European war and its predicted consequences that made the 1920s and '30s so different from other periods preceding an outbreak of war. At such times, when a major conflict was seen as possible, or even likely, such heightened levels of fear and foreboding were simply lacking. Instead, past wars, and certainly those of the last few centuries, were invariably seen as an opportunity to improve the nation's standing, by extending the empire or gaining some other specific advantage. Admittedly, this was not always the outcome, but most certainly it was the prevalent belief at their outset. As for the war that was being predicted in the 1930s, this was seen as something very different. In particular, Britain would no longer be in a position to rely on her island status for protection. Aerial bombardment and a possible invasion were the more likely and immediate outcomes. In either eventuality, the south coast would take the brunt, likely to be devastated by the former and, if the latter, turned into a battleground.

In preparing for this war, a number of important templates could be used by those given responsibility for ensuring that the south coast was ready to fight and survive. Of particular importance was the experience of earlier conflicts, especially those fought against the Emperor Napoleon and Kaiser Wilhelm II. In both cases these were major European conflicts that had also taken on a global importance. More significant for the south coast, these same wars had been accompanied by the very real threat of invasion, with the latter conflict, through the emergence of the aeroplane, introducing indiscriminate death from the air.

In assembling the means to survive a future European war, members of the Committee of Imperial Defence (the government body responsible for co-ordinating overall military strategy), together with various home defence committees, looked back to the Napoleonic and First World Wars. Therefore, that same template, of steps taken in previous conflicts, must be the starting point for this study. Without an awareness of how the south coast had confronted earlier wars, the context of the story would be lost. Decisions taken in the late 1930s were clearly rooted in actions taken and lessons learnt previously. Although a historical slippage to the late eighteenth and early nineteenth centuries might appear a flight of fancy, the similarity to developments undertaken in the 1930s will become readily apparent. And for once, so it would seem, the lessons from history were being learnt and, if somewhat parsimoniously, occasionally acted upon.

## Note
1. Hansard, 10 November 1932.

# 1

# Defence & Military Recruitment

In time of war the south coast was among those areas given prioritisation for improvements in the general state and efficiency of coastal defences. This was the time-honoured response to any external threat of invasion or attack, the coastline of the south being generously endowed with a considerable collection of castles, fortified towers and hastily dug entrenchments. Significant periods of threatened invasion, either real or perceived, often gave rise to a dramatic increase in the quantity, if not quality, of such additions to the shoreline. In particular, the quatre-foil castles of Camber, Deal and Walmer, the seventy-three Martello-style towers that stretch between Folkestone and Eastbourne, together with an intricate series of fortifications built around Portsmouth and at a number of other strategic points during the 1860s, all resulted from such threats.

The First World War ensured that further attention was given to the shore-line defences. Temporary gun batteries, pillboxes and entrenchments were placed around both smaller harbours and isolated beaches, existing defences were gen-erally strengthened, while barbed-wire entanglements and trenches dug on the upper part of beaches became commonplace. Dover and Folkestone in particu-lar came in for considerable attention, the surrounding hills covered with field works to give protection to troops embarking for the Western Front, and provid-ing a defence in depth should a concerted enemy effort be made to destroy these essential port facilities. Newhaven and Littlehampton, further embarkation ports, were also given upgraded defences during this period, with the former, during the first three months of war, witnessing troops and civilian labourers working on the open ground that lay in front of the fort, clearing gorse bushes from the field of fire, putting in place barbed-wire entanglements, and filling and carrying sandbags. Given that any successful landing would have as its ultimate objective the capital, a further line of defences was constructed inland. This consisted of pillboxes and entrenchments constructed in 1915 between Maidstone and the River Swale, and were reinforced in 1917 by a number of heavier guns to provide artillery support.[1]

Even during the last months of 1918, when the possibility of a German invasion had long receded, the various defences were still heavily manned, with the
future author Neville Shute among those who awaited the arrival of just such
an invader. Shute, one of whose later novels was to investigate the impact that a
future war would have on the south coast, had been posted to the Isle of Grain.
Situated in north Kent, and equally valuable for preventing an attack on the royal
dockyard at Chatham or an incursion upon London, this was a location that had
been heavily fortified in the 1860s and, in 1915, was honeycombed with barbed-
wire entanglements and communication trenches. 'For the last three months of
the war,' Shute notes in his published autobiography, 'I mounted guard at the
mouth of the Thames estuary against Germans who could hardly have invaded at
this stage of the war.'[2]

In times of national emergency, both the army and navy made huge demands
on the manpower of the south coast, undertaking significant efforts to draw
vastly increased numbers into the ranks. Over time, the methods of recruitment had varied, with enforcement, monetary reward or reliance on patriotism
among the approaches most frequently adopted. For those inclined towards the
colours, there were normally two available options: full-time commitment to
a long-term military career or enrolment into a part-time force that required
only limited commitment and relatively easy disengagement. Only at the outset
of war did these conditions of service markedly alter, due to the need to retain
those already enrolled while encouraging others to enlist. As a result, those
entering the army might do so for the period of hostilities only, rather than for
a fixed number of years.

Of those who chose to enter the professional army, the choice offered was
quite extensive and included a myriad of infantry and cavalry regiments, together
with a number of more specialised support regiments that included the Royal
Artillery and the Royal Engineers. Prior to the mid-nineteenth century, the connection between a county and a particular regiment was not especially strong.
Consequently, regiments were inclined to recruit from wherever they were situated at the time, with recruiting sergeants a familiar sight along the entire length
of the south coast, attempting to 'drum up' interest through the offer of a lump
sum of money.[3] Thus, a great many men from Hampshire, Kent and Sussex were
drawn into any one of a number of regiments that were situated in these counties.
It was not until 1881 that permanently mustered regiments acquired an undis-
puted territorial connection. Militia and volunteer companies, already closely
associated with particular counties, were merged with regular line regiments, so
achieving this local connection. Emerging at this time were the Hampshire, the
Royal Sussex, the Royal West Kent and the Buffs East Kent regiments. The purpose was to create local pride and thereby boost recruitment.

The navy also recruited in these counties, both for the Royal Marines and for
seamen on board warships. The latter, up until the introduction of a proper career

structure, were normally undertaken for either a wartime period or for the time a vessel was in commission and at sea. A feature of naval recruitment, up until 1815, was the use of the press gang, whereby captains of naval warships in need of crew-members would send out a gang of sailors under an officer with the purpose of forcibly taking any person deemed suitable for sea service. Those larger townships around the coastline and wider rivers were most likely to receive the attention of the press, although the artisans and labourers employed in naval shipbuilding and replenishment facilities were automatically exempt.

A wartime-only practice, impressment ceased to be used after 1815, with a shortfall in seamen at the outbreak of the First World War made good by patriotic volunteers, the 30,000 men of the Royal Naval Reserve and (from 1916 onwards) conscription. Impressment into the army had, at one time, also been permitted, but this had ceased in 1780. In contrast with the Royal Navy, impressment into the army had been restricted to 'able-bodied idle and disorderly persons'.[4]

Additional means by which the navy gained recruits included the payment of bounties, a county quota and magistrates giving a convicted felon or vagrant the choice of prison or joining the services. At the beginning of the French Revolutionary War, when the government used bounties, £5 was offered to a man rated as an able seaman, with £2 10s to an ordinary seaman and £1 10s to an inexperienced recruit who would be rated a landsman. To this might be added an additional sum provided by a local source such as a parish vestry or patriotic organisation. In Southampton, for instance, a 3-guinea payment over the royal bounty was offered to every able seaman recruited in the town, with 2 guineas for every ordinary seaman and 1½ guineas for every landsman.[5]

But even when combining volunteers with those impressed or avoiding a prison sentence, the numbers joining the navy did not match the numbers required. For this reason the government devised a new scheme to augment recruitment: that of the quota system. This obliged each county to recruit into the navy a specific number, with fines imposed upon those counties that failed to achieve its given target. To operate the new scheme, magistrates throughout each county assembled for the purpose of devising how many men were to be raised from each parish, with churchwardens and overseers of the poor specifi-cally tasked with finding the necessary individuals to fulfil the county quota. Under the quota schemes introduced in 1795 and 1796, Sussex was responsible for bringing 314 men into the navy, while Kent recruited approximately 800.[6]

Returning to the part-time militia and volunteer companies, it has already been noted that they had a much closer territorial association and were only mustered during periods of hostility. At other times, those who had been recruited into the militia and volunteers assembled periodically for drill and manoeuvres. The num-bers who freely joined usually fell far below that of actual need, with the majority during the French Revolutionary and Napoleonic Wars made up of conscripts chosen by ballot from each parish. For Kent, divided between the West Kent and East Kent militia, this resulted in the mustering of just over a thousand men spread over fifteen companies, while the South Hampshire militia was centred upon Southampton. The actual process of balloting was a public affair, usually undertaken in a superior hostelry in the larger towns and cities in and around the south coast. The balloting for the Rape of Chichester, one of the four divisions into which Sussex was divided, was undertaken at Chichester in the Swan Inn, with 772 names having to be drawn. Later, as the war became even more threatening and the fear of invasion intensified, a supplementary militia, to be held in reserve, was also formed. In Kent this secondary force was embodied in 1798, but in Sussex it was not raised until 1803. Again, the process of balloting was identical to that of the original militia force, with 772 men once again required from the Rape of Chichester. This supplementary force was to be called out only 'in case of actual invasion or appearance of the enemy in force'. To prepare them for this eventuality, they were mustered, for purposes of training, on two occasions every week between April and December:

> That they are liable to be called out to exercise on every Sunday from the 25th March to the 25th December or if they have any religious scruples concerning being exercised on Sunday, then they are to be exercised on some other day, to be fixed upon by their commanding officer but are not to receive any allowance for such Sunday or other days' exercise, and they are to be exercised at least one other day in each week to the amount of twenty days at least, and for such additional days not being more than twenty in a year, they are to be allowed one shilling per day provided they have been exercised on the previous Sunday or other day in lieu thereof.[7]

Although muster rolls were maintained as late as 1820, the compulsive element was abandoned, with the militia transformed into an entirely voluntary force. Men would volunteer and undertake basic training at an army depot, before returning to civilian life under the agreement to continue regular training and attend an annual two-week camp. In compensation, they received a retainer.

A further form of military service was that of the volunteer movement, with many patriots upon the outbreak of war in 1793 enrolling themselves into spontaneously formed companies of soldiery. In Sussex, the Duke of Richmond raised a voluntary yeomanry cavalry that was restricted to the most influential of the county. Only slightly less elitist were companies of volunteer infantry, usually formed of affluent merchants. Of the latter groups, there were few coastal towns that did not see such bodies raised in their midst, with William Pitt, as Lord Warden of the Cinque Ports and resident at Walmer Castle, during the time he was out of office as prime minister, raising three companies.

The volunteer movement once again emerged during the mid-nineteenth century as a result of a series of invasion scares. In 1851, for instance, a number of volunteer companies were formed but quickly disbanded. In 1859, however, due to a more serious perceived threat, those joining the volunteer movement were not only greater in number but were attracted to companies that took on a greater degree of longevity. The number recruited in 1859 along the south coast was in excess of 4,000, with more following over the next few years. Those who joined these county-wide rifle companies were normally expected to supply their own weapons and design of uniform. In addition, some companies admitted women as honorary members, their uniform a sash or scarf of the uniform colour.

Virtually every town or geographical area within the south coast region gave rise to a volunteer company, these bearing a variety of names, some of them quite fanciful. On the Isle of Wight, for instance, the volunteers became Princess Beatrice's Isle of Wight Rifles, a name they were permitted to take because of that particular royal personage's connection with Osborne House. For the most part, these volunteer companies were connected in some way with the War Office; an exception were those founded by the artisans and labourers of Chatham, Portsmouth and Sheerness royal dockyards – these were more closely connected to the Admiralty. As time passed, the independence of these volunteer companies was eventually forfeited through their merger into the county regiments and the creation of specific volunteer battalions.

The First World War saw a similar spontaneous movement towards the formation of volunteer bodies, these being primarily orchestrated by a central body in London, the Central Association of Volunteer Training Corps (CAVTC). Unlike the volunteer companies of the nineteenth century, membership was limited to those who, through either age or other restriction, were prevented from joining the regular army. In other words, it was not to be seen as an alternative to the colours, but as a means of giving support to the army by the more general populace. However, in common with those earlier volunteer movements, there were no government subsidies towards the cost of equipment, with local councils frequently asked to give their support to fundraising activities. In Brighton, where two Volunteer Training Corps were formed, they were known as the Home Protection Brigade and were only briefly affiliated to the central association. Instead, and as a means of securing financial support, both battalions were accepted into the 4th Volunteer Battalion of the Royal Sussex Regiment.[8]

The main tasks assigned to these volunteers involved replacing the army and regular police in the mounting of road patrols, guarding designated buildings and stretcher-bearing. They were also supposed to be available for service in the event of invasion, but some initial confusion existed as to their legitimacy. In Chichester, where the volunteers were known as the City Guard, the senior military officers of the area pointed out that their use in any military situation might result in them being seen as 'non-belligerents' and, if captured, 'not entitled to the same treatment as uniformed soldiers'. Most certainly it was an issue that could not be ignored, for in the first few months, those who joined were indistinguishable from any other member of the public. Only with the introduction of a red arm-band and the letters 'GR' (George Rex) in black was the situation regularised. In Kent, by March 1915, some forty-eight such companies had been formed, with another thirty or more in Sussex and littoral east Hampshire.[9] Later, in March 1916, the War Office took responsibility for administering the Volunteer Training Corps, and eventually provided army issue uniforms and weapons.[10]

The urban centres of the south coast saw particularly heavy recruitment into the volunteer movement. Here were large numbers of men employed in both the numerous naval facilities and munitions works, who were automatically exempt from military service. Indeed, the government actively discouraged them from enlisting as it was considered they were already undertaking essential war work. While it did not place these workers on the military front line, it did at least allow them to become more visibly committed to the national cause and under-mine some of the criticisms that were levied in their direction. The *Daily Sketch*, for instance, in December 1914, openly suggested that such workers, in failing to enlist, lacked patriotism. A remark clearly resented by those employed in the armaments industry, it naturally elicited an angry response from the central com-mittee of the General Labourers' Union. An apology was demanded from the *Daily Sketch*, it being pointed out that many of those employed in the dockyards at Chatham, Portsmouth and Sheerness had actually been refused the right to enlist. It was further pointed out that some had still left to join the army, but in doing so forewent both a relatively secure job and a future pension.[11]

Social standing was an important influencing factor when choosing the fight-ing force. Certain regiments were considerably more prestigious than others, with those of an aristocratic or more decidedly middle-class background being drawn to them. At the top of the tree were the guards and cavalry regiments while, decidedly lower, were the infantry regiments, including those that formed the basis of the county regiments of the south coast. The same was also true of the voluntary battalions. The militia raised at the time of the French wars, for instance, was very much an association of agricultural labourers, drawn in the ballot, who were not of such a background to be able to relinquish themselves of their duties through payment of £10 or £15, thereby exempting themselves for five years. For those of particularly high social standing there was the much more acceptable alternative of joining the yeomanry. The word 'yeoman' refers to small farmers, with the officers drawn from the nobility and the ordinary recruits made up of their tenants. Often characterised as play soldiers, they normally undertook a few hours of training each week and spent much of the rest of their time strut-ting around in expensive uniforms. Among these, of course, was the Duke of Richmond's voluntary cavalry, with those who joined required to provide their own horse and accoutrements.

The importance of class was a continuing factor in recruitment throughout the nineteenth century and into the twentieth century, with those who joined the ranks being overwhelmingly working class. Private C. Jones, a recruit to the Royal Sussex Regiment at the outbreak of war in August 1914, who in civilian life had been employed as a clerk, in letters regularly written to his mother commented on some of his fellow recruits, whom he first met at the barracks in Chichester and with whom he clearly felt socially distant:

> Their degree of intelligence was obviously of the lowest. They were just drink sodden, unclean and foul mouthed brutes lacking the mental capacity of even a decent dog – but you must by no means run away with the idea that this applies to the whole collection, some were of a very good class, others were poor and ill kept but yet decent fellows enough and anxious to do well. Again, there were the countrymen simply and badly educated but muscular and healthy who will, with training, make a better soldier than I can ever hope [to be].[12]

Recruitment into the county regiments in the late summer of 1914 was helped by the knowledge of friends and fellow townsmen or villagers also joining. Among early recruits to the 7th Battalion of the Royal Sussex Regiment, for instance, were virtually the entire membership of both Eastbourne Football Club and the Sussex Cricket Club. Indeed, playing on such homogeneity of membership were the very locally recruited 'Old Pal' battalions. One such example was the Southdowns, subsequently forming the 11th, 12th and 13th Battalions of the Royal Sussex Regiment. Conceived and sustained by Claude Lowther, Conservative MP and the occupant of Herstmonceaux Castle, they were recruited by local men working informally in their villages and encouraged by the idea of camaraderie. A further feature of the Southdowns was its distinctiveness from the more normal military tradition, with its endorsement of friendlier relationships between officers and men, greater opportunities for promotion and comfortable billets.

A patriotic surge of recruitment saw thousands of men from the towns and villages of the south coast volunteering into the army within six weeks of the First World War being declared. Enrolled into Kitchener's New Army, they were enlisting only for the duration of the war. Helping to bring about this high level of recruitment were hundreds of local meetings held in town halls, village centres and pubs. Among them was one held at Horns Cross, near Dartford, in September 1914, its typicality serving to represent the meetings held throughout this rural hinterland of the south coast:

> Arriving at the appropriate place shortly before the time announced, there was nothing to shew that only a few hundred miles away the nation with her allies was at death's grip with a powerful foe, while the gallant men of our Navy are as courageously yielding up their lives for the Motherland.
>
> A small knot of young men had assembled and an onlooker might have been excused for thinking that the great sacrifices that have been made were too

highly considered but as the time for the speaker's arrival drew near so the crowd increased, and quite a crowd, and an enthusiastic one, had assembled.

A glow of light some distance along the road presently announced the advent of a car, to be followed at a short interval by others adorned with words and posters bearing the words –

Kitchener's Recruiting Agency
Enlist Here and Now

Out of the car sprang several well-known gentlemen, accompanied by strangers, some in uniform. A car drew to the front and the Revd Recrore of the village invited the crowd to draw near. In impressive tones he explained the purpose of their meeting and he wished he had a dozen tongues to speak what was in his heart. Five hundred thousand men were wanted and were wanted at once.[13]

One village, not far inland from the eastern Kent shoreline, saw such a high level of recruitment that it was declared 'the bravest village in the United Kingdom'. This was the result of a competition held by *The Weekly Dispatch* to find the village with the largest proportion of men who had, by 28 February 1915, volunteered to serve. Over 400 villages entered the competition, with Knowlton deemed to win: from a population of thirty-nine, a total of twelve (31 per cent) had enlisted. Judged by Lord Birkenhead, the Attorney General, the prize given to the village was a 17ft-high cross of Aberdeen granite, with figures of a nurse, soldier and a casualty at the top and a roll of honour on the plinth. Unveiled on 1 September 1919, it is located just outside the village on the south side of the Sandwich Road.

Providing a dramatic boost to the numbers in khaki was the mobilisation of the reserve battalions of each regiment. Composed of the Army Reserve, the Special Reserve and the Territorial Force, these were part-time soldiers who were only called up during times of mobilisation. Their immediate value, of course, depended on levels of training, with the Army Reserve being the most highly trained. Consisting only of men who had formally served at least seven years in the regular army, it had been a condition of their original recruitment that they also serve in the Army Reserve for five years.

Separate to this was the Special Reserve, made up of men who need not have formally been in the regulars and who, upon first joining, had been given six months of full-time training followed by a further four weeks every year. The Territorials were a force first created in 1908, following reorganisation of the militia and volunteers; they received a limited amount of training each year. A particular condition of their service was that they were not obliged to serve abroad.

Despite the continuance of a high level of recruitment throughout the opening months of the war, it failed to keep pace with the high rate of attrition witnessed on the Western Front. In order to boost recruitment, the upper age limit for volunteers was raised from 38 to 40 in May 1915, but this was no real solution. Later, in October, following the appointment of Lord Derby as director-general of recruitment, a new volunteer scheme was introduced whereby those registering their names would only be called upon when necessary. Known as the 'Derby Scheme', it placed married men into separate groups from single men, with the inducement to the former group that they would only be called up when the supply of single men was exhausted. Call-up under the Derby Scheme began in January 1916, but overall the numbers coming forward were not as hoped, resulting in the Military Service Act of March 1916, which specified that all men aged between 18 and 41 were liable for military service. Within this there were several exemptions that included those who were married (or widowed with children) or were in a reserved occupation.[14] The act also permitted conscientious objectors to be absolutely exempted, allowing them to perform alternative civilian service or to serve as non-combatants in the army. However, to do so an objector had to prove their right not to fight by attending a tribunal, established by their local council, that assessed the sincerity of their claim. On their website, the Peace Pledge Union (PPU) says of these tribunals:

> The government meant well: these tribunals were intended to be humane and fair. But it was left to local councils to choose the people who actually sat on the panels, and they often selected themselves. They were a mixed bunch: businessmen, shopkeepers, landowners, retired military officers, civil servants and the like, most of them too old to be called up. Most were also strongly patriotic and therefore prejudiced against anyone whom they thought was not. Often they were people 'of not very great depth of vision or understanding', genuinely confused about their task and its complicated guidelines.[15]

In their choice of language, the PPU is clearly making an attempt to understand the savagery that assailed the conscientious objector when he stood before one of these tribunals, and is defending their choice not to fight in a country that had always prided itself on preservation of individual freedom. Standing as a single example of what could beset such a claimant is the example of Walter Abnett. An 18-year-old who appeared before a tribunal in Gillingham in March 1916, Abnett was seeking full exemption from military service. He gave as his primary reason his conscience, believing 'that war was against the teachings of Christ'. Unfortunately for Abnett, he considerably weakened his case by adding a further reason, that of working with his father as a boot maker, a business that he suggested was in the national interest. Nevertheless, this was no excuse for his treatment by those who attended the tribunal, and especially by its two leading members, Alderman Featherby and William Henry Griffin, the Mayor of Gillingham:

*The Mayor:* I do not think that any of us believe that war is taught by Christ. I am myself definitely a Christian believer and I hold that this war is the war of the devil, and a Christian has to fight the war of the devil.

The young man, in reply to questions, said he was himself the proprietor of his business and it was in the national interest that it should be kept on, as it enabled people to economise by repairing their own boots (laughter).

*Alderman Featherby:* You don't refuse to work for soldiers and so enable them to fight?
*Applicant:* I can't very well help that (laughter).
*Alderman Featherby:* You can just as well as you can refuse to fight.
*The Mayor:* Would you join the RAMC [Royal Army Medical Corps]?
*Applicant:* If I did it would cause someone else to join the infantry.
*The Mayor:* But your refusal in any case would mean that another would have to fight for us. Men engage on warships to secure food for you and if you object to the services you must object to eat their food.
*Applicant:* We have no alternative (laughter).
*The Mayor:* Then you speak of conscience?

Although Abnett was a member of the Gospel Union and held devout religious beliefs, he was given no chance to explain these. Instead, it was simply assumed that the reason for his appeal was his wish to remain in the business of boot making. Quite simply, those who were members of the appointed tribunal had little understanding of Abnett's conscientious objections, but had a good understanding of business. Indeed, if Abnett had appealed entirely on grounds of business, his appeal might well have proved successful. Most certainly, that same tribunal allowed full military exemption to several local businessmen, but not one single Christian on grounds of conscience. As regards Abnett, he was permitted to take his appeal to the next level, that of the West Kent Appeal Tribunal. However, by that time he had rethought his position, recognising the inflexibility of those who composed the membership of such bodies, indicating that he would no longer object to serving with the RAMC. As a result, he was given partial exemption, required to enlist with that particular military body.

Apart from their harshness towards those who appealed on grounds of conscience, these tribunals often lacked consistency. Portrayed in comical terms, the *Southampton Times* reported on the failure to gain an exemption by one appellant:

A man told the court that a girl could not do his work. He could shift very heavy weights.
*General Shone* [a member of the tribunal panel]: Just the man for heavy guns![16]

Only five months later, the same tribunal gave exemption to two engine drivers of the South Hampshire Water Company, when it was revealed that their muscular strength was required for shifting heavy drainpipes.[17] Were they not just the men for heavy guns, too?

The First World War also saw the recruitment of women into the services, permitting the movement of more men to the front line. By the end of the war, all three fighting services had separate female units, namely the Women's Auxiliary Army Corps (WAAC), the Women's Royal Air Force (WRAF) and the Women's Royal Naval Service (WRNS). Primarily, the work they undertook was that of driving, office work and cooking. In addition, many women served in the military as nurses, through the Queen Alexandra's Nursing Service, the Territorial Force Nursing Service, Voluntary Aid Detachments and the more aristocratic First Aid Nursing Yeomanry (FANY).

Parodying the employment of women through the establishment of specialised military units were the foreign labour corps, which were made up of non-British citizens who would work alongside the army undertaking general labouring work. Many, for instance, were recruited in China and based at Folkestone in a large camp beside Cherry Garden Lane. From here, they were employed in local hospitals, labouring in the docks or redirected to France for similar work. In all, 94,000 Chinese labourers passed through the town of Folkestone between 1915 and 1919.[18]

A problem attached to the rapid expansion of the military at a time of emergency was that of the pressures placed upon both available accommodation and the need to quickly train the new intake. Prior to a major scheme of barrack construction during the French Revolutionary War, troops had been billeted at local inns and hostelries. However, when large numbers of troops were involved, it not only ensured that all accommodation was taken, but led to a dramatic rise in the price of local food stocks. Innkeepers and local inhabitants throughout Kent and Sussex submitted petitions to the Home Secretary, Henry Dundas, requesting that proper military barracks be built. One, submitted from the innkeepers of Chichester, read as follows:

> Your petitioners have suffered exceedingly by the experience attending thereon and the very insufficient allowance established for the supply of forage, they therefore most earnestly entreat, that the very heavy burden they are subject to may be taken into consideration of His Majesty's ministers and they may be indulged with barracks sufficient for the accommodation of cavalry and such other forces of the kingdoms which may be thought necessary to be stationed in this part of Sussex.[19]

Similarly, from Southampton, a petition from the town publicans requested a barracks for their relief, as 'they were oppressed by the number of soldiers quartered at their houses, while their families suffered considerably'.[20]

Dundas, for his part, was not unsympathetic to such petitions, declaring that he had received 'many applications' and was 'sensible [that] the subject must undergo the consideration of government in a general point of view'.[21] A barrack department had already been created with the task of either renting or overseeing the building of new barracks. This resulted in the establishment of military accommodation at a number of south coast locations, including Brighton, Chatham, Chichester, Portsmouth and Walmer, together with a large number of more temporary structures and training camps at additional points along the coast. Other barracks, such as those of the Royal Marines at Chatham and Portsmouth, together with the Royal Engineers at Brompton, were to be of significant value for the recruiting, training and assembly of troops in future periods of emergency. To these, over time, additional barracks were also established, including one for the Royal Marines at Deal and further facilities in the main military towns, especially those of Portsmouth and Chatham.

Upon the outbreak of the First World War, despite the existence of a sizeable number of barracks along the south coast, accommodation was clearly inadequate. Primarily, this was due to the high level of enlistment that was witnessed during the first months of the war. In addition, however, the south coast, because of its proximity to France, served as a focal point for the training and transhipment of troops, while a reserve of men had to be held in the area for coastal defence. Private Jones, the already mentioned recruit to the Royal Sussex Regiment, provides a glimpse of a not uncommon experience for those arriving in the various barracks of the area:

> The barracks [at Chichester] are old fashioned consisting of a large enclosed space with numerous erections built bungalow style sufficient for the comfortable accommodation of 500 men. In all there were about 1,200 in the barracks on the day of our arrival, all raw recruits. There were only about six n.c.o.'s to take charge of the whole lot. Needless to say the place was in a hopeless confusion.[22]

With the barrack canteen having run out of food, Private Jones and many of his fellow recruits had to seek out local hostelries:

> We went back to Barracks immediately as we had been strongly advised to be in early to get 'b----y blankets'. I fell in with an awful mob at 8pm and, as luck would have it I & all with me were handed a blanket apiece. Fifty-three of us; we then lined up & told we were to sleep in the library for the night. It sounded all right and we were marched along with light hearts anticipating a refreshing night's sleep after a tiring day. We were quickly undeceived – the library we found to be quite a small room covered with dirty hay on which we had to sleep packed like sardines with one of the noisiest and obscene collection of

human beings it has ever been my misfortune to meet and the smell of them packed into a small building after a hot day was truly sickening.[23]

To help alleviate pressure on regimental barracks, it was recommended by the War Department that new recruits should only remain in these depots for approximately a week before being dispatched elsewhere for training. This was no real solution, as the training grounds were equally ill-prepared. In this respect, 700 new recruits to the Royal West Kent Regiment fared particularly badly when sent from their regimental barracks at Maidstone on 12 September 1914 to training grounds at Shoreham. Arriving at the station during a heavy downpour, they discovered no arrangements had been made to receive them, and they were marched instead to a field where they were left to shelter under trees. Eventually, tents and blankets were made available.[24]

To help remedy these problems, the barracks staff turned to the local authorities, church organisations and residents for assistance in housing the huge overflow of recruits. By mid-September, in Gillingham, 'it was estimated that quite 5,000' were billeted in the borough, with 'recruits by the hundred' arriving daily.[25] Of particular value was a hall belonging to the local Co-operative Society, used to billet 160 under one roof. In Lewes, 'there was scarcely a house in the town without its complement of troops' following the arrival, for training, of 11,000 new recruits from the north.[26]

A more permanent solution involved establishing hutted encampments alongside the training grounds – a decision approved by the Army Council in mid-August. Each established encampment was to be of a sufficient size to accommodate an infantry battalion at war strength. At Shoreham, for instance, new huts on the plans as approved were under construction in mid-October. At Seaford a total of 750 huts had been completed by December 1914, intended to accommodate 20,000 men who had previously been sent there for training and who had been housed in Hastings, St Leonard's and Eastbourne. Also, in East Sussex, at Cooden near Bexhill-on-Sea, a further hutted camp was built for the volunteer battalions of the Royal Sussex Regiment.

C.S. Forester, in one of his earliest novels, *The General*, drew attention to this particular failing, which he blamed in part on the War Office:

The new armies were left unclothed, unhoused and unarmed. Units rotted through the winter of 1914–15 under canvas on the bleak exposed hills and plains, which had been passed as suitable for summer camp. They shivered on seas of summer mud; they ate food prepared by inefficient cooks and ineffective apparatus.

Forester also extended his criticism a little further, questioning the nature of wartime skills being gained at such camps, telling of how these new recruits were 'practiced in the evolutions of 1870 by sexagenarian non-commissioned officers' using 'make-believe guns under the coordination of make-believe staffs'.[27]

In general, while the south coast had an overall military preparedness for war, it was never at a level sufficient to meet the actual demands of conflict. The infrastructure was present, but invariably needed a degree of restructuring and modernisation. Various extended periods of peace resulted in government-fostered economies and a deterioration of existing facilities. This was certainly the situation following the ending of the First World War, with considerable attention, particularly from 1935 onwards, directed towards the recreation of defences and the rebuilding of the necessary manpower for both fighting a war in Europe and ensuring that the south coast was adequately defended from the possibility of invasion.

## Notes

1.  Andrew Saunders, *Fortress Britain: Artillery Fortifications in the British Isles and Ireland* (Oxbow Books, 1995), p. 213.
2.  Neville Shute, *Slide Rule* (Pan Books, 1983), p. 32.
3.  In 1805 the bounty offered to a new recruit was 12 guineas and equivalent to four months' wages for a farm labourer. Out of this they later had to purchase their kit – a point frequently left unmentioned at the time of recruitment.
4.  Edward E. Curtis, *The Organization of the British Army in the American Revolution* (Humphrey Milford, London, 1926), p. 63.
5.  Bernard Knowles, *Southampton, the English Gateway* (Hutchinson & Co., 1951), p. 62.
6.  ESRO QAN/EW1 (Sussex) Record Book Navy Act, 1795–97; KAO Q/AN4 (Kent) Navy Act Returns, 1795.
7.  TNA HO50/88-311 Correspondence of the Sussex Militia.
8.  H.M. Walbrook, *Hove and the Great War* (The Cliftonville Press, 1920), p. 9.
9.  S.V. Hurst, 'The Volunteer Movement in Kent', in *Bygone Kent* (1996) 17:12, p. 722.
10. In December 1918 the VTC forces were stood down, with members required to 'return their rifles, bayonets, gas masks [and] steel helmets'. See Hurst, 'The Volunteer Movement in Kent', p. 722.
11. *Chatham News*, 19 December 1914. The General Labourers' Union was one of several unions that represented those employed in the munitions factories or the dockyards.
12. IWM Private C. Jones Mss ff.14. Re-quoted in Keith Grieves (ed.), *Sussex in the First World War* (Sussex Record Society, 2000), p. 15.
13. *Bexley and District Times*, 22 September 1914.
14. In May 1916 conscription was widened to include married men, while by April 1918, the age of conscription had been raised to 51.
15. Peace Pledge Union website, www.ppu.org.uk/learn/infodocs/cos/st_co_wwone.html, accessed 3 August 2009.
16. *Southampton Times*, 24 March 1917.
17. Ibid., 8 September 1917.
18. Michael George, *Dover and Folkestone During the Great War* (Pen & Sword reprint, 2007), p. 55.
19. TNA HO42/27, November 1793.
20. Knowles, *Southampton*, p. 62.
21. Ibid.
22. Ibid.

23. IWM Private C. Jones Mss ff.14. Re-quoted from Grieves (2000), p. 9.
24. Lieutenant-Colonel H.J. Wenyon & Major H.S. Brown (eds), *The History of the Eighth Battalion, the Queen's Own Royal West Kent Regiment* (London, 1921), p. 2.
25. *Chatham News*, 12 September 1914.
26. *Brighton Advertiser*, 19 September 1914.
27  C.S. Forester, *The General* (Penguin, 1936), p. 27.

# 2

# The Civilian Dimension

The need to keep the civilian population on side is essential in any wartime situation. Particularly important is ensuring a sufficiency of food and other basic needs. In respect of food production – an often neglected aspect of war – the south coast played an incredibly important role, with large swathes of cultivatable farmland immediately adjacent to the coast proving of inestimable value for securing homeland food supplies. However, despite the existence of such extensive farmland, food supplies in the opening years of the French wars proved extremely scarce. Many of the larger south coast towns witnessed food riots, a result of poor harvests in both 1794 and 1795. In consequence, the price of wheat soared, leading to a similar increase in the price of bread. In September 1794, before the crisis had taken effect, wheat at one of the chief Sussex coastal markets – Chichester – sold at approximately 42s a quarter. Twelve months later it had reached 80s. Furthermore, it was to remain at this high level until March 1796 when, despite the risks of interception at sea, large imports of wheat were secured from Canada and the Baltic.

Although the nation managed to survive that particular wartime-induced food crisis, the danger never completely disappeared. Food shortages remained a continuing feature of that entire war, with a range of alternative approaches taken to alleviate it.

Undoubtedly the most important was that of increasing food production at home, with a particular concentration on the production of wheat. A particularly essential crop with high nutritional value, production from 1800 to 1814 rose by approximately 1.7 million quarters, an increase of 25 per cent. Apart from the ploughing of land, either previously unused or given over to grazing, a major contributory factor was the more efficient use of land through the enclosure of fields, which were still subject to the medieval system of being open and cultivated in strips. Primarily market driven, the government's role was to ease such progress through encouragement rather than direct intervention. Similarly, food squandering was recognised to be an important contributory factor to shortages and resulted in appeals to the general populace not to waste food. In 1800, the seventh year of the war, George III was persuaded to issue a proclamation that most earnestly 'exhorted and charged' all:

> Of our loving subjects who have the means of procuring other articles of food other than corn, as they tender their own immediate interests and feel for the wants of others, to practice the greatest economy and frugality in the use of every species of grain.

And, as for the heads of households, they were asked to:

> Reduce the consumption of bread in their respective families by at least one thirds of the quantity consumed in ordinary times, and in no case to suffer the same to exceed one quarter loaf for each person in each week, to abstain from the use of flour in pastry, and moreover carefully to restrict the use thereof in all other articles other than bread.[1]

A not dissimilar state of affairs was reached during the bleakest years of the First World War, when a shortage of many basic food items led to a massive increase in prices. Although supported by a good many other strategies, the inducement to economise was again resorted to, George V issuing an almost identical proclamation to the one that had been issued by George III over a hundred years earlier:

> Our Royal Proclamation most earnestly exhorting and charging all those of our loving subjects the men and women of our realm who have the means of procuring other articles of food other than wheaten corn, as they tender their own immediate interests and feel for the wants of others, especially to practice the greatest economy and frugality in the use of every species of grain.[2]

On this occasion, the food shortage had been brought about by the intensity of the German U-boat campaign and the destruction of large amounts of European farmland. Lord Milner, a member of the five-man War Cabinet, estimated that the price of foods had approximately doubled by early 1917.[3]

Increasingly the government became involved in the distribution chain, introducing the office of Food Controller in December 1916 and establishing localised Food Control Committees. The latter had the authority to monitor and restrain prices, introduce localised rationing and seize food stocks.

The value of the Food Control Committees came to the fore during the winter of 1917/18, when supplies of dairy products and meat were especially difficult to secure. In the Medway Towns, the various borough Food Control Committees were proactive, seizing 4 tons of margarine at Chatham in February 1918 and sharing it around various shops in the area where 'people had been waiting for hours'. In Gillingham, where one large shop was refusing to sell margarine to non-regular customers, it was only the direct intervention of the chairman of the borough Food Control Committee that prevented the escalation of a serious disturbance. On that occasion, he ordered that the shop supply all in the queue with margarine in ½lb packets. Also, in that same month, due to a shortage of cattle being brought into the market at Rochester, no meat was available for the butchers of Chatham and Gillingham. As a result, the two area committees were given a government priority to secure cattle from the markets in East Anglia.

The Food Control Committees of north Kent faced particular difficulties as they oversaw an area with a population that was subject to a constant increase throughout the war. With the government calculating food supply levels on estimated populations of 1915, there was always a potential for a shortfall. In addition, as the chairman of the Chatham Food Control Committee bemoaned, there were additional problems inherent in being both a port and a military town; 'a man could come ashore with a Board of Trade certificate entitling him to purchase 35lbs of meat but there was not 35lbs to purchase'. To this, he added, 'the difficulty of patients in hospital who were authorised to receive 4¾lbs of meat' when the diet available to local inhabitants was considerably less.

Brighton and Hove were further boroughs with a particularly active and effective Food Control Committee, with much of their work undertaken by specialised subcommittees. Of particular importance was the Meat Advisory Committee, which 'purchased each week the whole of the meat required for the two towns, and sold to each butcher the exact quantity required for his registered customers with absolute fairness to the quantity'.[4]

According to Walbrook:

> It was the only scheme of its kind in the country organised exactly on these lines, and worked most smoothly, saving the retailers a great deal of trouble, and securing the maximum of public convenience possible in those difficult times.[5]

As a result of these food shortages, queuing for lengthy periods of time became a way of life. The slightest indication of a commodity in short supply becoming once again available at a certain shop, resulted in queues being formed well before the shop was due to open.

In Southampton, queuing had also become normality, made worse by a number of essential products failing to reach the city by expected dates. In early December 1917, grocers within the city were still waiting for the previous month's cheese allocation, while they had also been without matches for the past two months. In a meeting of the Master Grocers' Association, members expressed a lack of confidence in the workings of the local Food Control Committee, with one speaker summarising the numerous and recent shortfalls, referring to a recent 'tea distribution fiasco, the sugar muddle, the butter famine [and] the bacon, fat and lard troubles'.[6]

For those forced to queue, the experience was less than enjoyable. However, there were occasional acts of charity that helped alleviate the daily unpleasantries. A vicar in Rochester wrote of one such incident:

> I noticed with pleasure the other day a woman very near the door of a shop where there was a large crowd, when a delicate woman with a baby came along. 'Here', said the first woman, 'you take my place and I'll go behind'. And she did.[7]

In Gillingham, those in another long queue found themselves in receipt of hot tea and cocoa supplied thoughtfully by those living nearby.[8] Unfortunately, these same queues in the Medway Towns led to tragedy when a young child, having just secured ½lb of margarine for a family that had gone without for two weeks, stepped into the path of a butcher's van and was killed. The vastness of the queuing crowd had prevented the driver from seeing the boy in sufficient time to stop.[9]

The introduction of a nationwide scheme of rationing helped reduce the time many spent in shop queues while ensuring a more equitable distribution of those essentials in short supply. Initially, it was only sugar that was subjected to rationing; a nationwide restriction on the purchase of sugar was introduced in December 1917. This caused a problem for one chain of shops in Southampton, those of the Co-operative Society. In an effort to reduce queuing, it was decided that sugar would only be supplied to those customers who left their ration cards with the shop. All those who did so were then guaranteed their sugar allowance without having to join long queues. Unfortunately for the Co-op, this was viewed as illegal and the Society was subsequently fined.[10]

Following the rationing of sugar, meats and fats were rationed a few months later, with this initially restricted to London and the Home Counties. The allowed weekly levels for an individual were fixed at 15oz of beef, mutton or lamb, 5oz of bacon, 4oz of fats and 8oz of sugar. A factor that had helped ensure the introduction of rationing was the pressure placed upon the government by organised labour and, in particular, trade unions.

Greater efficiency in the use of farmland during the First World War was mainly achieved through the creation of a War Agricultural Committee within each county. An idea subsequently readopted upon the outbreak of the Second World War, these committees were composed of farmers, labourers and others interested in agriculture. Their object was to ensure that farms worked to their highest levels of output. In this regard, the agricultural workers of the south coast must be seen as of equal importance to those serving on the front line. However, that was not quite the way the government saw it. During the first few years of the war, farm labourers were generally encouraged to enlist, with few being later protected from conscription. In a classic piece of muddled thinking, the army was then forced to make large numbers of its recruits available to the War Agricultural Committees that then directed them to the farms that had formerly been farmed by those forced into the army.

As well as distributing army recruits into various farms, the War Agricultural Committees were also empowered to use existing labour more effectively, moving individuals with particular skills to those farms where they were most needed. The West Kent district committee, for instance, moved skilled ploughmen upon request. At the same time, the War Agricultural Committees had a female workforce at their disposal – the Women's Land Army (WLA) that had been formed in 1915. In Kent and Sussex, by 1918, some 200 members of this body were working in the two counties, with several hundred more women also employed on the land but not members of the Land Army. Further additions to the agricultural workforce of the south coast, and whose distribution the War Agricultural Committees determined, was that of prisoners of war, schoolteachers and civil servants.

Schoolchildren also found employment on the land. Although full-time education was supposed to be until the age of 14, it was possible for those aged 12 and upwards to be allowed a reduction in the number of hours of schooling and to work up to 33 hours per week. In coastal Sussex, this clause was liberally used, with many boys employed on farms and girls as 'little mothers'. In this latter role, they looked after the young children of the home, allowing mothers to gain employment on a nearby farm. It was also in Sussex that children might be excluded from school at an even lower age, with one school log book – Chidham School's – recording a 10-year-old being given a certificate that allowed him to begin work in his father's market garden.[11] In contrast, Kent was a little less generous with its interpretation of the rules, issuing certificates only to boys rather than girls, with 638 recorded as being released in January 1917.

To further help ease the food crisis, the government fostered the idea of National Kitchens. Established from May 1917 onwards, they provided cheap basic meals outside of the ration system. However, their adoption was neither universal nor particularly rapid; the Southampton City Corporation only gave reluctant consideration to their introduction in early 1918. In the Medway Towns, at about the same time, a correspondent to the *Chatham News* implored that Gillingham Borough Council set about establishing such facilities, suggesting that at least six were needed. If they 'came forth', he argued in a letter that was published in January 1918, 'half of this disgraceful queue business would disappear'. The writer further noted that 'anyone who dines in a canteen or mess knows that even in these times a substantial meal can be supplied at very reasonable costs'. In Brighton, where a National Kitchen was established in Livingstone Road, a fairly typical menu was as follows:

Lentil soup            2*d*
Stewed mutton and peas   4*d*

| Cold roast beef | 6d |
| Blancmange and fruit | 2d |
| Jam roll | 2d |
| Baked potatoes | 1d[12] |

These prices, as it happened, compared most favourably with some of the local hotels of the town, which were then charging 7s 6d for a very similar fare.

> The kitchen itself [in Livingstone Road] and the selling counters were on the ground floor, while the large room upstairs, which was formerly a rifle saloon, was equipped as a dining room for the convenience of the laundry and factory girls of the neighbourhood by whom it was greatly appreciated. Forty of them could sit down together and appreciate a good meal. The kitchen catered impartially for all classes and was impartially used by all.[13]

Adding to these shortages, especially of everyday manufactured items, was the fact that many factories abandoned their normal products and diversified into war work. Perhaps Reginald Wells, a designer and manufacturer of pottery and ceramics, undertook the most extreme example of such diversification. In 1915 his manufacturing efforts were directed towards aviation and the temporary establishment of the Wells Aviation Company. From Chelsea, where pottery had been his main interest, a move was made to Chidham, near Chichester. Here, following the purchase of Cobnor Estate, an airfield was created and work commenced on the construction of one aeroplane. Fortunately, the airfield was also put to the alternative use of training pilots for the army and navy. Much more typical, however, were developments in Brighton and Hove, where a large number of local firms made an easier conversion into the production of military supplies. Henry Walbrook, a wartime resident of Brighton, refers to an organ builder producing shell cases, a window blind manufacturer turning to the construction of fittings for collapsible boats and other locally based engineering companies producing aircraft undercarriages, fuse caps and hand grenades.[14]

A particularly important aspect of the south coast wartime economy was that of a series of military-industrial complexes that were scattered at various locations along the coastline. Very much at the heart of most of these were the royal dockyards at Chatham, Portsmouth and Sheerness – all of them government-owned sites and responsible for the building and maintaining of ships for the Royal Navy. Even at the time of the French wars of the late eighteenth and early nineteenth centuries, they already possessed amazingly long histories, with both Portsmouth and Chatham having been established under the Tudor monarchs. At one time these yards represented the largest employers of civilian labour in the country, with the three south coast yards between them employing a staggering 7,800 artisans and labourers in 1814, the year in which Napoleon was exiled to Elba.

Nevertheless, the naval dockyards of the south coast were only one aspect of maintaining and employing warships at sea. Once out of dockyard hands, a warship would require munitions, food supplies and a crew. All this had to be catered for, a range of additional facilities having to be developed in unison with the dockyards, including the employment of a sizeable number of civilian workers. At Chatham and Portsmouth gun wharves, used for the supply of munitions and repair of armaments, stood next to the dockyards, while nearby a naval barracks had been opened in 1903. At Sheerness, victualling and ordnance facilities were also developed.

Replicating some of the work of the royal dockyards, both in the construction of warships and in repair and maintenance work, were a number of private shipbuilders along the south coast. At the time of the French wars, the Medway (especially the Frindsbury Peninsula), the Thanet Towns, Dover, West Itchenor, Southampton and Beaulieu had all shared some aspect of this work. Few of those concerns survived beyond the second decade of the nineteenth century, often forced into closure because of the long period of peace that followed upon the defeat of Napoleon. In turn, however, new and more specialised companies emerged, these, by the early twentieth century, concentrated upon the east Hampshire littoral and Isle of Wight. Among the largest and most noticeable of these was J. Samuel White at Cowes, J.J. Thornycroft at Southampton and Vosper at Portsmouth.

Located at Faversham was a further arm to the south coast military-industrial complex: a number of sites engaged in the manufacture of gunpowder and other munitions-related materials. One of the largest and certainly the oldest of these was the Chart works, nationalised in 1759, but subsequently falling into the hands of private ownership. By the outbreak of the First World War it occupied a site a mile in length that stretched between Faversham Creek and the village of Ospringe. A great number of additional companies had, at varying times, also undertaken munitions production at Faversham, these frequently attracted by the existence of experienced personnel already engaged in the manufacture of explosives. Among those that came to Faversham in the years leading up to the First World War were the Cotton Powder Company (CPC) and the Explosives Loading Company (ELC). The CPC established itself in 1873 on the Uplees Marshes alongside the Swale, and was, by 1914, occupying a 500-acre site. The ELC also established itself alongside the Swale, acquiring a 100-acre site in 1912. Obviously it goes without saying that such work was dangerous, a case proven in April 1916 when stored TNT at the ELC works exploded, leading to the destruction of several buildings and the loss of 108 lives. Another explosives factory existed at Cliffe-at-Hoo. Owned by Curtis and Harvey, it was first planned in 1901 and was developed over a 60-acre site. By 1917, it was employing a workforce in excess of 2,000.

An aspect of south coast military-industrialism that emerged immediately prior to the outbreak of the First World War was that of aviation. In Rochester, Short Brothers established a sizeable factory for the manufacture of aircraft in January

1914, located on the Esplanade close to the road bridge. It was here that the firm constructed their highly successful Types 184 and 310, both used by the Royal Naval Air Service as a general reconnaissance and torpedo bomber. While the Rochester works produced seaplanes, a second and earlier factory in Eastchurch produced a small number of landplanes.

Elsewhere in north Kent, aircraft were also produced, albeit in very small numbers, at Port Victoria and Eastchurch, both under the supervision of the Admiralty. Along the east Hampshire littoral, a number of other aircraft manufacturers also existed at this time, with Supermarine perhaps the most significant. First established at Woolston, on the east bank of the Itchen River in September 1913, but not adopting the name until 1916, the company, at that time, was building seaplanes for the Royal Naval Air Service. At Hamble, from 1915 onwards, the Fairey Aviation Company was involved in assembling seaplanes that had been previously built at a factory in Hayes, Middlesex; while at Hythe, the May Harden & May Company were assembling seaplane hulls. At Gosport, the Gosport Aviation Company was also producing marine aircraft, having an additional assembly area at Northam Bridge in Southampton. Finally, on the Isle of Wight, both J. Samuel White and S.E. Saunders were constructing aircraft in the Cowes area, these mainly built under contract for the Royal Naval Air Service.

The ease with which many of the south coast manufacturers were able to expand during the First World War was achieved only through the employment of large numbers of women. The naval dockyards and other Admiralty facilities were large employers of women, as were most of the other war-related manufacturers spread along the south coast. At the Kingsnorth airship station on the Hoo Peninsula, which also served as a factory for the assembly of airships, a number of women were employed not only as clerks and messengers, but also as seamstresses who worked their skills on the cotton fabric that enclosed the gasbags. Florrie May, then a young girl straight out of school and employed at Kingsnorth, remembers that among her duties was that of helping weigh down the airships as they came in to land. For this she had to wear a special pair of heavy lead boots and take hold of the landing ropes that were thrown out by those in the airship. Fortunately, she may not have been aware of the potential danger of such a task: if all of the landing ropes were not secured in unison there was a possibility of the airship being caught by a gust of wind and taking with it any who failed to let go.[15]

Occasionally, and encouraged by the peculiar hardships of a nation at war, the both male and female workers within these military-connected complexes combined to demand better conditions. A particular concern was the escalating price of food. In Kent, during 1917, the Workers' Union, which had over 200,000 members in the county, held a series of packed meetings in Faversham and Gillingham. The message on each occasion was the same: the government needed to do more to control prices and prevent profiteering. In that June, for instance, the meeting at Faversham held in the marketplace passed a resolution demanding that 'the government should purchase all essential food stuffs, commandeer and control all home-grown food products and regulate, on a family basis, at reasonable prices, the distribution of food to rich and poor alike'. A demand of revolutionary proportions, the Workers' Union at that time was also petitioning for local parliaments and full representation on borough Food Control Committees.[16]

Within the Southampton military-industrial complex a similar process could be witnessed, with a series of meetings, protesting the price of food, held throughout the city in 1917. With speakers drawn from the Independent Labour Party, the British Socialist Party and various churches, resolutions were passed that called on the government to bring about an equal distribution of food and to make profiteering illegal. One speaker, at a meeting held during the summer of that year, explained how the one was linked with the other:

Who were holding back shiploads of bacon and other stuffs? The profiteers. Cargoes were sold over and over again even before they reached this country. Each man who stepped in between the producers and consumer snapped up his profit and some who had never seen the vessel's cargo had made large sums of money by what they call 'enterprise'.[17]

Possibly these meetings had the desired impact; only five months later Frederick Miller, the owner of a Shirley Road meat shop, was fined in the police court for profiteering.

One additional union to be found in Southampton was the National Federation of Women Workers (NFWW), which was formed to give support to the many hundreds of women employed in the local wartime economy. For those who supported this union, a major concern was that of pay being rarely comparable to that of men undertaking the same work. Making the situation worse was the Munitions Tribunal, a government body for enforcing labour discipline, which did not support the payment of higher wages or allow women to move between factories to take advantage of better pay opportunities.

The existence of so many war-related industries on a coastline so close to the Continent created the possibility of some sort of enemy action that would damage production levels. In the seventeenth century the Dutch had deliberately sent a squadron of ships into the River Medway for the purpose of destroying both Sheerness and Chatham dockyards.[18] In 1770 a French plan was developed that would have seen 10,000 men marching across Kent and Sussex to besiege those same dockyards. Napoleon, in his own planned invasion of England, had also targeted north Kent, informing Marshal Louis Berthier, his chief of staff, that Chatham, with its dockyard, could be easily taken.[19]

It was the fear of such a possibility that led to the military lines that defended Chatham from landward attack being strengthened at the beginning of the nineteenth century, through additions to Fort Amherst and the construction of Fort

Clarence. By the time of the First World War, the military-industrial complex of the south coast, including both Southampton and Portsmouth, was even more vulnerable, being open to aerial bombardment by both Zeppelins and heavy bombers. To help reduce the threat, and apart from the introduction of anti-aircraft guns, the military officers commanding those industrial areas asked the various town councils to dim or reduce their street lights. In addition, the chief constables were informed that every effort should be made to convince local shopkeepers 'that no objection is taken to any lighting arrangement that they may make to the interior of their shops, provided that no reflection there from is thrown either upon the ground or the sky outside'. It was as a result of this, and its subsequent enforcement by the Rochester constabulary, that one Strood butcher was among the first to be fined for showing a light in an area that should have been dimmed. Warned by a police officer that lighting from his shop was reflecting on to buildings across the road, he failed to make adjustments and was subsequently fined £1.[20]

Only a few weeks after the fining of that particular butcher, north Kent found itself subjected to the first bombing raid of the war. Having already dropped a single bomb on Dover, a Rumpler Taube bomber then passed over Cliffe-at-Hoo, dropping a further bomb close to the Curtis and Harvey gunpowder factory. The *Chatham News*, in covering the event, told of how the enemy aeroplane had come under fire from guns sited at Chattenden, Upnor, Chatham and Lower Hope Point, thereby revealing to all and sundry the exact location of every anti-aircraft gun in the area. From Cliffe, the Taube proceeded to follow the line of the Thames, coming to within 5 miles of the Royal Arsenal. At that point it was deterred from going any further by a Vickers Gunbus of the Royal Flying Corps that had taken off from Joyce Green. Hotly pursued, the Taube was brought under machine-gun fire as it once again passed over the village of Cliffe. Those below were now able to credit themselves with watching the first aerial 'dog-fight' ever to be fought in British skies. The outcome, however, was indecisive, the Taube eventually escaping back to its own airfield.

Over the following four years, the military-industrial complexes of the south coast became a frequent target for aerial bombardment. Initially it was the Zeppelin that was most feared, these having a range in excess of 1,000 miles and an endurance of several days. As a result, Zeppelins tended to roam widely at night, able to drop several strings of bombs over towns widely dispersed. Although a number of these raiders passed over the south coast, the bombs that were dropped rarely caused much damage; but there was always the potential for panic.

Maybe the factor that saved the south coast from serious attack was the more regularised system of blacking out major towns when it was known that a raider was in the area. This was achieved by notifying the suppliers of electricity who subsequently cut the power. Most certainly it was the failure of this system, combined with the lack of adequate shelter, which ensured Chatham received one of the most devastating raids of the entire war. On this occasion it was not a

Zeppelin but a Gotha bomber, with the raid occurring on 3 September 1917. Dropping a 110lb bomb, the enemy aeroplane scored a direct hit on the naval barracks, which resulted in the death of 136 naval ratings. That the bomber, in company with three other aircraft, had located Chatham so easily was a result of the town lights not having been switched off. Although the warning had been given, it was not acted upon, as those responsible had believed it to be part of a practice alarm carried out earlier in the evening. Contributing to the considerable loss of life was the fact that the bomb hit the drill hall, used to provide additional sleeping quarters. Having, as it did, a glass roof, the thousands of flying shards greatly added to the number of victims.

The locating of such an extensive amount of war-related industry in this highly vulnerable area of the country is something that might well have been corrected as soon as the wars with Napoleon were brought to an end in 1815. In particular, it was these wars that had, once again, demonstrated the ease with which the south coast could be attacked if an enemy felt so inclined, with there being little sense in loading the area with munitions factories and naval dockyards. It would not, of course, have been necessary to dismantle every component of the various complexes, merely those which offered nothing to the direct support of military or naval operations. In this respect, therefore, both Portsmouth and Sheerness dockyards, used for the repair and maintenance of operational warships in the Atlantic, North Sea and English Channel, were of considerable strategic value.

Gun wharves and victualling yards were also a useful requirement, allowing ships to be quickly replenished. Similarly, the army needed barracks and hospitals to ensure that the coastal defences were adequately manned and supported. However, the bulk of the military-industrial complex, consisting of gunpowder factories and a major naval shipbuilding facility at Chatham, were less than usefully positioned. Far from having learnt the earlier lessons of war, the late nineteenth and early twentieth centuries simply saw an expansion in the overall size of the complex, with new facilities being added. It was not until the mid-1930s and the threat of a further major conflict that serious thought was given to the dispersal of this industry. However, by that date, and with so little time in hand, only a limited degree of reallocation was possible.

As well as ensuring that those who lived in the two counties were adequately fed and the industrial complex was secure, there was also the need to provide sufficient protection to the civil population in the event of invasion. The possibility of invasion, a threat that was very real during both the French wars and the First World War, led to the creation of various plans for the evacuation of the areas most likely to be attacked. In 1798 questions went out to the churchwardens of the various parishes of Sussex from the Duke of Lennox, in his role as Lieutenant of the County. They mainly related to the mobility of the population and the potential need for evacuation in the event of invasion. The information required concerned livestock, wagons, mills and their capacity, baking ovens and their capacity, bridges, boats and barges, men capable of active service, people unable to move themselves, arms, implements, drivers of teams and stock, and men serving in the army. Similarly, in 1916, plans were also developed for the evacuation of that same coastal belt. Initially, only those areas immediately threatened were to be evacuated by the military authorities, with most people to be advised to 'stay quietly in your houses'. However, it was also recognised that many might choose to leave the coastal belt without being ordered and thereby could cause additional problems. For this reason, posters and leaflets were circulated, for those living in East Sussex, carrying the following instructions:

> Leave on foot or by private transport.
> No railway trains available.
> Proceed northwest over the Downs and take to the fields when necessary.
> Special constables at cross roads will direct you.
> Carry with you money, food and a blanket.

The development of the aeroplane led to a focus on how the civilian population might be defended against aerial bombardment. While the military-industrial complexes of the south coast may have been extremely attractive targets, no stretch of the coastline was really safe from attack. That first air raid on Christmas Day 1914 might have been mainly directed towards the north Kent armaments industry, but it had been initially signalled by that same Rumpler Taube dropping a bomb on Dover. Although the castle appears to have been the intended target, that particular bomb landed without causing any real damage beyond a few broken windowpanes and slight bruising to a man who fell out of a tree while collecting holly. In the four years that followed, Dover, together with nearby Folkestone and the Thanet Towns, would be frequently raided. Undoubtedly, the most serious of these was a bombing raid by a squadron of Gotha bombers upon Folkestone, on 25 May 1917, causing seventy-two deaths. As with the Chatham raid later that same year, the high number of casualties was a result of inadequate warning; the chief constable, who should have been contacted with a clear warning, was given no notice of enemy bombers in the area. A daylight raid was carried out during the Whitsun weekend, when the town was especially busy with visitors and day-trippers, many of them in the crowded shopping centre. Tontine Street was especially busy, with a queue having formed outside Stokes, a greengrocer, where a fresh supply of potatoes had arrived. Oblivious to any danger, those who noticed the aircraft passing overhead assumed them to be British, with only the fall of bombs and a series of explosions proving them to be German. It was Tontine Street that took the brunt of the damage, with many of those queuing outside Stokes being simply blown to pieces.

Even when knowledge of a raid was communicated to the areas most threatened, the system lacked rigidity. In particular, any form of centralised direction was missing, with each local borough authority having to devise its own individual scheme. The system in operation at Hove, given here as an example, was no better or worse than anywhere else:

1. That in the event of information of impending raid by aircraft or bombardment from the sea being received by daylight, a signal consisting of three double explosions at intervals of about ten seconds will be given from the Corporation-yard, Sackville Road, on hearing which the public should return home and keep to their houses until the 'all clear' signal is given.

2. On the notification 'all clear' being received, constables on bicycles will be dispatched with whistles and placards intimating that immediate danger of attack has passed.

3. Night Warnings. In the parish of Hove the electric light will be appreciably lowered and kept lowered until the danger is past. In the parish of Aldrington, owing to the different system under which the electric current is supplied, the electric light will be cut off until the danger is passed.[21]

Unlike both Chatham and Folkestone, Hove was never subjected to an air raid during these years, so the system remained untested.

## Notes

1. TNA PC2/156, 3 December 1801.
2. TNA PC2/431, 2 May 1917.
3. Alfred 1st Viscount Milner, House of Commons, 21 May 1917.
4. H.M. Walbrook, *Hove and the Great War* (The Cliftonville Press, 1920), p. 129.
5. Ibid.
6. *Southampton Times*, 8 December 1917.
7. *Chatham News*, 16 February 1918.
8. Ibid.
9. Ibid.
10. Ibid., 8 & 15 December 1917.
11. Ibid., 1 April 1915.
12. Walbrook, op. cit., p. 126.
13. Ibid., p. 127.
14. Ibid., pp. 24–33.
15. Author's interview with Florrie May, September 1979. The danger alluded to was very real, with a leading mechanic at Kingsnorth plunging to his death after being taken some 200ft into the air.
16. *Faversham and North East Kent News*, 30 June 1917. While provision allowed for organised labour to have representation on the borough Food Control Committees, those in Faversham and the Medway Towns strenuously fought such demands.
17. *Southampton Times*, 7 June 1917.
18. Philip MacDougall, *The Story of Chatham Dockyard* (Rainham, 1982), pp. 40–2.
19. John Cookson, 'What if Napoleon had Landed', in *History Today*, Vol. 53 (September 2003).
20. *Chatham News*, 12 December 1914.
21. Walbrook, op. cit., p. 85.

# Part Two

## Preparing the Passive Defences

# Introduction

In previous wars, or in periods leading to a possible war, virtually the entire expenditure of British governments in preparing for hostilities was directed towards supporting the active defences of the nation: the weapons of war and the men who would be using them. With the predicted future European war likely to be very different to any previous war, an entirely new approach to defending the country had to be adopted. In particular, attention needed to be given to Civil Defence, the means by which non-combatant elements of the population could be protected from injury or death. At first, through a desire to avoid financial commitment, the government gave only relatively little attention to such needs. A government committee, entitled the Air Raid Precautions Subcommittee, was certainly established in 1924, but was allowed to bumble on for a total of eleven years before any of its recommendations were acted upon. This was in 1935, when the government informed local authorities, as a result of one such recommendation by this particular subcommittee, that they were to be given responsibility for the co-ordination of Civil Defence. It was, for the government, a fortuitous recommendation, as it allowed the central authority to shelve its own responsibility for Civil Defence and the need to underwrite much of the resulting costs.

It was the air raids of the First World War that first alerted the civilian population of Britain to the horrors of bombing, with the south coast among the areas most frequently attacked. In the years that followed, with bombers having both a greater range and a greater bomb-carrying capacity, the threat of aerial bombardment simply increased. Indeed, the occasional visit, as occurred in the First World War, of a few raiding bombers was no longer the feared scenario. Instead, it was felt that a vast fleet of heavy bombers that could destroy whole cities would initially attack southern England. It had even become accepted that there was no adequate defence against such an attack. In the House of Commons on 10 November 1932, Stanley Baldwin, a future and former prime minister, warned 'the ordinary man in the street' of something of which he must be made aware: 'the bomber will always get through'. Baldwin's speech is worth looking at more closely, as it influenced the subsequent thinking of those charged with defending the country:

> any town which is within reach of an aerodrome can be bombed within the first five minutes of war from the air, to an extent which was inconceivable in the last war, and the question will be whose morale will be shattered quickest by that preliminary bombing? I think it is well also for the man in the street to realise that there is no power on earth that can protect him from being bombed. Whatever people may tell him; the bomber will always get through.[1]

Of towns and cities along the south coast, a number were inescapably regarded as first-line targets in any concerted bombing campaign. These, in some cases, were the same population hubs that had received the attention of Zeppelins and Gothas in the earlier war. Particularly vulnerable was north Kent, approximately forty minutes' flying distance from the Continent. Here, the royal dockyards of Chatham and Sheerness, crucial in their support of the seagoing navy, remained as vulnerable as ever; a beckoning target for any determined enemy. Furthermore, and resulting from expansion during the First World War, both yards were surrounded by an even larger number of tightly packed, small working-class houses that ensured the predicted bombing raids would result in huge loss of life.

In addition, Chatham, together with neighbouring Gillingham and nearby Sheerness, possessed a number of additional naval facilities, these also drawing into the area a very large number of civilian workers. Despite this known vulnerability, little attention had been given to the dispersal of this large military-industrial complex and its supporting workforce to areas more remote and less vulnerable to bombers that might emanate from the Continent. The government had stood by and permitted the area to become even more attractive to enemy bombardment by allowing Short Brothers both to continue and expand their manufacturing of aircraft in Rochester. From their original Rochester site, immediately adjacent to the Medway and very close to the centre of the city, the firm had acquired a second factory, at the airport to the south of the city. While the riverside complex from 1937 onwards was engaged in the construction of Sunderlands for RAF Coastal Command, the new airport factory, beginning in 1938, was building Stirlings for Bomber Command.

In Faversham, dominated during the First World War by the munitions industry, a dramatic change had resulted, much of this work having disappeared. Both the CPC and the ELC had moved away from the town due to an overall reduction in demand for the materials they produced. This still left a sizeable portion of the industry within the Faversham area, which, in 1926, became part of the ICI conglomeration. This was a most fortuitous development as that company took a somewhat forward-looking view, noting that at Faversham such works were dangerously close to the Continent. So, unlike the British government which seemed to ignore such risks, ICI was determined to find a more isolated area upon which to centralise the manufacture of explosives. In 1934, to the sadness of those it employed, ICI moved much of the machinery it possessed at Faversham, together with a number of key workers, to the Ayrshire town of Ardeer, where it was already engaged in the manufacture of explosives.

Moving along the coastline, the port towns of Dover, Folkestone, Newhaven and Shoreham were also likely targets because of their actual or potential roles in the transhipping of troops, reception of war materials or general use by the navy. Of these, Dover was especially vulnerable, only 21 miles from Calais with its harbour having a clearly designated role as a naval port that was essential to the support of merchant shipping passing along the Channel. As well as these four port towns, which by their very nature possessed sizeable populations that would need protection from air attack, there were a great number of other towns that opened on to the coast. Among them, of course, were the leading resorts of Brighton, Margate and Southsea, but to these can be added a further twenty or thirty resort towns that were equally open to attack. Magnifying the danger was the fact that some of these towns could be considered legitimate military targets, possessing as they did various barracks, small manufacturing industries or were close enough to RAF airfields as to be caught up in raids for which they were not the real target.

The military-industrial complexes of the Portsmouth Harbour and Southampton Water areas dominated the east Hampshire littoral. Although more distant from the Continent, but still less than an hour's flying time, they were within easy range of bombers operating from European airfields. While Portsmouth possessed the largest and most important naval dockyard in the country, Southampton had one of the country's leading commercial ports. Between them, these two cities were of unequalled importance to the nation when at war. At Portsmouth, the naval dockyard not only engaged in the construction and maintenance of warships, but also served as a base for the Atlantic and Channel fleets. In addition, and within the area of the city, a naval barracks, gun wharf and other naval facilities remained, while on the south-east side of Portsea Island, the Airspeed Company were manufacturing twin-engine Oxford aircraft for the RAF which were used for training pilots. On the Gosport side of the harbour were the Haslar naval hospital and the Royal Clarence victualling yard, together with a submarine base and a Royal Navy ordnance depot. In turn, the Southampton area was not far behind. Apart from its commercial port facilities, the area of Woolston possessed both the aviation works of Supermarine, responsible for the production of Spitfires, and the Thornycroft yard that specialised in the construction of destroyers. A few miles along Southampton Water is Hamble, the location of several aviation companies that included Armstrong-Whitworth and Folland. A valuable fuel oil terminal for shipping also existed at Hamble.

On the Isle of Wight, the military-industrial complex that existed at Cowes had continued to expand, J. Samuel White's shipyard remaining the single most important component. A major constructor of naval warships, White's was responsible for the launching of eight destroyers and four sloops during the period 1935–39. With workshops on both sides of the River Medina, the firm's thirst for both skilled and unskilled workers ensured that this part of the island was as densely populated as anywhere in Portsmouth or Southampton. Also based around Cowes was Saunders-Roe (previously S.E. Saunders), whose factory at Somerton, prior to the outbreak of war, was engaged in the construction of Supermarine-designed Walrus amphibious aircraft for the Fleet Air Arm.

While those who lived in these vulnerable south coast towns, as well as those in less threatened areas, might fear the damage that could well be inflicted upon them, there was also the question of what these bombs might contain, the dread being that they held mustard gas. Although banned under the Geneva Convention of 1925, it was believed that both Italy and Germany might not be deterred from its use. It was for this reason that in 1938 the government widely dispersed details of the means by which poison gas might be delivered:

> Air bombs containing gas may be small or large, but the effects produced will be similar. In the case of non-persistent gas the whole contents of the bomb will form a cloud near the point at which it strikes the ground and this cloud will drift along the wind. The size of the cloud when first formed will be small, but the concentration of gas in it will be very great. As the cloud is swept along by the wind it will become diluted with more air, but its size will increase.[2]

Alternatively, it was suggested:

> Mustard gas or other persistent gas can be sprayed from aircraft. The liquid falls in fine drops over a fairly wide area. The drops may indeed be so small as not to be noticed by persons upon whom they may fall. Such a spray may be a source of very great danger, because it may fall on the face, neck, and any exposed parts of the body, in addition to the clothing, without being noticed.[3]

Even without the addition of gas, there was increasing evidence of the willingness of some nations to use the bombing of civilians as an overall war-winning strategy. Put to deadly use by the Japanese in Manchuria, the Italians in Abyssinia and the Germans in Spain, the devastation that might be wreaked on an unsuspecting and undefended town was all too clear. For those who wished to know more, there was plenty of literature available, describing the effect of such raids and their toll on the ordinary people who were sitting underneath the bombs. Of raids on the crowded working-class quarters of Barcelona, readers of one *Penguin Special* were informed:

The explosives seemed to be about as twice as effective as those used in the last war, but evidence on this point is difficult to get. During twenty-three bombardments of Barcelona 528 bombs were dropped causing 916 deaths, 2,500 wounded, and destroying 863 houses. The subsequent attacks in March and April were relatively more severe, but in no case has there been evidence of any specific objectives except the general target of an industrial area.[4]

This fear of the bomber led to increasing attention being given to the protection of civilians against aerial bombardment. Much lower key was the attention given to ensuring the country could survive a long, drawn-out war that would involve maintaining an adequate food supply. While the bomber had certainly gained a reputation during the First World War, it had not exactly brought the country to its knees. On the other hand, the food shortages that were witnessed in 1917 and early 1918 had very nearly brought the country to a point of crisis.

It was, therefore, the issue of maintaining adequate food supplies that had to be resolved before the outbreak of any future European war. Unlike matters relating to Air Raid Precautions and the immediacy of death from the air, this was not an area of high visibility. Much of what happened with regard to food preparation was carried on behind the scenes. In particular, a series of government initiatives were taken to ensure the infrastructure was in place and would only become operational once war was declared. To this end, therefore, the government established a trained but inactive female agricultural labour force and planned for a general increase in wartime production. For the south coast this would have important future application, but few signs of this infrastructure existed until the actual declaration of war. Underlying these initiatives, which also included the establishment of non-operational Food Control Committees, was the intention that a food shortage crisis, which was certainly witnessed by several south coast towns during the First World War, would not be repeated in the next European war.

The Munich crisis of September 1938, more than anything else, shocked attitudes within Britain as to how it was to fight the future war. For approximately fourteen days there were few within the British population who did not rightly fear the outbreak of an imminent war. In that same period, towns, cities and villages throughout the country were placed on a full wartime footing. Boroughs throughout the entire length of the south coast set about digging trenches, sandbagging municipal buildings and preparing first-aid posts. From newly available regional government reserve stocks, each Civil Defence authority was able to order gas masks, with teams of volunteers setting about both assembling the masks and distributing them locally. At the same time, airfields, dockyards and barracks were hastily camouflaged, while soldiers, sailors and airmen were recalled to duty, the expectation being that air raids were a likely threat.

The immediate cause of the crisis was Hitler's ambition for an area of Czechoslovakia – the Sudetenland – to be ceded to Germany. Mainly populated by ethnic Germans, with Nazi propaganda deliberately fermenting disorder and violence, a justification for invasion was established. By 12 September, mobilisation along the Czech border was complete, with Hitler making a speech at Nuremberg that he was ready to support the Sudeten Germans in their demand for freedom. At that time, Czechoslovakia had an alliance with France and the Soviet Union, thereby ensuring that a major European conflict, and one that would inevitably include Great Britain, would result from any such invasion.

For his part, Neville Chamberlain, the British prime minister, believed that he could defuse the situation through direct talks with Hitler. The outcome, an agreement struck in Munich, was that Hitler could take immediate possession of all Czechoslovakian territory that had a population of more than 50 per cent ethnic Germans. The French also went along with the agreement, leaving Czechoslovakia with the alternative of either agreeing to the arrangement or opposing, without British and French support, the invading German army. Since the latter option was an impossible task, given the relative size of the Czechoslovakian army compared to that of the Germans, the Czechoslovak government, with considerable reluctance, also accepted the outcome of the Munich agreement. In return, Czechoslovakia received a guarantee, backed by Britain and France, that the future boundaries of this newly truncated country would be fully protected. Yet, within six months of the agreement being struck, the Third Reich, Hungary and Poland dismantled the remainder of Czechoslovakia.

If nothing else, the Munich agreement brought about a miniscule period of breathing space. It permitted some of the local authorities along the south coast of Britain to build on what they had already started, by introducing more shelters, training the numerous Civil Defence volunteers that had now come forward and continuing to develop realistic Civil Defence schemes.

## Notes

1.　Hansard, 10 November 1932.
2.　Air Raid Precaution Handbook No 1: Personal Protection against Gas (HMSO, 1938), p. 13.
3.　Ibid., p. 15.
4.　G.T. Garratt, 'Air Raid Precautions', in *The Air Defence of Great Britain* (Penguin, 1938), p. 117.

# 3

# Perception

During the 1920s and 1930s the experience of the First World War came to dominate many aspects of life along the south coast. It was something that was completely unavoidable. Kent, Sussex, the Isle of Wight and the east Hampshire littoral, as a direct result of the recent war, had probably witnessed the deaths of approximately 20,000 former inhabitants.[1] While most were either enlisted or conscripted members of the armed services, the dead also included a number of civilians killed in air raids or undertaking work in connection with the war.[2] To this number should be added a possible 60,000 or more who suffered wounds of sufficient severity as to hospitalise them at some point during the war or immediately after.

For the most part, the apocalyptic horseman of war had taken his toll primarily from the youthful – the lost generation. Surviving mothers, sons, daughters and wives would remain stricken in grief for the remainder of their lives. One Kentish mother, Charlotte Fullman, sometime of Chatham, was particularly heartbroken, having endured the loss of five sons. Juliet Nicolson, author of a recent book, described the plight of her and the myriad other families who had suffered the carnage of these four years:

> Formal occasions of remembrance designed to comfort often produced the reverse effect. Private anniversaries of the day someone was reported missing, the day a final telegram was delivered, wedding days and the day you last saw them all prompted memories so similar to the moment of actual loss that the healing cycle was derailed.[3]

Added to this was the equally disturbing sight of those who had been maimed and disfigured. The men themselves, scared of public ridicule, often found it difficult to enter open streets during daylight hours. The most disfigured might find themselves institutionally protected, temporarily or permanently resident in a hospital or charity home. At Westgate-on-Sea, hideously blinded and face-scarred former soldiers walked hand upon shoulder, snaking their way towards the beach where deckchairs were laid out in readiness. Those who came too close would turn away in horror, telling their children not to look.

With these deaths and casualties mainly affecting males born between 1875 and 1901, it seriously skewed the post-war demographic composition of this corner of southern England. In its wake, the First World War left a disproportionately large number of widows and young women who would never have the future opportunity of a male partner. In Kent and Sussex, the immediate pre-war census of 1911 showed these counties to have a slight gender imbalance, with women forming 52.8 per cent of the population, but this had increased to 54 per cent by 1921.[4] For women in search of husbands, and there were a great many, the advice from a certain Walter Gallichan, author of *Sexual Apathy and Coldness in Women*, was that the seaside towns of Sussex were best avoided, as women of marriageable age far outnumbered eligible men.

The massive loss of life, combined with grief and bewilderment, inevitably led to a reaction. Wars, which for over a hundred years had been fought at a safe distance and had taken a relatively limited toll on people's lives, had led to a national misunderstanding regarding the dangers of war. Upon the outbreak of the First World War in August 1914, the predominant view was that the fighting would not only be over quickly, but would have little impact upon the nation as a whole. The lessons learnt during the time of Napoleon had simply been forgotten. Possibly it was during the late spring and summer of 1916 that the bitterness and horror of what was taking place finally registered. Jutland, in May, accounted for over 7,500 British lives lost, while in July, the Somme on its first day claimed 20,000.

Throughout that summer, the guns of the Western Front were clearly audible along the south coast, with local papers overflowing with the news of local lives lost. Those in the naval towns of Chatham, Sheerness, Gosport and Portsmouth were particularly devastated by the losses at Jutland, with several hundred residents reported as killed. Even Chichester, a coastal town but with more limited naval associations, had losses estimated at eighty. To this horrendous news would be added the seemingly endless flow of deaths from the Somme, with the *Chichester Observer* recording in August over fifty deaths a week. As for north Kent, the *Chatham News* was recording as many as a hundred lives lost per week, with Sittingbourne and Faversham newspapers listing a further fifty or sixty. This was also a time when wounded soldiers were first becoming a familiar sight. Caroline Playne, a leading pacifist, following a visit to Brighton in early 1917, wrote: 'the sight of hundreds of men on crutches going about in groups, many having lost one leg, many others both legs, caused sickening horror. The maiming of masses of strong young men thus brought home was appalling.'[5]

The contrast between the idealism of the young men who went to war in 1914, and the terrible toll of death and injury to no great end, was to permanently haunt those who had survived. For most it created an intense fear of future war, with increased numbers wishing to ensure that no similar arena of slaughter would ever again be possible. Only by placing the interwar period into this context is it possible to understand the reluctance by many to prepare for any future war. The likelihood, so most assumed from the evidence of the First World War, was that any second war of comparable nature would simply destroy civilised society. To do anything other than work for peace would be a simple denial of that earlier war. Those who talked of the need for rearmament were often seen as warmongers, intent on creating a situation where war would be inevitable. Only in the late 1930s, with Hitler firmly entrenched in Germany, did a new reality take hold.

It was the shock of what had happened during the First World War, and the need to ensure that the fallen were not forgotten, that caused over 3,000 memorials to be put in place within the numerous south coast towns, villages and hamlets.[6] Indeed, throughout the nation as a whole, the demand for memorials was so great that foundries in the immediate post-war years were working flat out to meet the demand. For the most part, these memorials represented a desire to record the names of those who had given their lives in the national conflict, irrespective of social class and background. Where there was the slightest hint that this was not the case, those contributing to a memorial were likely to demand the return of their original contribution.[7]

Part of the democratising influence of the recent war, previous generations had rarely recorded names unless they had been drawn from those families who controlled the local communities: the squire, vicar and those of affluence. It is a theme pursued by Keith Grieves in a paper published in the *Sussex Archaeological Collections*. He refers to these controlling groups within each community as a 'self-elected secondary elite' and details how, in Sussex, they frequently controlled the post-war process of commemorating the dead by placing themselves at the head of parish war memorial committees. In doing so, they controlled the design and positioning of the memorial, together with the overall message. Admittedly, Grieves indicates that a more open debate took place in some parishes, but even in such cases, the hand of this controlling elite was still evident.[8]

The recording of names on a plaque that was placed either in the church or on a grander memorial in close proximity to the church was the normal outcome of the decision to erect a parish memorial. In listing the names, a minority of memorials made a distinction between officers and men, but most simply placed names in alphabetical order. The families of the elite, however, still reserved for themselves the right to erect individual memorials to their own sons, explaining why the number of post-war memorials so clearly exceeds the number of parishes lying either along or in proximity to the south coast.

While in future years the simple listing of names would be a poignant reminder of the folly of war, this was not the underlying reason for the erection of these memorials. The names were there to personify the notion of sacrifice, and provide relatives with the comfort of knowing that the sacrifice made had been recognised. However, at this point there was a parting of the ways. While a listing of all names was usually agreed upon, not all were happy with the means of general representation. A not uncommon style was that of a cross with an affixed sword. Some parishes were even more nationalistic in the given message, choosing to make a connection with the ideal of the soldier saint and the notion of it having been a just war, fought with God's approval.

The choice of those who were invited to unveil the parish memorials reflects the viewpoint of those who had overseen the erection of the memorials. Larger parishes were anxious to obtain a high-ranking military officer together with a military band. In some cases it was a simple matter of local pride. When the War Memorial Committee at Worthing discovered that the neighbouring parish of Chichester was to have its memorial unveiled by Field Marshal Sir William Robertson, it was thought only right that 'some equally distinguished soldier could be induced to honour Worthing in such a manner'. As a result, they too invited Robertson to unveil their memorial.

As for the speeches offered, these varied quite considerably. Some simply saw the memorials as an opportunity to reflect on the tragedy of the war, while others used the occasion to hammer home the importance of sacrifice and patriotism. Robertson, in his speech at Chichester on the evening of 21 July 1921, fell into the former category, the field marshal referring to the huge amount of 'sorrow in many hearts'. In conclusion, so the reporter of the *Chichester Observer* noted, Robertson made the suggestion that 'on every anniversary of that day or on armistice day, they should come to that monument and bring their children'. In so doing, they would be showing 'honour to those great men'.[9]

In contrast to the mild and reflective tone of Field Marshal Robertson was the approach taken by Major-General Thuillier, commander of the Thames and Medway area, when unveiling a joint memorial to the fallen of the two east Kent villages of Doddington and Newhaven. This was altogether a much more formal military-style event, with Captain Alered de Laune of Doddington marshalling and parading the sixty returned ex-servicemen of the two villages. In his address, Thuillier indicated his own view of the message that such memorials should give to future generations. In essence, his speech was reported in the *Faversham and North East Kent News*:

And what was it these memorials would say to those who came after? They would remind them that in the beginning of the 20th century the manhood of the British nation was in no way decayed, but that in the great virtues and qualities of patriotism, endurance, grit and self sacrifice the men of this period were fully equal to those of the past. The memorials would remind them that when war came men came forward from every town and village and every walk of life, without compulsion, to endure hardness and face dangers, and alas! In the case of many of them – as of those whom they commemorated upon this cross – to give their lives so that others might live in freedom.

Thuillier then proceeded to use the lost generation as a means of exhorting future generations to perform a similar duty if the need arose:

Although the war was over, the need for patriotism, courage, endurance and self-sacrifice was not past. It was idle to imagine that war might never occur again. We could wish it might be so but a glance at the state of Europe and the world generally dispelled any such idea. Even now enemies open and concealed threatened the peace of our country; industry and the finance of the country had not recovered; and the great problems of unemployment and of consequent distress were not yet solved.

While the unveiling of memorials often contained speeches that reflected on the importance of patriotism and sacrifice, this was less so with regard to the act of remembrance associated with Armistice Day. Dedicated by George V as a time to commemorate members of the armed forces who had been killed in war, it had a stronger degree of solemnity than that of the unveiling ceremonies. Centring as they did upon a two-minute silence, they encouraged individual reflection on the terrible toll of injury and death in a conflict that gained so little. Typical in its creation of an all-pervading air of sadness was the Armistice Day ceremony at Chichester, which took place in November 1923:

Two minutes – and what memories and what thoughts were crowded in to that brief space of time! As one stood erect with one's thoughts resting reverently on the memory of that great Army that lay in Flanders fields, one could not help wondering what effect the silence had elsewhere.

Those wonderful two minutes were being kept throughout the length and breadth of the country; how many mothers, widows and sweethearts were thinking, with an awakened ache at their heart, of the men who had left with a laugh on their lips and full of life and youth to die for their king and country in the battlefields of France. How many men were thinking regretfully of the pals with whom they had once fought side by side?[10]

***

In common with the nation as a whole, the Anglican Church, upon the outbreak of war in 1914, had possessed an ambivalent attitude. The Lambeth Conference, a gathering of bishops in communion with the Church of England, held approximately every ten years, might have been seen as the body most likely to determine the future direction of the Church. However, in the immediate pre-war conferences of 1897 and 1908, there was no outright attempt to condemn war. Quite the contrary. In 1897 the conference admitted the inability of the Church to prevent war, while going on to suggest that wars between nations could sometimes be considered just.[11] As for the 1908 conference, there was a drawing back from even this fairly weak stance, the conference 'frankly acknowledging the moral gains sometimes won by war'.[12]

In taking a decidedly unethical stance, the Church had clearly allied itself with the nation at war and showed little inclination to support those who would not fight. Although Lord Kitchener and Archbishop Davidson had both expressed that the pulpit should not be used for recruiting, individual clergy certainly pursued such a course of action. In Chichester and its immediate locality, the clergy at all levels were unhesitant in the encouragement of their parishioners to get into uniform. In a Christmas sermon in 1914, the Bishop of Chichester, Dr Ridgeway, posed the question: 'What then is our duty?' His answer, quite simply, was that 'we must be prepared to fight at any cost'.

Another leading churchman of the city, the Dean of the Cathedral, would stand on a wagon as troops marched out of the city, beseeching them to go forward into battle. At the outset of the war, in August 1914, young men attending St George's church in Chichester were urged to ask themselves the question: 'Why am I not fighting on the front for my country?' If they could not give a good answer, they were told: 'The sooner you enlisted the better.' In nearby Bosham, the vicar used the parish magazine to appeal for recruits, while the vicars of Arundel, Littlehampton and Selsey all appeared at recruiting meetings. As for the Rev. Henry Green of Climping, he went so far as to list the goodness that could come out of war. In this he included unifying the home population, creating sympathy for those who suffer and providing a sense of dependence on God.

Among those who were committed to the carving out of a new and more ethical pathway for the Anglican Church were Canon Hugh Richard Shepherd, Dean of Canterbury (known to all as Dick Shepherd), and George Bell, Bishop of Chichester. Both, in their day, were highly controversial figures intent on not only working towards a more peaceful world, but convinced that the Church could play a major role in the achievement of that ambition. Shepherd, in a book published three years before the conference, set out an argument in which he questioned the dual stance of a Church that proclaimed the tenderness of Jesus while upholding state violence. To this end, Shepherd proposed a specimen resolution that the brotherhood of all could not be reconciled with an ideal 'that requires men to slay their brother men'.[13] However, it was words from a further book written by Shepherd, 'that Christianity and war are not compatible', that were to be taken forward by the Bishop of Chichester to the 1930 Anglican Church conference. Passed as resolution 25, the conference agreed that 'war, as a method of settling international disputes, is incompatible with the teaching and example of our Lord Jesus Christ'. Although not subsequently endorsed by the Church Assembly (at that time the legislative and governing body of the Anglican Church) until 1937, it was a powerful message and clearly gave authority to those members of the clergy who wished to work for a world order founded on unity rather than disunity.

Dick Shepherd, himself a former wartime chaplain, was determined to translate the words of resolution 25 into some form of action. To achieve this, and to gauge levels of support, he wrote to a number of newspapers in October 1934, asking that those 'who wish the repudiation of methods of violence' should send him a postcard. He indicated that at some point in the 'near future', they would be called together to vote on a resolution that stated: 'We renounce war and never again, directly or indirectly, will we support or sanction another.'[14]

Within a few weeks he had received over 100,000 responses. From this, and a packed meeting held at the Royal Albert Hall, emerged the Peace Pledge Union. Along the south coast, the Union was as well supported as anywhere else in the country. Throughout the area there were more than forty groups established, with those at Brighton and Dover among the largest and most active.

In Chichester, Bishop George Bell was focusing on another important facet of the peace movement, that of creating the framework that would enable Christians in different countries to act and speak together. It was his view that on any occasion when war threatened, the churches, through being united, would be able to bring pressure on their respective governments to accept the settlement of disputes by peaceful and judicial means. Bell also believed that the Church should be taking a central role in establishing ethical principles. As chairman of the international church conference focusing on life and work, held at Geneva in 1932, Bell explained the principles that underlined his thoughts:

> We are not here to look round for a good social programme which the Christian community can adopt as its own. Nor are we to content ourselves with appealing to other authorities, international or national to end some social evil. We wish to show what the Christian conscience commands. We believe that the Christian religion has distinctive principles and distinctive standards, which it should be the aim of the church to discover and set forth.[15]

So passionate was Bell in his commitment to world peace that the Bishop's Palace in the cathedral city of Chichester became an important centre for internationalism and progressive thought. Over the years, a great many famous names were drawn to the palace, not least of them Mahatma Gandhi. In turn, Bell sent out emissaries, with the Dean of Chichester, the Rev. A.S. Jones, securing an ultimately unsuccessful meeting with Adolf Hitler in Berlin. In January 1939 in his New Year message to the people of Sussex, Bell, still clinging to a desperate hope for peace, confided his belief 'that the great masses of people in every country are lovers of peace and desire friendship with the people of other countries'.[16]

Eventually discredited through its inability to prevent a series of aggressions committed by Germany, Italy and Japan, the League of Nations had originally been established as the international body that would ensure the settlement of international disputes. One of the few positives to come out of the Versailles Treaty, the League of Nations was widely supported in Britain, with individuals able to register their support through membership of the League of Nations Union (LNU). By the mid-1920s the LNU had over a quarter of a million registered subscribers, with its membership peaking in 1931 at 407,000.[17] Among the activities it undertook was the Peace Ballot of 1935. An unofficial referendum in which over 11 million people participated, it provided strong support for the aims and objectives of the League of Nations. Along the south coast of Britain there were at least fifty independent LNU branches, these having a combined membership in excess of 10,000 people.

Particularly active in support of the LNU were the various churches, which were often at the forefront of setting up local branches. In Lewes, a packed meeting of the LNU in 1934, organised by the Society of Friends, voted overwhelmingly against the use of force. At Chichester, the first meeting to discuss the establishment of a branch of the LNU in the city was organised by the Free Church Council. Held on 4 October 1920 in the council assembly rooms, the chairman of this meeting, H.A. Sydenham, made it clear that, in his view, the only way to prevent war 'was by the combination of all religious forces' for the purpose of opposing war. The Bishop of Chichester gave his public support to the LNU when he presided over a meeting held at Chichester in January 1921, while later that same year the churches came together in the city to organise a recruiting meeting. This was held in Eastgate Square and was presided over by the Archdeacon of Chichester, with the Methodist minister of Selsey in attendance. At this meeting, the archdeacon made clear his belief that any future war would have a truly unimaginable outcome:

> If ever a war was carried out in the world on the same scale as the past one it would mean the practical destruction of civilisation altogether. It was not a foolish thing for people to believe this and we have to take proper precautions.

In calling for the establishment of a Chichester branch of the LNU, those who joined would be 'united in a great federation' that is working 'to preserve themselves from an appalling disaster'.[18]

The PPU and LNU were two distinctly different organisations. While the former totally rejected violence as a means of solving the world's problems, the LNU accepted the use of force if sanctioned by the League of Nations. In the case of the latter, the mere threat of such force, so members of the LNU believed, would result in no nation failing to present its grievances to the League for final adjudication. However, on one important issue the two organisations were in total agreement. If a future major war did break out, it would almost certainly destroy the current level of civilisation.

Outside of the PPU and LNU, a large proportion of the population seemingly agreed. The National Peace Ballot of 1935 sought from 11 million voters in the population their views on a number of questions relating to the use of force. On the possibility of all-round disarmament by international agreement, over 9.5 million (92 per cent) were in favour; on whether nations, through the use of economic sanctions, should combine to stop one nation attacking another, over 10 million (94 per cent) were in favour. However, 6.7 million (74 per cent) did agree that if economic sanctions failed, they would favour a resort to military measures.

The Peace Ballot was organised by the LNU between February and May 1935, with half a million of its supporters asking those over the age of 18 to vote on a total of five questions.[19] While the outcome of the ballot was strongly suggestive of anti-militarist opinions, the results have to be treated with care. For one thing, in 1935, there were over 25 million people aged over 18 in the population, with the majority not voting. In addition, the questions themselves were conducive to answers that the LNU particularly desired. As regards the south coast, the return of ballots was generally lower than in other areas of the country.

Having demonstrated the limitations of the National Peace Ballot, it was, nevertheless, a considerable achievement on the part of the LNU, with some areas, including parts of the south coast, witnessing a voting turnout that exceeded that of local elections. To do this, local committees of the LNU, which were based on parliamentary constituencies, arranged for their supporters to canvass door-to-door for the purpose of encouraging everyone in each household to vote in the ballot. In Dover, with its large and extremely active LNU branch, this involved 400 volunteers each calling on approximately 100 local families. If nothing else, it encouraged an open debate, which took place between husbands, wives and older children. According to one Sussex volunteer: 'I was delighted the other day when a man told me he had answered "yes" and his wife "no" to all six questions.'[20]

The effect of the First World War was clearly the root cause of such strong support for the ideas of the LNU and, to a lesser extent, those of the PPU. However, an additional factor was undoubtedly the general fear of what outcome a future war might bring. To re-quote the words of the Archdeacon of Chichester, there was every certainty that it would result in the 'practical destruction of civilisation'.

The Munich crisis, while galvanising much of the nation into more extensive preparations for a future war, led the LNU to intensify its own efforts for obtaining peace. For this reason, an increased number of meetings were held, often involving a number of leading peace activists, among them the Bishop of Chichester. In November 1938 the Brighton LNU passed a resolution at one of its meetings that supported the agreement reached in Munich while seeking out implementation of an international conference. In its preamble, the resolution praised the efforts of Prime Minister Neville Chamberlain, and through his efforts alone it was believed 'that Europe is not at war today'. Also in Brighton, Lloyd-Williams, a leading local activist, told members of the LNU youth group that 'war is silly and unreasonable'. He then went on to call for a mobilisation of public opinion to 'work together to stop war', irrespective of whether they were 'Conservatives, Socialists, Liberals [or] Communists'.[21]

However, following the Munich crisis, as the weeks dragged on, an element of despair within the peace movement clearly becomes discernible. Certainly the two main organisations, the PPU and LNU, begin to witness a fall in their south coast membership, while cries of despair are heard. On the Isle of Wight, in July 1939, one isolated pacifist felt constrained to write in the visitors' book of St John's church, Sandown: 'Thou shalt not kill. Down with conscription.' It was, as it happens, the same week that Sandown first tested out its newly installed air-raid sirens, a procedure that was now to become a weekly event, continuing until the outbreak of war some seven weeks later.

Although equally committed to peace, one additional organisation did not necessarily share the views of either the pacifist PPU or the LNU and its emphasis on collective world security. This was the British Legion, the voice of the ex-service community. Most of their members, of whom there were over 2,000 along the south coast, had directly witnessed the carnage of the First World War and this was very much at the heart of Legion policy and branch activities. In Chichester, during the summer of 1938, the branch in that city had controversially held out an olive branch to German ex-servicemen. In what was viewed as a valuable exercise, men who had fought in the kaiser's army were invited to Chichester to meet with local legionnaires. The Germans, for their part, had proved most amiable 'and without doubt held out the hand of friendship'. Upon their return to Germany, the Nazi-controlled press chose to vilify those who had participated in this visit to Chichester.[22] In pursuing its desire for peace and that of not forgetting their fallen comrades, the Legion was a major participant in the annual Armistice Day services and was determined that a major festival, similar to that held at the Royal Albert Hall, should take place at Brighton.

That the organisation was as committed to peace as the PPU and LNU is unquestionable. At Brighton, where the debate over the potential future war was being vigorously conducted, Lady Edward Spencer Churchill, chair of the National Executive of the British Legion Women's Section, told a packed meeting that no organisation was working harder than the Legion for the cause of peace. To which she added that this was because those who formed the British Legion were the ones who had personally seen 'the horrors of war' and witnessed the sight of 'slaughtered bodies'.[23]

In general, while peace was considered the first objective, the British Legion was also strong in its belief that a national military force was essential for deterring an attack by a potential enemy. Admiral Phipps Hornby, whose family had long settled in the Sussex village of Compton, in addressing his local branch of the Legion, turned his focus on how they should be directing themselves:

> No one is more qualified than we of the Legion to bring home on what I look on as one of the most important things to be done at the moment, and that is to get the man in the street to realise that in the future a war is going to be brought home to every man, woman and child in this island. And unless we are organised in key staff so that every man and woman is able to take their part if that calamity does come, then we shall find that we shall have a very rough time in the next war.
>
> Another thing, which those who had served in the last war could do, was to impress on the young people how much it was up to them to qualify themselves to take up arms should war come upon them.[24]

Despite their philosophical differences, these three heavily subscribed organisations, the PPU, the LNU and the British Legion, all had one common viewpoint – that of a universal hostility to a future pan-European war. Where they differed was in the means by which such an eventuality could be prevented. In the case of the PPU, it involved opposition not just to the concept of war but to the weapons of war and anything that was suggestive of war. The LNU, on the other hand, wished to see a stronger League of Nations and a move away from individual state forces, seeing the League as an international police force. Finally, the British Legion, equally opposed to a future European war, saw deterrence as the only reasonable solution. By building and maintaining a powerful unilateral military force, firmly controlled by the government, no nation would dare pick a fight with Great Britain.

At the risk of oversimplifying the strongly held beliefs of those who inhabited Britain in the 1920s and '30s, these three approaches more or less encapsulated the overall attitudes of the nation at that time. Furthermore, it helps to explain why the preparations for that future war, long recognised as having certain inevitability, remained sluggish and blatantly lethargic. Those who attempted to warn the nation of the impending conflict, and the need to suitably equip the country, were seen as warmongers and likely to encourage other countries to similarly prepare. In so doing, it was argued, they were in fact making war an even more likely outcome. Then there was a possible fourth group: those who gave little thought as to where the nation was going, but were happy with a status quo that did not involve a rise in taxation or interfere with life in their own small world.

While the government of the day might have overruled all this, it was, nevertheless, dependent on those same individuals if it was to remain in power. A government intent on heavy military expenditure had to be sure that it had the support of those who would be casting their votes in the next election. Even after the arrival of Hitler on the European scene, this could not be assured. In reality, it was events in the late 1930s, especially the threat and eventual entry of the German army into Czechoslovakia, which really brought about a sea change – thereby permitting a last-minute dash to shore up the nation's passive and active defences.

## Notes

1. The arrival at an exact and more precise figure is impossible. The figure of 20,000 is based on a severe downward rounding of the estimated 2.19 per cent loss suffered by the entire population of Great Britain. That the figure given for the area is substantially correct can be supported by reference to the names presented on memorials along the south coast and records of the Commonwealth War Graves Commission. See also, PP (1921) xx *The Army Council General Report of the British Army 1912–1919 [Cmd 1193]*.
2. Here must be included the 72 deaths resulting from the Folkestone air raid of May 1917 and the 108 killed in the Faversham explosion of April 1916.
3. Juliet Nicolson, *The Great Silence* (John Murray, 2009), p. 5.
4. In real terms, it meant that an additional 11,000 women from those south coast counties were likely to remain unmarried, the war having culled their potential partners.
5. Caroline Playne, *Britain Holds On* (George Allen Unwin, 1933), p. 76.
6. United Kingdom National Inventory of War Memorials.
7. In Worthing, where such a threat seems to have emerged, a number of correspondents to the *Worthing Gazette*, during the summer of 1920, made clear that a return of contributions would be demanded.
8. Keith Grieves, 'Rural parish churches and the bereaved in Sussex after the First World War', in *Sussex Archaeological Collections* 139 (2001), pp. 203–14.
9. *Chichester Observer*, 27 July 1921.
10. Ibid., 14 November 1923.
11. Rev. Dr Clive Barrett, *The Lambeth Conference – a Vehicle for Christian Peacemaking* (unpublished draft document), p. 2.
12. Ibid.
13. H.R.L. Shepherd, *The Impatience of a Parson* (London, 1927), p. 216. Re-quoted from Barrett, op. cit., p. 3.
14. Sybil Morrison, *I Renounce War* (London, 1962), p. 100.
15. Ronald Jasper, *George Bell Bishop of Chichester* (Oxford, 1967), p. 99.
16. *Chichester Observer*, 7 January 1939.
17. John T. Callaghan, *The Labour Party and Foreign Policy: A History* (London, 2007), p. 69.
18. *Chichester Observer*, various dates. As evidence of local support given to the LNU by churches in the Chichester area, the Anglican Church in Bognor recruited forty members into the Bognor branch in February 1921. The WSRO holds the Chichester congregational church records and these show that the church enrolled on 26 March 1927, receiving a corporate membership certificate.
19. The questions on the ballot paper, together with the votes on each question, were as follows: Should Great Britain remain a Member of the League of Nations? Yes: 11,090,387. No: 355,883. Are you in favour of all-round reduction of armaments by international agreement? Yes: 10,470,489. No: 862,775. Are you in favour of an all-round abolition of national military and naval aircraft by international agreement? Yes: 9,533,558. No: 1,689,786. Should the manufacture and sale of armaments for private profit be prohibited by international agreement? Yes: 10,417,329. No: 775,415. Do you consider that, if a nation insists on attacking another, the other nations

should combine to compel it to stop – (a) by economic and non-military measures? *Yes*: 10,027,608. *No*: 635,074; (b) if necessary, by military measures? *Yes*: 6,784,368. *No*: 2,351,981. Details taken from Adelaide Livingstone, *The Peace Ballot* (London, 1935), pp. 9–10 and supplementary sheet.

20. Ibid., p. 21.
21. *Brighton and Hove Gazette*, 29 October & 5 November 1938.
22. *Chichester Observer*, 25 February 1939.
23. *Brighton and Hove Gazette*, 29 October 1938.
24. *Chichester Observer*, 25 February 1939.

# 4

# Air Raid Precautions

If a new European war broke out, a clear worst-case scenario existed for the south coast. This was invasion, with any number of beaches and undefended bays between the north shore of Kent and Southampton likely to be subjected to hostile attack. Yet it was not this which preoccupied the minds of those responsible for the defence of this area of the nation. Instead, overwhelming concern was directed towards that new weapon of war – the bomber.

In reflecting upon the experiences of the First World War, the bomber was not something to be totally ignored. After all, the south coast area had seen some of the worst raids of the war, both Chatham and Folkestone witnessing attacks that were especially devastating. Yet all sense of reality appears to have deserted those responsible for influencing public opinion. Instead of dwelling on the south coast as a possible future battleground – the actual and planned landing point for many past invaders – attention turned primarily to aerial bombardment. While an invading army would clearly devastate huge swathes of southern England, the maximum damage likely to be inflicted by bombing, although severe, would be relatively limited by comparison.

In part, the fear of aerial attacks was generated by a huge exaggerated belief in the power of the bomber and what it might achieve. This is not to say that aerial defence, both active and passive, should not have been developed, only that it should not have totally dominated the government's plans at the expense of defence against invasion. Nevertheless, while defence against air attack was much talked about, in reality surprisingly little was actually achieved.

Helping to bolster the fear of the bomber were a number of novels published during these years which often described, in graphic detail, the supposed effects of bombing. Most frequently, the object of these books was to reinforce the importance of peace by demonstrating the perceived nature of a future war. One such example was *Invasion from the Air* by Frank McIlraith and Roy Connolly. Subtitled *A Prophetic Novel* and published in 1934, it describes an attack on England by the combined air fleets of Germany and Italy. Kent, in particular, was marked down as receiving a number of raids:

> Over Woolwich, with the Arsenal as an objective [following an earlier raid on Gravesend], bombs were raining like hail … Nearer to the mouth of the river petrol storage-tanks [the Isle of Grain] were bursting, sending up thick plumes of heavy black smoke shot with crimson.[1]

Since London was the main target of these raids, large numbers fleeing the city looking for a safe haven would attempt to find this on the south coast. It was part of the scenario developed by McIlraith and Connolly:

> Along such highways as the Colchester, Canterbury and Brighton roads, the traffic swelled to torrents of vehicles. Over the fields tramped the pedestrian fugitives. Like a vast sack London was being emptied.[2]

According to an article published in the *Daily Telegraph*, and acknowledged by McIlraith and Connolly as an influence on their novel, it had been suggested that, following a series of intensive air raids, some 80 per cent of the population of the metropolis would have left the city within a week. In further developing this aspect of the future war, McIlraith and Connolly depicted a subsequent break-down in law and order:

> Towards evening, refugees, hungry themselves, but driven to desperation by cries of children, looted eggs, vegetables or anything else edible. Farmers who attempted to defend their property were attacked and roughly handled. They looked in vain for police protection.[3]

Other published 'future war' genre novels were *The Shape of Things to Come* (1933), *The Poison War* (1933), *The Black Death* (1934), *Menace* (1935), *Day of Wrath* (1936), *War Upon Women* (1934), *Chaos* (1938) and *Air Reprisal* (1938). Of these, it is possibly *The Black Death* that has a particularly frightening content, depicting a cloud of poison gas wiping out the entire population along the south coast, together with much of the rest of the country. However, it was H. G. Wells' *The Shape of Things to Come* which achieved a particularly wide audience, it being turned into a film and shown in cinemas along the south coast in March 1936. Taking a more encyclopaedic view of the world, Wells correctly predicted the cause of war as being a clash between Nazi Germany and Poland, with France and Russia also being drawn in. But he incorrectly predicted that Britain would remain neutral. As for the film, this vividly portrayed the gas bombing of civilians.

Reinforcing the believability of these novels was the ever-increasing use of air power against civilians in a series of widely reported events. Mussolini's illegal invasion of Abyssinia in 1935 involved the dropping of mustard gas on civilians and the systematic bombing of hospitals and Red Cross field units.[4] Similarly, in September 1937 the Japanese indiscriminately bombed the Chinese cities of Nanjing and Canton, with their bombers specifically targeting crowded railway stations and hospitals. Most infamous, if only because it received greater publicity, was the bombing of Guernica, an ancient Basque town, by the aircraft of both Hitler's Condor Legion and Mussolini's Aviazione Legionaria. Carried out in April 1937, the atrocity was not only widely reported in newspapers, but was the subject of a great deal of film footage that made its way into British cinemas. Certainly by the second week of May 1937, there would have been few filmgoers in the major towns of the south coast who would not have seen a Gaumont newsreel that told of hundreds of men, women and children being killed in the raid. According to the commentary, 'four thousand bombs were dropped out of a blue sky into a hell that raged unchecked for five murderous hours'. And just to underline the point, viewers were reminded that 'this was a city and these were homes, like yours'.

Neville Shute, who we first met as a soldier defending the beaches of north Kent during the final year of the First World War, was one who was aware of the bomber's increasing use against civilians. Himself a popular writer, with a string of novels to his name, Shute chose to add to that growing list of future war novels. In *What Happened to the Corbetts* he concentrated on one particular family, looking at how they would survive the problems of being bombed out of their home. Written in 1938, the book focused entirely on south coast England. Indeed, Shute felt that this would be the focal point of any war, with nightly bombing raids upon major towns of the area. Among these he certainly included Chatham and Portsmouth, together with their naval dockyards, and the larger south coast resort towns like Brighton.

The plight of the Corbett family, who lived in Southampton, is of seminal importance in its realistic demonstration of the need to protect the civilian population better in the event of war. Unlike other books, and most of what was being written in the press, this gave much closer consideration to how the infrastructure of a city would stand up to heavy aerial bombardment. At that point in time, with the real war against Germany less than a year away, Shute has the Corbetts hurriedly creating their own air-raid shelter by digging a trench in the garden and quickly assembling a small stockpile of tinned products. Other than that, Peter Corbett is uncertain as to exactly what he should do:

> Like most Englishmen of that time, he had read something about Air Raid Precautions in the newspapers. He knew, vaguely, that he has been advised to make a gas proof room, and he knew with certainty that he had done nothing about it. There had been something about buckets of sand for incendiary bombs, and something about oilskin suits for mustard gas. And there had been a great deal about gas masks – in newspapers at any rate.[5]

As for those gas masks, a man wearing a Civil Defence armlet supplied them on the day following the raid:

'Gas masks,' he said. 'How many in your household?' There was a lorry going down the street, with men going from house to house.

'Good work,' Corbett said, impressed. 'There's my wife and myself, and three children.'

'How old are the children?'

'Six and three. And a baby.'

The man went back to the lorry, and returned with the masks. 'Here you are – be careful of them. Don't use them unless the gas is really there. When you've used them for ten hours, come to the Civic Centre and exchange them for fresh ones. There. One large for you, one medium for your wife, and two small ones for the children. We can't do nothing for the baby.'[6]

Upon being questioned as to how they were to protect the baby, Corbett was informed that it would be necessary to create a gas-proof room. Given that the house in which the Corbetts were living, in the Portswood area of Southampton, had already received extensive bomb damage, Corbett replied:

'That's not so easy, with the windows in this state.'

'I know. You might be able to screen off a bit of the cellar with wet blankets, or something of that.'[7]

As the raids continued, more and more of the local roads became unusable, electricity and gas supplies were lost throughout the city and instructions were issued for the boiling of water following damage to both the mains and sewage piping. In turn, local medical centres were unable to keep abreast of the number of casualties needing hospitalisation, while the breakdown in the sewage system led to serious health problems. Corbett learnt of this last problem when talking to his neighbour, Mr Littlejohn:

'You've heard the news?'

'No,' said Corbett.

'Cholera,' said Mr Littlejohn.

Corbett stared at him wide-eyed.

'There's been an outbreak of cholera, down Northam way. Over seventy cases, so they say. They've got patrols on the roads. Nobody's got to leave the city till he's been inoculated.'[8]

Within the city, the availability of anti-cholera vaccine was insufficient to meet the demand, with a surgeon friend telling Corbett: 'But keep it under your hat and don't go spreading it around. We don't want to start a panic or anything like that.'[9]

The publishers, William Heinmann Ltd, on bringing out *What Happened to the Corbetts* in April 1939, also distributed a thousand free presentation copies to workers involved in Air Raid Precautions. This tied in closely with Shute's motive for writing the book. Through the work of his wife, a doctor of medicine who was working with local authorities to prepare them for gas attacks, he felt that there was an inadequate awareness of what really might happen. Indeed, he questioned the emphasis that was being placed on gas and felt that more attention should be given to the effects of high-explosive bombs. These, apart from destroying considerable areas of housing, would also break open sewage and water pipes.

Shute, in common with other 'future war' writers, was not particularly realistic with his description of what would happen to the south coast in the event of war. Nowhere in the world at that time was there a nation with an air force of sufficient strength to carry out a series of nightly raids that would see such a level of devastation over such a wide area. As an aeronautical engineer and a director of Airspeed, an aviation company based at Portsmouth, Shute must have known this. However, in writing the book his point was not to discuss the potential might of one country over another, but to highlight the inadequacies of passive defence. From this point of view, a certain amount of exaggeration becomes acceptable. In taking Southampton, he admitted that he had no great knowledge of the city, but he wanted to give a real example 'of what may be coming to us'. His book, therefore, was directed towards those officials who ran that city, or indeed any city on the south coast, who were responsible for protecting the citizens in the event of a raid. Of those particular officials in Southampton, Shute specifically stated in the epilogue to his book:

> Your Mayor and your Town Clerk will be grieved with me, your Medical Officer of Health will be a very angry man, and your Engineers of Electricity, Gas, Sewage, Telephone and Water – especially Water – will be considering what action they had better take.[10]

The attention that Shute gives to borough officials needs some explanation. Quite simply, the government had devolved matters relating to Air Raid Precaution into the hands of second-tier authorities – the borough and district councils. This had resulted from a proposal made by a government subcommittee that had been first established in May 1924. The purpose of this subcommittee had been to look into the whole issue of ARP, a matter of concern following the air raids of the First World War. In particular it gave attention to the prevention of damage, provision of shelters and gas masks, together with plans for evacuating areas vulnerable to bombing. Chaired by Sir John Anderson, Permanent Under-Secretary of State at the Home Office, it seems to have reached a conclusion at a fairly early stage that local authorities would be best suited to undertaking this role, with the government providing the necessary support and encouragement. However, this was not communicated to those various authorities until July 1935, when a fairly innocuous circular was issued.

As no form of consultation with the authorities had preceded the arrival of this circular and no reference had been made to a financial settlement, few chose to give any detailed consideration to the content of the memorandum or heed its message. Further discouraging the authorities from spending out on Civil Defence schemes was the fact that legally they were not financially empowered to do so, the authorities being strictly controlled on exactly where money raised from rates might be directed. Despite the declining international situation, which the government was more than aware of, nothing was done to remedy this situation for exactly two years. In July 1937 the Local Authority Association, which acted as the voice of the local government sector, was invited to confer with the Home Secretary on the financing of ARP schemes. Out of these talks emerged the Air Raid Precaution Act, passed by Parliament in December 1937, which provided both the necessary legal authority and a £2 million pot of money that was to be made available in the form of grants for suitable local Civil Defence schemes.

An immediate consequence of the nation's 1,440 authorities all being given responsibility for Civil Defence was the dramatic growth in red tape and bureaucracy. In fact, it created an organisational explosion. At the pinnacle of this empire was a new government department with twelve regional offices, while at a more local level a new administrative branch had to be created within each and every local authority. As for the new government department, an outgrowth of the Home Office, this was the Ministry of Home Security, which had as its sole purpose the overseeing of all local Civil Defence schemes. For purposes of keeping its eye on developments along the south coast, the two significant regions of the new ministry, each headed by a separate commissioner, were Southern (No 6 Region) and South Eastern (No 12 Region). Whereas the former, with its head office in Reading, took in the east Hampshire littoral, the latter, with its office in Tunbridge Wells, was responsible for the whole Kent and Sussex coastlines.

The second-tier authorities along the south coast were encouraged to develop their own individual air-raid schemes from July 1935 onwards. Included within such schemes was a plan for protecting the public through the creation of a coherent Air Raid Precaution service, and for the integration of other existing emergency services. Within this plan, thought was to be given to the need for air-raid shelters and the supply of gas masks, together with the sufficiency of hospitals and medical care, and the availability of emergency housing and coffins required for the resulting fatalities. Attention would also have to be given to the co-ordination of police, ambulance and fire services, as well as those bodies responsible for maintaining and repairing the infrastructure of the borough. In any air raid, such essential facilities as gas, electricity and water supplies were likely to be affected, while roads and railway lines would also be damaged. Collectively, the combination of all these services, when directed to the defence of a borough against an air raid, was known as Civil Defence.

Upon being advised in July 1935 of their new responsibilities, few councils chose to react. Having neither the finances nor the expertise, most ignored the requirement for as long as possible. In Portsmouth, it was not until January 1937 that the city council appointed a committee to even consider the matter, while an ARP officer and chief air-raid warden were not to be appointed until the following year. Nevertheless, one of the city's officers, Stephen Allchurch, the superintendent of the Transport and Cleansing Department, did choose to pursue his own independent line, converting one of the city council refuse-collecting lorries into a fire-fighting and gas decontamination unit. Unveiled at the central depot in June 1936 to delegates of the Institute of Public Cleansing, the vehicle had been converted to carry water and, through the addition of suitable machinery, could pump this water through hosepipes and jets. As the City Corporation itself recorded:

> During experiments, water had been played to a height of 60 feet. The mobility of the vehicle, it is claimed, would enable it to proceed quickly from one fire to another, while other equipment would enable it to spray the roads and houses and thus act as a gas decontaminator.[11]

Although seeming somewhat unorthodox, the experiment became a model for a number of south coast authorities, with several boroughs choosing to similarly convert refuse lorries.

Elsewhere, and lacking the forethought of their own sanitation departments, most key south coast authorities, including Sheerness, Brighton and the Thanet Towns, continued to drag their feet, all failing to make key ARP appointments until 1937. Indeed, without the necessary finances and legislative support there is little that such officers could have done. Instead, those various authorities simply contented themselves with acting as government megaphones, through which government advice was usually disseminated. As a result, posters and leaflets were circulated in abundance advising on what to do in the event of a gas attack or how to protect houses against blast and splinter from bombs. The effect was negligible.

Peter Corbett, in the Shute novel, admits that he had read and basically discarded such information. He was far from unique. In a survey carried out by the *Kentish Express* in September 1938, few of its readers appeared any more knowledgeable. Most could not even remember receiving any of the numerous leaflets that had been distributed, or showed any real interest. A resident from Saltwood, near Folkestone, proclaimed: 'I have received no instruction whatever. If a raid occurred, I should send all my household staff into the woods with the orders to scatter.' From Hythe, a mother of a young family admitted: 'We were all measured for gas masks but beyond that I know nothing.' Others were simply complacent. A Whitstable resident felt that he did not need to worry, as 'they didn't bomb [Whitstable] in the last war'; while in Dymchurch, another man reported that an ARP meeting was meant to have been held by the parish council but nobody attended.[12]

A south coast defence exercise held in July 1937 served as the first real proof of how little had been achieved since the issuing of that first circular some two years earlier. Although primarily a military exercise in which the cities of Portsmouth and Southampton were to be attacked by the hostile forces of a notional 'Blueland', it was also decided to test out the Air Raid Precaution schemes along this area of the coastline. One ward in Portsmouth and two in Southampton were chosen for full dress rehearsals, but the whole of the Hampshire coast and the Isle of Wight were voluntarily darkened between midnight and 3 a.m. on the night of 16 July. On hand to observe events was a reporter from *Flight* magazine:

> I elected to visit Portsmouth, and at midnight officials of the A.R.P. Department conducted a party of privileged spectators, including many Chief Constables, from the Guildhall to the scenes of damage and tragedy. Actually six exercises, or tableaux as they were called, were carried through in Portsmouth that night, and others in Southampton, but in the time it was only possible to visit two.

Of the drive through Portsmouth that night, the invited reporter was clearly impressed:

> Having been severely raided and shelled that morning, the good people of the city were very air-raid-conscious, and practically all householders had darkened their houses completely. Only one shop, where there was a sale of ladies' underclothing on, had its electric lights in full blast. There was no traffic in the streets except our two omnibuses and a few cars of people connected with the exercises, and they were feeling their way along with only sidelights showing.[13]

Claimed as a particularly spectacular incident was the exploding of a high-explosive bomb, which supposedly made a crater of 15ft in diameter; it damaged gas and water mains, and sewage pipes, and set fire to an adjoining house. Repair squads were summoned, and first-aid and ambulance parties dealt with a total of twelve 'casualties'. Given that the fear at this time was a massive series of air raids that might continue for several weeks, the ability of Portsmouth to meet such a raid was far from proven. Nevertheless, Sir Samuel Hoare, the Home Secretary, in attending the exercise, congratulated 'Portsmouth and Southampton upon being two of the pioneer municipalities in this work. Their example, I am sure, will be followed by other cities of the country, and I offer my thanks to all those who helped make the exercise useful.'[14]

More realistically, he should have commented on an even greater number of shortcomings that included a complete lack of public air-raid shelters, the unavailability of gas masks and a combined Civil Defence and casualty evacuation service that numbered no more than 500 volunteers. Furthermore, these were issues to which local authorities would soon find themselves having to give greater attention following legislation that would be introduced over the next two years.

The increasing interest being taken in Civil Defence, although relatively low key when compared with the post-Munich crisis period, can be seen from the inclusion of that particular coastal defence exercise in a contemporary children's novel, *Winged Might*. Written by Percy F. Westerman, a writer of stories for older boys, the heroes of the book, Alleyne and Frayne, are on a yachting holiday and are temporarily moored in Tipner Lake on the north-east side of Portsmouth Harbour; from here they observe the blackout:

> Thousands of feet above the ground a pale bluish light was slowly dropping. Almost immediately a score of searchlights was switched on.
>
> High above the city [of Portsmouth], unseen and unheard, a squadron of raiding aircraft had pierced the aerial defences. The dropping of that blue light was the signal to the squadron commander that, in theory, a hail of bombs had been released upon the first naval port of the British Empire.
>
> 'They were through that time,' remarked Alleyne thoughtfully. 'Altitude gives them immunity; but it's a dead certainty that in the real thing most of those bombs would fall, not on the dockyard, but on the town. The search-lights seem useless.'
>
> 'Worse than that, I should say,' added Frayne. 'The raiders have only to take up position towards the centre of the ring of searchlights and they know they are over their objective.'[15]

In the event, Westerman, a former Portsmouth dockyard clerk, was chillingly correct in his prediction as to the likely outcome of future air raids on the dockyard: in the coming Blitz, many houses near to the dockyard were destroyed by bombs falling 'not on the dockyard, but on the nearby town'.

Of particular importance, and something to which the second-tier authorities were ideally suited to achieve, was the recruiting of volunteer air-raid wardens. They were to be the backbone of borough ARP schemes, available to help, assist and advise, both before, during and after air raids. Although the role of ARP wardens had been under general discussion from the early 1930s, the government did not officially unveil the concept until the beginning of 1937, with further details included in that year's Air Raid Precautions Act. At that time, local authorities were required to recruit and train some 800,000 volunteers into the role. To oversee the work of wardens, each borough was to appoint a chief warden, with the authority divided into sectors that would each be under the control of an area warden. The initial requirement was one ARP warden for every 500 residents of a borough, and the individual wardens were to operate from designated posts. At these posts would be stationed a post warden, to whom all incidents and requirements to meet these incidents were to be reported. The ARP warden, of course, was the man on the ground. Their training included rescue work, organisation, first aid and bomb-protection procedures. They also had a number of additional roles such as the enforcement of blackouts and the overseeing of public shelters.

As with much else connected with the development of ARP schemes in the period immediately before the Munich crisis, local authorities viewed the recruitment of wardens as less than urgent. Portsmouth, for its part, was not inclined to appoint a chief air raid warden until early 1938, as was the case with Sheerness, the various Medway authorities and Brighton. This was partly due to a desire not to panic members of the public, but it also meant a call on local resources, which was considered best to delay. Inevitably, this further impeded the recruitment of wardens and their subsequent training. Many south coast authorities were certainly reporting a huge shortfall in the numbers they had actually recruited, which proved especially serious in September 1938 when there was a clear belief that the nation would soon be at war. Gillingham, one of those three Medway boroughs without a chief warden, needed over 600 more volunteers to bring its numbers up to strength, while Lewes in Sussex was recording a shortfall of 100.

The provision of gas masks, noted to be lacking for the citizens of Portsmouth in that ARP exercise of July 1937, was something that the government had technically already solved. Indeed, it was possibly the one area that was completely resolved, millions of gas masks having already been manufactured and held in storage. Although gas had been used on the Western Front in the First World War, it had subsequently been prohibited under the Geneva Protocol that had come into force in 1926. Nevertheless, Italy, seen as a potential future enemy, had since deployed mustard gas during its illegal invasion of Abyssinia through both aerial bombardment and specially designed artillery shell canisters. It was therefore possible that Germany, too, might unleash the weapon in a future war.

To meet this possibility, and even before its use in Abyssinia, the government had utilised the Porton Down chemical research laboratory to design what became known as the General Civilian Respirator. With manufacturing beginning in 1936, the respirators were at that time placed into storage to be issued when the time came. By September 1938, a total of 38 million had been manufactured, with most of these distributed to borough ARP sections for distribution to the public. In the south coast counties, something approaching 3 million were to be distributed; but, as noted by Shute in his novel, nothing was available for young children.[16] Instead, as Peter Corbett was informed, a gas-proof room had to be created. Only in September 1939, a few weeks after war had actually been declared, were suitable masks available for babies and very young children.

Generally, it has to be said that with the government handing over direct responsibility for Civil Defence to towns and boroughs, it was creating a problem rather than solving one. With most boroughs of a fairly diminutive size, it led to that huge outgrowth of bureaucracy that has already been described. More forethought would certainly have curbed this outcome through encouraging authorities to work together or making the higher-tier authority, the county councils, ultimately responsible for Civil Defence.

A classic example of where unification of a Civil Defence programme would certainly have reaped great benefits was with regard to the Medway Towns, home to a particularly important naval dockyard and a likely target for bombers. Here, three relatively small metropolitan boroughs, those of Rochester, Chatham and Gillingham, were nestled so closely together as to be indistinguishable from each other. However, when calls were made for these three boroughs to work together, zealous councillors, tied to the concept of the parish-pump, quickly overruled such ideas. In February 1938 a scheme mooted to employ just one chief ARP officer to oversee the three boroughs was soundly rejected, leading to each of these boroughs creating their own separate departments, each with their own chiefs. In Chatham, one councillor who despaired of this arrangement put it all into a nutshell: 'history is still repeating itself; we are still worshipping our parish-pump and will have nothing to do with our neighbours'.[17]

Yet in the joining together of the three towns, an ideal unit for Civil Defence planning would have been created. All three towns were part of the same military-industrial complex that was supported by a large workforce whose homes straddled the area. Irrespective of whether these workers and their families lived in Rochester, Chatham or Gillingham, all had needs that were exactly the same and their chances of getting bombed only differed according to their proximity to the naval dockyard or the factories of the Short Brothers.

The Medway Towns also serve to illustrate a further problem in regard to this disorganised approach to Civil Defence. Whereas Rochester, due to it possessing a number of wealthier middle-class houses, was able to raise a significant sum from the rates, this was not the case for poorer, working-class Chatham. As a result, Rochester, when pushed to act by the Munich crisis, was able to develop a scheme that required an expenditure of £25,000. Incorporated into this were the acquisition of land for fixed ARP posts and the purchase of buses for conversion into emergency first-aid mobile units. Neighbouring Chatham, on the other hand, which possessed a much less wealthy base but a greater population, could only afford an expenditure of £5,000. For this sum, Chatham was able to provide itself with forty-five street surface shelters. In theory, a more equitable distribution of expenditure would have been more appropriate.

Throughout the south coast area, there were authorities that would have benefited from shared Civil Defence links, resulting in efficiency savings and ensuring a fairer distribution of monies available. The Isle of Sheppey, a significant target because of its dockyard together with a military airfield at Eastchurch, was divided into three Civil Defence authorities: Sheerness, Queenborough and a rural district council. In the council chamber of the island's rural authority, which was responsible for the entire island outside of Sheerness and Queenborough, the arguments against a triple-zone authority were carefully rehearsed in April 1939. As one councillor noted:

> They had one medical officer [for the entire island]. Why three ARP offi-cers? They would certainly have one man in charge in wartime. They had three officers receiving three lots of letters on the same subject, and with so much overlapping he considered they should appeal for a united policy for the entire island.[18]

To this was added the comments of a further councillor, who felt it was 'abso-lutely ridiculous' to have three ARP officers for such a small island and each receiving an annual salary of £250.[19]

Adding a further level of Civil Defence bureaucracy, and to be added to the newly created Ministry of Home Security and its regional administrators, was that of the county councils also being given a range of responsibilities. In fact, it was often not clear as to where the role of one authority began and the other ended. However, it certainly made sense for the county councils to be involved, given that they were already responsible for a number of strategic services that had Civil Defence implications, including public health, policing and education. Indeed, it might well have made sense for the county councils to be given overall authority, so eliminating the need for each borough to have separate and expen-sively trained ARP officers.

Instead, the county authorities were simply forced to create their own sepa-rate bureaucracies that overlaid those which had been created by the boroughs. In Kent, this took the form of dividing the county into six areas, each with its own officer and a typist. Interestingly, and recognising the strong need to create greater unity in particular areas, the Way ARP division amalgamated the entirety of Sheppey, Medway and Sittingbourne – a move that, in itself, made a great deal of sense. Within this division, ten authorities continued to work their own separate pathway, each incensed by the idea of co-operating with their immediate neighbour. Rev. Morgan, an elected Kent county councillor, simply stated the obvious when he observed: 'I think we are going to have more organisation than output.'[20]

A clear example of where the newly created bureaucratic structure lacked the ability to seek out cost-effective solutions was with regard to air-raid shelters. Along the entire south coast, the county authorities for Kent, Hampshire, the Isle of Wight and East and West Sussex pursued a programme of building air-raid shelters within school premises. For Kent it required an overall expenditure of £100,000. Available for all children and teachers while within the grounds of the school, they were entirely unavailable for these same individuals once the schools were closed in the evenings and at weekends. Seemingly, the county authority was responsible for children and teachers if it was a weekday raid but not if the sirens sounded after 4 p.m.

Health and the evacuation of casualties was another area of bureaucratic confusion that was not helped by the creation of second-tier councils by the primary Civil Defence authority. In particular, this was because the boundaries of these authorities did not line up with those of the health authorities. Instead, and this was not until early 1939, emergency medical facilities and the provision of ambulances was transferred to the Ministry of Health. Although this was to reap a number of benefits during the period of the war, it saw no real expansion of hospital facilities prior to September 1939. In Hastings, the only way to ensure a sufficiency of space upon the declaration of war was through the process of removing 400 existing patients to their homes. Even this made little impact, as 180 of those spaces were immediately taken up by stretcher cases evacuated into the area from London. Other hospitals along the south coast witnessed similar use of their ward space, thereby creating accommodation in London hospitals for those who might become victims if the capital was bombed. This, of course, was no comfort for those living on the coast if they too were subject to a bombing raid. As for the additional personnel who would be needed to work in these hospitals, a register was compiled of those who would be willing to serve. The procedure adopted was later explained by the then Minister of Health, Walter Elliott:

> In August [1939], before the war, the register covered 10,000 trained nurses, 4,000 assistant nurses, and 55,000 auxiliaries (14,000 trained). By 1940 the numbers were 15,000 trained nurses, 6,500 assistant nurses, and 100,000 auxiliaries (26,000 trained). This figure includes 12,000 members of the St John Ambulance Brigade and the British Red Cross Society who had already received training from those bodies.[21]

In terms of providing training opportunities, the involvement of county councils was especially important. In March 1936 attention in Kent had turned to the danger of gas bombing, with the county hall in Maidstone hosting a training course. Those present, of which there were over a hundred and many of whom had drawn from the coastal boroughs, were to return to their respective authorities and set up their own training courses. In that same year, and as part of the concern that gas might be used in aerial attacks, Kent County Council oversaw the setting up of specialised facilities in the county police station at Ramsgate, which was used as a countywide training facility. Following the Munich crisis, and the realisation that insufficient numbers of ARP wardens were being recruited, Kent County Council began a cross-county National Service Committee that had as its objective the stimulation of recruitment into both military and Civil

Defence organisations, and the provision of impartial advice. It was chaired by the Marquis of Camden, who accepted that 'the crisis of last September' had revealed 'some serious shortages in volunteers', with the committee designed to 'bring numbers up to strength'.[22]

Indeed, it was the Munich crisis that was to radically alter attitudes towards ARP and Civil Defence in general. Prior to 1938, most were aware of the dangers of bombing, but few individuals or authorities were prepared to commit to the necessary actions that would help reduce death and injury during a sustained bombing campaign. From September 1938 onwards, only eleven months away from the outbreak of a second twentieth-century pan-European war, the needs of south coast Civil Defence schemes began to be prioritised.

## Notes

1.  Frank McIlraith & Roy Connolly, *Invasion From the Air: a Prophetic Novel* (London, 1934), p. 119. There were several petrol storage tanks on the Isle of Grain.
2.  Ibid., p. 289.
3.  Ibid., p. 247.
4.  Ian Patterson, *Guernica and Total War* (London, 2007), p. 122.
5.  Neville Shute, *What Happened to the Corbetts* (London, 1938), p. 9.
6.  Ibid., pp. 31–2.
7.  Ibid., p. 32.
8.  Ibid., p. 57.
9.  Ibid., p. 69.
10. Ibid., p. 234.
11. V. Blanchard (ed.), *Records of the Corporation* (Portsmouth, nd), p. 15.
12. *Kentish Express*, 30 September 1938.
13. *Flight* magazine, 22 July 1937, p. 96.
14. Blanchard, op. cit., p. 15.
15. Percy F. Westerman, *Winged Might* (Blackie & Sons Ltd, 1937), p. 77.
16. The Air Raid Precautions handbook, issued by the Home Office in March 1938, addressed the lack of masks for children with the simple phrase: 'a special means of protection will be provided'. Given that it was far from being available at the time of the Munich crisis, and not even available on the outbreak of war, this must have been most reassuring.
17. *Chatham News*, 11 March 1938.
18. Ibid., 14 April 1939.
19. Ibid.
20. Ibid., 19 May 1939.
21. Walter Elliott, 'Medicine and the State', in *British Medical Journal*, 29 December 1945, p. 434.
22. *Chatham News*, 17 February 1939.

# 5

# Trenches, Sirens & Blackouts:
# The Munich Crisis

On his return from Munich on 30 September 1938, Prime Minister Neville Chamberlain, while waving his famous scrap of paper, uttered the words: 'I have returned from Germany with peace in our time.' Later that same day, he not only reiterated these same words but also recommended to an assembled crowd waiting in Downing Street, 'to go home and sleep quietly in your beds'. Ultimately, of course, Chamberlain had bought, at some cost to the Czechoslovakian nation, a mere eleven months of peace, with the invasion of Poland eventually bringing Britain and Germany into a situation of total war. While the Civil Defence and military preparations that had been spurred by the crisis of that September were now abruptly curbed, this work did not cease. Britain, as a result of the crisis, had finally realised that it was not well prepared for the future war, which was now seen as all but inevitable. The belief held by increasing numbers was that Hitler would make further claims on Europe and that continued appeasement would only encourage his ambitions. If nothing else, Munich had bought just a sufficiency of time to ramp up the country's readiness for war.

The one thing that the month of September 1938 had demonstrated was that despite several years of planning, Britain's Civil Defence was in no position to meet the devastation that might be inflicted by German air raids. The tardiness of the government was primarily to blame, having only given second-tier authorities full sanction to spend money and apply for grants at the beginning of that same year. Faced with the possibility of imminent war, and with the fear of air raids suddenly uppermost in the minds of those who lived on the south coast, panic set in. Instead of being able to turn to a carefully honed plan of Civil Defence, the authorities were forced into a knee-jerk reaction. Along the south coast, each and every borough was suddenly directing its manual workforce, often joined by older schoolboys as in the case of Hastings, to the construction of slit trenches, the erection of sandbag blast walls and the distribution of gas masks.

In Chatham, to take a fairly typical example, it was reported: 'The authorities have commenced an extensive programme of trench construction in selected portions of the area [Chatham], more than 700 unemployed labourers being engaged to assist in the work of excavation.'[1]

To this it was added: 'The trenches are constructed in a zigzag plan, and vary in size according to the ground available. When completed they will be protected by some form of covering.'[2]

In contrast with the *Chatham News*, which provided considerable detail, the *Kentish Express*, which reported happenings on the south coast of Kent, adopted a more reserved approach to what it was prepared to tell its readers, concerned that such information might get into the hands of the enemy:

> The highest authority are against any press reference to the location where trenches are being made against air raids, and for that reason the *Kentish Express* is giving no pictures or referring to gas mask distribution. No one knows what future value this information may be to an enemy. But we can assure our readers that during the past few days those who are responsible for war preparations have not been idle. The protection of our historical buildings has not been lost sight of. We must wait to see, but it is for everybody's sake that we keep cool and feel every confidence in those who are at the head of affairs.[3]

The efficiency of local authorities along the south coast varied greatly, with some carrying out a rapid construction of slit trenches and making air-raid shelter arrangements, while others appear to have done very little. Some residents of Hythe and Lydd seemingly felt that their respective authorities fell into the latter group. On being interviewed by the *Kentish Express* at the time of the Munich crisis, a shop assistant from Lydd forthrightly stated:

> Months ago they came and asked us how many gas masks we should need, but they haven't been near us since. And it's about time that Lydd ARP woke up, because bombs were dropped within three miles of us in the last war. They have given no instruction to the civil population.[4]

To this, a young mother from Hythe felt able to add: 'We all measured up for gas masks but beyond that I know nothing.'[5]

In Worthing, criticism of local ARP arrangements went considerably further than a few random comments to a local newspaper. While the Munich crisis was at its height, a *Worthing Gazette* columnist, using the pseudonym 'Trifler', admitted the town to be 'definitely slow in these matters' and called for the digging of tunnels in the Downs. Elsewhere, and in the same edition, it was noted that little had been done in the town to develop an ARP fire-fighting service, the town having few volunteers and lacking equipment. In October, with the crisis out of the way, the *Worthing Gazette* was inundated with letters criticising the poor response of the council. Among the first letters to be published was one from the town's chief ARP warden, Commander E.M. Lockwood, accusing the council of having no interest in the matter:

> A very large number of aldermen and councillors have not the slightest knowl-
> edge of what the ARP scheme is or what it means to the safety of the town in
> case of an air raid. We have had in our office to all intents and purposes no visits
> or enquiries from members of the council as to the true purpose of the ARP
> department here in Worthing.

Other correspondents to the *Gazette*, in supporting Lockwood, indicated that several months prior to the September crisis they had attempted to enrol as war-dens but had received nothing more than a letter from the town clerk thanking them for their interest. A further correspondent even went so far as to suggest that because of the lack of any initial planning, the sum of £4,500 spent by the council during those crisis weeks was nothing less than wasted money. To this end, therefore, he suggested that those on the council should be surcharged, forcing them to pay this money out of their own pockets.[6]

Herne Bay was another council heavily criticised for its ARP arrangements, the local Residents' Association accusing members of the Herne Bay Urban District Council of doing little in comparison to other authorities. In particular, it was noted that the Herne Bay ARP Committee failed to meet at any time during the crisis, that a full inventory of gas mask needs had not been under-taken and that no attempt was made to construct new shelters. Undoubtedly, what lay behind Herne Bay's shortcomings, together with those of Worthing, was its failure to appoint a specialised officer, all ARP work falling upon an already over-burdened clerk of the council. To underline its criticisms, the Herne Bay Residents' Association pointed to the nearby authority of Deal, indicating that this authority had got things right and should be looked to as a model that Herne Bay might follow.

At the time of the Munich crisis, Deal certainly appeared to have achieved for itself a reputation of excellence. Of particular significance was its appointment of a chief ARP officer. Few other towns had such an officer, allowing Deal to put in place, at a much earlier stage than other authorities, a skeletal ARP organisation that worked reasonably efficiently. Beyond this, however, the town was little better prepared than the rest of the south coast. What made the difference was having an administrative structure already in place, which meant that the digging of public shelters and trenches, together with the distribution of 25,000 gas masks, went ahead with greater rapidity than in many boroughs. In addition, the Deal ARP Committee was able to undertake a survey of cellars beneath public buildings, with decisions taken as to which would prove suitable for air raid purposes. In particular, people living near Walmer and Deal castles were informed that these could be used in the event of an air raid. Although well short of what would be required on the outbreak of war, the *East Kent Mercury* was quite happy to flag up the achievements of Deal, claiming that the town 'has not in vain boasted one of the best organisations for Air Raid Precautions in the country'.[7]

Perhaps it was the issuing of gas masks that really demonstrated the amateurish approach taken by a number of south coast authorities at the time of the crisis. Although the distribution of masks from regional storage centres to boroughs was conducted with reasonable efficiency, few boroughs had a plan for their assembly and onward distribution. With regard to assembling the masks, the face piece had to be attached to a metal container using special tools. A time-consuming task, it required the rapid recruitment of volunteers, often achieved through the use of loudspeaker vans touring the various streets. In Hastings, volunteers assembled the masks at the municipal bathing pool; in Herne Bay, the Pier Pavilion at Kings Hall; in Folkestone they were assembled by shop assistants from some of the large stores in the town, and on the Isle of Wight, assembly was at the old Electric Lights Work at Skew Bridge.

The council at Worthing, however, already heavily criticised, took an approach that almost beggars belief. Rather than call for volunteers, they imposed the work on schoolboys, who were drawn from a local school and taken to the hastily designated ARP headquarters at Beach House. Due to the lack of wardens, there was no one to supervise them, leading to a scene of absolute chaos. As one potential ARP volunteer recorded, on visiting Beach House: 'crowds of boys [were] throwing empty gas mask cases from the first floor at boys on the ground floor.' Assuredly, it was this approach to the assembly of the gas masks that resulted in a demand for all respirators in Worthing to be recalled due to them being 'in a very poor condition'.[8]

Southampton was another authority that viewed itself as particularly advanced in ARP matters, described by Bernard Knowles in an official wartime history of the city as 'a model of its kind'.[9] With Neville Shute having already used the city as a generic example of just how little had been achieved by late 1938, it is valuable to look at Southampton in reality. Shute, in *Whatever Happened to the Corbetts*, noted the existence of a partially developed ARP organisation and a citizenry that was fundamentally confused as to how they should react under bombardment. In addition, little had been done to expand the workforce or resources of those who would be responsible for the repair of roads or the maintenance of water, gas and electricity supplies. Finally, Shute describes a complete breakdown of the town's medical services: the hospital unable to cope with the number of casualties and those made sick by a subsequent outbreak of cholera.

While those responsible for organising the city's Civil Defence scheme were scathing in their criticism of the novel, it seems clear that Shute was fundamentally correct in his description of Southampton at this time. All that the city had achieved by the time of the Munich crisis, and coincidentally the time of the book being written, was a workable organisational structure. Since 1936, an ARP co-ordinating officer had been in place, with a medical officer for ARP casualties appointed two years later. While numerous wardens had also been appointed, both their numbers and levels of training were inadequate. As part of its pre-war planning, the city had been divided into three Civil Defence zones (western, central and eastern) and sites selected for a number of planned warden posts. Only in one respect had the city authorities excelled themselves, and that was with regard to the new Civic Centre, which began construction during the 1930s and contained an underground (and presumably bombproof) central control room for those responsible for managing ARP services during an air raid.

In general, and with the exception of the control room, the City Corporation had given little thought to the physical protection of the citizenry, to the expansion of the essential maintenance and repair services or to the provision of an adequate ARP team. Only through the shock of the Munich crisis did Southampton even begin to get to grips with the situation, the long-delayed warden posts mostly constructed by August 1939 and a War Emergency Committee established four months earlier. However, it was all too little too late. The war that was declared in September 1939 left the city fathers with too much still to do.

When the raids eventually came, during the autumn and winter of 1940, Shute was again proven correct as to the level of destruction that would be inflicted upon the city. Among the worst was a six-hour blitz on the night of 30 November/1 December 1940, leaving the city with 137 dead, 250 seriously injured and 1,169 properties destroyed. Bernard Knowles attempted to describe the scene that was revealed on the morning of 2 December:

> The town itself presented a grievous spectacle. A reeking mass of calcined brick and blackened stone, it had become a smouldering catacomb. Traces of the tremendous struggle were everywhere visible. It was as though the town had been the victim of a savage and brutal assassination. Every thoroughfare was blocked – actually thirty were completely impassable – by fallen buildings. Many were still blazing. The water shortage – seventy-four mains had been brought out of action – had long ago precluded any real hope of saving them.[10]

Unquestionably, the number of deaths and the extent of the damage would have been considerably reduced if Southampton had been better prepared and better served. In a visit made to the city three days after the weekend blitz, Wing Commander E.J. Hodsoll, Inspector-General of ARP, was heavily critical of how the city was organised. In particular, he highlighted internal petty jealousies that prevented departments from working together, while naming a number of officials whom he viewed as unsuitable for the tasks they undertook. Among these were both the chief constable and the town clerk, and he particularly castigated the mayor, who he described as 'a poor creature' whose 'sole concern was to be out of town as soon as possible in the afternoon'.

So serious was the situation in Southampton that at Whitehall's insistence, responsibility for ARP was taken out of the hands of the corporation and handed over to the regional ARP control centre based in Reading. As for the effect of the raids on those living in Southampton, foreshadowed by Peter Corbett who took his family to Bursledon, countless numbers, seemingly led by the mayor, fled to the safety of the countryside. Many were so totally demoralised that they were recorded in the files of the Mass Observation organisation as sharing 'a fairly general feeling that Southampton was done for'.[11]

It was the Munich crisis that destroyed the earlier complacency towards Civil Defence. Most authorities attempted to improve upon what they had already started. Some went considerably further, while others, such as Southampton, continued to make heightened, if still limited, progress. But the real point was that few authorities were to be put to the test in the way that Southampton was, and, because of this, other south coast schemes were rarely to be found wanting.

The first sign of a real change following the Munich crisis was the dramatic increase in the number of volunteers joining the Civil Defence organisations. In addition, the general attitude of ordinary members of the public rapidly changed. An ARP warden in Brighton had found that in early 1938, when collecting information about gas mask needs, the public had been far from sympathetic: 'When we began our house-to-house census we sometimes had the door slammed in our face by people who refused to have anything to do with gas masks.'[12]

Now, in total contrast, he found himself greatly welcomed when handing out gas masks.

Even after the Munich crisis, however, the desire to undertake any meaningful expenditure continued to dominate the thoughts of locally elected councillors. This was so in Rochester where, despite having a robust scheme of Civil Defence that had been finalised many months earlier, the need for a 2s 1d increase in rates was regarded as unacceptable. In February 1939, with the clock rapidly running down, a Rochester councillor informed his colleagues:

> 'I don't believe there are any businessmen in this City who would begrudge a 2s 1d rate if they thought it was going to be for the safety of the citizens', he said. 'They would urge us to get on without further delay; so that once it is done we can forget about it.'[13]

In East Sussex the county council, responsible for the construction of shelters in schools, was not in a position to begin this work until the summer of 1939. From then onwards, matters proceeded at a breakneck speed, with a concentration upon the construction of shelters in the playground of schools located closest to the coastline. In Brighton, a photographic record was maintained, making it particularly easy to track the progress of this work. It shows that many of the shelters in Brighton were under construction by late summer and were not to be completed for several months. All were of a common design, brick-built, oblong in shape, with benches that lined bleak interior walls. Among schools receiving shelters at this time were Coombe Road, Elm Street, St Luke's, Standford Road, Pelham and St John's. Shelters were also built in the grounds of Xavier College and the School of Art.[14]

Other heavily delayed local ARP schemes that failed to get under way until after the Munich crisis included the construction of deep shelter tunnels by the metropolitan boroughs of Ramsgate and Dover. That the two towns should come up with such an elaborate scheme was due to their genuine fear of air attack that resulted from their proximity to the Continent. The Dover tunnel, which received final government approval in February 1939, was cut into Coombe Valley and had its entrance in Noah's Ark Road. When finally completed, it had an effective length of 954ft and an extreme depth of 100ft. Able to accommodate 850 residents, it cost approximately £8,000 to construct. An extension to the tunnel, with an estimated additional cost of £8,560 and the possibility of accommodating a further 1,275 residents, was proposed but never constructed.

The Ramsgate tunnel had a much greater capacity than the one built at Dover, designed to allow 60,000 people to take shelter. To achieve this, an extensive tunnel with numerous entrances and several spurs was dug under the main area of the town between Ellington Park in the south and Dumpton Park Drive in the north. First submitted to the Ministry of Home Security for a grant in early 1938, it was at that time rejected as premature. Following the October crisis, a further grant application was made, but once again the plan was rejected. Only with Hitler's entry into Czechoslovakia in March 1939 was a grant finally made available, with excavation work beginning shortly afterwards. The most extensive series of deep air-raid shelters to be constructed anywhere in the country, work on the project was undertaken by Francois Cementation Co. Ltd, with final costs amounting to £60,000. Included within this work was the installation of seating, lighting, ventilation shafts, chemical toilets and loudspeakers for the relaying of messages and wireless programmes. An important feature of the tunnel, which was between 50ft and 90ft in depth, was that of an entrance immediately aligned to the borough hospital, to facilitate the easy movement of patients into the tunnel and casualties into the hospital.

Returning to Brighton, it was here in October 1938 that Professor Haldane, author of a then recently published book on the subject of ARP, made a call for the government to pursue a general policy of building deep shelters. Speaking at a meeting of the Left Book Club held at the Friends Meeting House in Ship Street, he indicated that Brighton was a likely target for bombers. This, he said, was 'owing to its large population' now 'that terrorization of civilian populations was the aim of the military men'. For Brighton, he specifically indicated that shelters could be cut into the surrounding chalk hills, these being 'ideal for building underground shelters', and he estimated the cost as being approximately £2,000.[15] Professor Haldane was a significant critic of the government, and generally attacked its policy of relying on gas masks and refuge rooms. As he further said at the meeting held in Brighton: 'underground shelters, giving 100% protection, could be provided for the whole of Britain at a cost of between £400 million and £500 million, which was only a quarter to a third of the sum being spent on armaments.'[16]

At the time of the Munich crisis, all that had been achieved in Brighton in the way of public shelters was the opening of these under some of the arches in King's Road, Grand Junction Road and Madeira Drive, while sandbags protected part of Lower Marine Drive.[17]

Other highly vulnerable south coast authorities would certainly have benefited from similar shelter schemes as adopted by both Dover and Ramsgate. In Southampton, attention was only given to the creation of deep shelters in August 1939. By that time, of course, it was too late to undertake any real excavation work, with the City Corporation turning its focus on existing stone cellars that were to be found under a number of substantial medieval buildings within the city. According to the *Southern Daily Echo*:

> One of the Norman vaults under the Walls has been converted into a shelter for 200 people. Undercroft in Simnel Street has also been converted for 120 people. Altogether, 100 basement shelters providing accommodation for 10,000 people have been opened in this area. These basements once housed wines and spices ... One basement under Quilter's (an old hostelry at the lower end of the High Street) had not been opened for 15 years. Another, under Scrases' old brewery, is a vast labyrinth of cellars capable of accommodating 900 people – a weird world this one, with curious old pipes and even a covered-in well of unknown depth.[18]

In the meantime, the only shelters available were the slit trenches that had been dug during the time of the Munich crisis; luckily, Southampton was not raided during the first weeks of war.

Folkestone was another borough that might well have prioritised the digging of deep tunnels into the surrounding cliffs. Indeed, at the time of the Munich crisis some tunnelling was under way, but this was for drainage rather than for protection from falling bombs. By the outbreak of war in 1939, Folkestone was yet one more south coast town that was without any public shelters, other than the hastily dug slit shelters left over from September 1938. Instead, arrangements had to quickly be made with the owners of the Royal Pavilion and Norfolk hotels for the public to use their basements, together with underground cellars in two Martello towers and Sandgate keep. All this, of course, comes as an even greater surprise when the disastrous daylight bombing of Tontine Street during the First World War is recalled.

The failure to provide deep shelters in Portsmouth was to be clearly regretted during the winter of 1940/41. With few safe places in which to take cover, many residents, in common with those in Southampton, simply fled each night into the surrounding countryside. Eventually, in June 1941, the city's War Emergency Committee sanctioned tunnels to be dug into the chalk pits on Portsdown Hill. Once completed, these would have sufficient room to accommodate over 3,000 people. Unfortunately, though, Portsmouth had already seen the worst of the bombing, with almost 1,000 killed and a further 3,000 casualties during the winter raids. How many might have been saved by an earlier decision to build those deep shelters? Not surprisingly, there was considerable anger in the city that many had been left to face the Portsmouth blitz in only hastily erected surface shelters. It was this sense of anger that was captured by the Mass Observation organisation during a series of interviews carried out in Portsmouth in the summer of 1941. Of the new shelters, one 55-year-old female dockyard worker complained: 'They're still building them. But what I say is didn't they do all that sort of thing before the war. They knew we was going to be bombed, didn't they?'[19]

A male dockyard worker added in a similar vein: 'They ought to have done it all before. They knew we was going to have a war didn't they? They could 'ave got the whole population of Portsmouth in the 'ill. Made an underground city of it.'[20]

A similar situation to that of Portsmouth arose in Hastings. During the Munich crisis, zigzag trenches were dug in many of the town's municipal gardens, but little further work was subsequently undertaken. This meant that by the time war was actually declared, Hastings lacked any solid shelters, whether subterranean or above ground. Even those being constructed in school playgrounds were not as robust as those being built in Brighton, many of them being the open slit shelters dug a year earlier and now covered over by railway sleepers and given the addition of entry point anti-blast sandbag walls. Given that German bombers frequently visited Hastings, with the first raid on 26 July 1940, it was not surprising that residents were soon demanding a greater level of protection. After many delays, the council adopted the same solution as that of Portsmouth, belatedly adapting nearby caves. In fact, the initiative at Hastings pre-dated that of Portsmouth but not, of course, that of Dover or Ramsgate. By October 1940 the St Clement Caves had been effectively converted, with an entrance in Croft Road. Able to accommodate 300–400 people, the caves also served as a hospital and school. Later, a further deep shelter was added by tunnelling into the hill at Torfield.

It was the Munich crisis that had also given a greater level of attention to the need for purpose-built shelters, with only a few exceptional authorities having previously given any real thought to the issue. In part, this was because the government itself was laying stress on each family, individual or employer to create refuge rooms within their own houses and places of work. Behind this concept was the belief, as fostered by the government, that 'any room with solid walls is safer than being out in the open'.[21]

This individualised do-it-yourself approach to Air Raid Precautions had been firmly pursued by the Home Office from March 1938 onwards. In that month it had published a 36-page booklet that was eventually distributed nationwide to all homes. Entitled *The Protection of Your Home Against Air Raids*, it made no reference to the need for any form of external shelter. Instead, full emphasis was placed on individuals identifying a place of refuge within their own homes and then setting about improving its ability to withstand the impact of high-explosive bombs. In choosing a refuge room, residents were advised:

> Almost any room will serve as a refuge room if it is soundly constructed, and if it is easy to reach and get out of. Its windows should be as small as possible, preferably facing a building or blank wall, or a narrow street. If a ground floor room facing a wide street or a stretch of level open ground is chosen, the windows should if possible be specially protected. The stronger the walls, floor, and ceiling are, the better. Brick partition walls are better than lath and plaster; a concrete ceiling is better than a wooden one. An internal passage will form a very good refuge room if it can be closed at both ends.[22]

More information was offered on how to strengthen the room through the addition of scaffolding and how to ensure that glass splinters from the windows were not blown in. Householders were also advised to provide the room with tinned food, washing facilities, chamber pots and a simple first-aid kit.

A heavy class bias was attached to this advice. One writer saw it as emanating from a middle-class belief that 'an Englishman's home is his castle'.[23] For those who lived in detached or semi-detached houses with structurally reinforced brick walls, it might have been halfway reasonable advice. For the working class, many of whom still lived in single-partition-walled properties, to have stayed in such a house during an air raid would have been near suicidal. G.T. Garratt, who witnessed first-hand the bombing of working-class quarters in Madrid, deplored the advice:

> It is difficult for anyone who has seen the condition of a bombed industrial area to take the protection of individual houses very seriously. The high explosive bombs shatter and crack all except the first-class steel-framed buildings within a considerable area.[24]

The crisis of September 1938 completely threw the refuge room concept out of the proverbial window. Few families had attempted to create such rooms and most preferred to take their chances in the open. The second-tier authorities further undermined the government's approach through a nearly universal programme along the south coast of digging emergency slit trenches. Following on from this, many of these same authorities chose to submit ARP schemes that included grant requests for the construction of public shelters.

The government, in choosing to react to this situation, determined upon an entirely new approach, seeking out a suitable design for small family shelters that could be erected in gardens. This was the famous Anderson shelter, named after Sir John Anderson who had joined the Cabinet in October 1938 as Lord Privy Seal and now had general responsibility for all issues connected with Air Raid Precautions. It was shortly after his appointment that Anderson had sought a suitable design and one that could be put into immediate mass production. Consisting of six galvanised corrugated-steel panels that formed the main body of the shelter, together with further panels to give it both height and secure ends, the whole could be easily assembled through the use of bolts. Buried 4ft (1.2m) into the soil, they had then to be covered with a minimum of 15in (0.4m) of soil. Once erected, each Anderson shelter could accommodate up to six people. Available from February 1939 onwards, those local authorities located in areas thought likely to be bombed were provided with shelters on demand and then took responsibility for distributing them. To householders earning more than £250 per annum, a charge of £7 was made. Those on lesser incomes made no payment. Along the south coast, despite the likelihood of attack, not all authorities were seen as in danger of being bombed; this included the Isle of Wight. Such authorities, therefore, were not initially allowed to take possession of Anderson shelters for distribution.

The arrival of Anderson shelters was only a partial solution to the protection of citizens during an air raid and did not take away the obligation of authorities to build public shelters. In the case of many householders, particularly in the more built-up areas of the south coast, their homes were without gardens or sufficient space for these shelters. In addition, and reflecting back on the Folkestone raid of 1917, adequate protection needed to be provided for shoppers, pedestrians and others going about their daily routine outside of the home. For this, more public shelters were required. For towns such as Southampton, Portsmouth and Chatham, which proved to be particular targets of the Luftwaffe, soundly built public shelters would have been of inestimable value. It was certainly the case that some south coast areas did reflect on this possibility, with Rochester among those councils that decided to explore the adaptation of existing tunnels for use as air-raid shelters.[25] In the event, Chatham pushed forward with the construction of forty-five surface shelters for general use, while in Portsmouth, which had long neglected the problem, a number of surface shelters were built. However, as far as Portsmouth was concerned, these were insufficient in number by the time war was declared. Instead, in streets where houses were unsuitable for Anderson shelters, it was found necessary to erect, on the immediate outbreak of the war, street communal shelters made out of sandbags.

A further outcome of the Munich crisis was that air-raid sirens began to be introduced as the means by which the public should be notified of an impending air raid. In a circular dated 26 September, the Home Office instructed that public warning systems be established in each borough, with the BBC first broadcasting the standard siren notes during the middle of September. Most authorities at that time had to make recourse to a local arrangement, often using workplace sirens. As and when the electrically operated sirens became available, they were installed throughout the length of the south coast. At Herne Bay and Whitstable, and in many other places, the approved government–pattern sirens were affixed to the local fire stations, with gas-work sirens the favoured stand-in until the installation of the correct device.[26]

Hand in glove with the policy of providing air-raid shelters, the government should also have enforced a solution to the homeless refugee problem. If public shelters proved effective, it would ensure the survival of householders but not their homes. Along the south coast, and especially in the many densely packed towns of this area, hundreds of houses could see potential destruction but with the survival of their occupants. Garratt, drawing on his knowledge of the bombing of Madrid, felt it essential that 'people whose homes have been suddenly destroyed' should not feel that they will now suffer 'for having been part of the passive defence of the country'.[27] Instead, every administrative area should be ready with centralised facilities – a clearing house – composed of medical staff, midwives, nurses and the means to evacuate the newly homeless into the countryside. In the summer of 1938, several months before the Munich crisis, Garratt was pleading for facilities that never actually emerged, even when the bombing of Portsmouth, Southampton, Brighton, Hastings and the Medway Towns was at its height. Of the required clearing houses, he indicated that they:

> Should be able to deal with four or five thousand people, and should be chosen with an eye for easy evacuation to the country, and not too far from the congested and dangerous areas. It is possible to house a very large number of refugees on a limited floor space, if, but only if, the other arrangements for cooking, etc., have been made in advance.

It was a matter that Garratt considered to be of great urgency:

> The work of assigning clearing houses to areas should be done at once, and each individual should know now that in case of air attack which left him alive, but homeless, his first port of call, for himself and his family, should be some building where he can get food, attention [and] lodging for the night.[28]

Centres for those people bombed out of their homes were slowly established and brought into use, and were initially seen as a further aspect of ARP work. Into this, however, was factored the Women's Voluntary Service for Civil Defence (WVS). An organisation that originated in May 1938, it came about when the Home Secretary, Sir Samuel Hoare, invited Stella Isaacs, the Marchioness of Reading, to form a body which would bring women more centrally into ARP work. Specifically, the WVS had as its objective 'the enrolment of women for Air Raid Precautions Services of Local Authorities, to help to bring home to every household what air attack may mean, and to make known to every household what it can do to protect itself and the community'. A voluntary organisation that recruited from among the ranks of mothers, housewives and those keen to contribute to the future-war effort, it was to take on a vast range of duties. In particular, members of the WVS were to work with the evacuated homeless through organising accommodation, food, clothing and mobile laundries.

Unlike other voluntary organisations, there was a general requirement placed on local authorities to ensure that each should have a branch of the WVS within its boundaries. To aid the efficiency of each locally organised body, second-tier authorities were expected to provide, from January 1939 onwards, both office space and clerical assistance. As with local authorities, the WVS was organised at both a county and borough level, with Evelyn Emmett of Amberley Castle the county organiser for Sussex and whose given offices were in County Hall, Chichester. Initially, membership of the WVS was open to all women aged between 17 and 70, with a square white metal badge, inscribed with 'WVS for Air Raid Precautions' – later 'WVS for Civil Defence' – given to all who had completed sixty hours of service. The familiar grey-green and wine-red uniform was usually worn only by those undertaking specific responsibilities, with the cost of the uniforms borne by the member herself.[29]

The impetus created by the Munich crisis led to a general improvement in Civil Defence that slowly became apparent throughout the months prior to the outbreak of the Second World War. Underlying the change in government attitude to the provision of shelters was the Civil Defence Act, passed by Parliament in July 1939. This considerably increased the power of local authorities, allowing them to designate buildings (or parts of buildings) as public shelters or for ARP use, while also permitting the construction of public shelters on highways or underground. Authorities were also required to provide, free of charge, the necessary scaffolding materials for buttressing the basement of houses, while also carrying out the installation work.

A further aspect of the Civil Defence Act was that owners of factories, mines and commercial buildings had to provide adequate shelters for those they employed. Although it did not affect the entire country, it was certainly obligatory for all in the south coast counties employing more than fifty. Of course, the major defence contractors along the south coast, Short Brothers in Rochester (manufacturing the Stirling bomber and the Sunderland seaplane) and Supermarine of Southampton (at one time the only manufacturer of the

Spitfire), together with the shipbuilding concerns of Vosper, Thornycroft and White's, and the naval dockyards of Chatham, Portsmouth and Sheerness, had already gone to great lengths to provide shelters for employees. However, a number of other major employers had made considerably less progress, with the coal-mining companies of east Kent, the locomotive workshops at Ashford, larger retail outlets and the various utilities now beginning a more vigorous effort to ensure that workers would be relatively secure if predicted air raids should take place.

As for the ARP service itself, the post-crisis months witnessed a considerable expansion in numbers volunteering. The *London Times*, while admittedly referring to the country in its entirety, noted that recruitment at this time was 'steady' but becoming 'spectacular' from March 1939 and following further aggression by Hitler when he marched his forces into Czechoslovakia.[30] A direct result was that local authorities, while long having recognised the need for more specialised units, were now in a position to establish these without risk of diluting the efficiency of the entire body. Authorities along the entire south coast greatly expanded units that now included decontamination, rescue and demolition teams, together with first-aid parties. Decontamination squads, basing themselves on the system first developed at Portsmouth in 1935, normally consisted of seven men and a driver, these drawn from borough cleansing or county highway staff. As regards the demolition and rescue units, they had to have a very high level of training and were normally drawn from among those in the building trade. As for the model upon which they worked, this had been developed out of procedures adopted during an earthquake in Tokyo in 1931, with levers, crowbars, jacks and ropes their standard equipment.

To help test out the newly expanded Civil Defence organisation, a number of practice exercises were carried out during the summer of 1939. Sometimes they were very locally based and at other times they involved two or more authorities working together. On the Isle of Wight, in March of that year, two of the authorities on the east side of the island, Ryde and Bembridge, combined to stage one of the earliest post-Munich crisis ARP exercises. With a district report centre established in the unmanned gun battery at Puckpool Park, incidents were reported and ARP units dispatched to both clear 'wrecked buildings' and treat mock casualties. As part of the exercise, newly installed air-raid sirens were sounded, flares were used to demarcate the fall of bombs and streets were cleansed of gas by decontamination units. Although the blackout was not officially enforced, most shopkeepers agreed to extinguish exterior illuminated signs while members of the public were asked to see that 'as little light as possible [was] visible from the outskirts of their houses'.[31]

The holding of a fairly elaborate ARP exercise on the Isle of Wight at this point in time seriously conflicted with the government's own assessment of the future course of a likely war. As demonstrated by its designation as a reception

1. Hythe Martello tower forms a backdrop to troops undergoing training at the Hythe School of Musketry, established in 1853. This is how the coast in this area of Kent would have been defended in the event of a French invasion in the mid-nineteenth century. (*All images are the author's collection unless otherwise stated*)

2. The key to protecting the south coast was the navy, the nation's first line of defence. Here, at the entrance to Portsmouth dockyard, layers of fortifications are firmly implanted along the shoreline.

3. Chichester was a major receiving centre for those enlisting during the First World War. Here, a squad of new recruits is in the process of learning the ways of the army.

4. Lydd, one of the many camps along the south coast used for the training of soldiers for the Western Front.

5. Trenches on the Isle of Grain. During the First World War, areas along the south coast vulnerable to invasion were given the protection of wire entanglements and Western Front-style trenches.

6. Chatham dockyard, 11 November 1918 – celebrating the end of the First World War. Here, artisans from the ropeyard are seen beneath a display of various ships' flags.

7. Damage to the Bull & George Hotel in Ramsgate, Kent. The bomb that caused the damage was one of fifty-three dropped by Zeppelin LZ38s on 17 May 1915. The raid cost the lives of two Ramsgate residents.

8. A commercial refinery on the Isle of Grain. Despite the lessons of the First World War, little effort was made to disperse the more vulnerable factories and military sites.

9. The Airspeed Oxford, an important training aeroplane for the RAF. These were manufactured in Portsmouth, thereby increasing the risk of the town being bombed.

10. A half-scale mock-up prototype of the Stirling bomber at the Short Brothers airport factory immediately to the south of Rochester.

11. The floating bridge on the Medina at J. Samuel White's military-industrial complex in Cowes, Isle of Wight. White's was a major constructor of Royal Navy destroyers, but the various workshops and sheds made White's a highly visible and vulnerable target.

12. Portsmouth dockyard, possibly the ultimate target for any raiding bomber.

13. On 20 July 1921, the Chichester War Memorial was unveiled in the town's Eastgate Square. Hundreds of other memorials were erected immediately after the First World War.

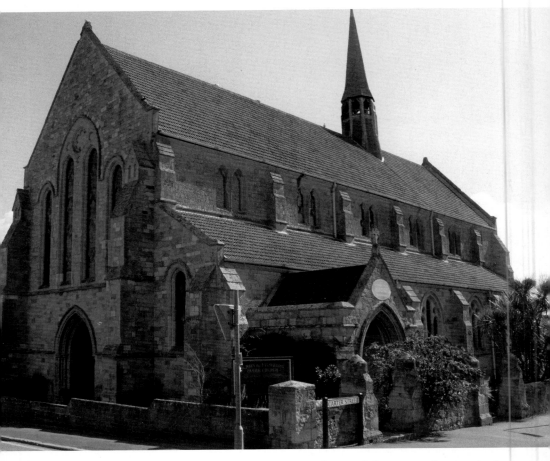

14. St John's church, Isle of Wight, where one desperate pacifist scrawled a message for peace in the visitors' book.

15. The Portsmouth City Corporation's experimental decontamination lorry – converted from a dustcart – is seen here in a practice exercise. (*Portsmouth Museums*)

16. The 1930s civic centre in Southampton – the base for those who would oversee civil defence operations during a bombing raid. To ensure their safety, the building included an underground bombproof office for ARP wardens.

WILLS'S CIGARETTES

THE CIVILIAN DUTY RESPIRATOR

17. 'The Civilian Duty Respirator' card from the Wills's tobacco company's collection. Official government publications to raise awareness of ARP failed to spark enough interest, so the Home Office used the imaginative approach of working with tobacco companies to produce a series of collectable cards devoted to ARP.

18. Volunteer fire fighters of the Chatham AFS are engaged in a practice exercise during the period immediately before the outbreak of war. (KM Group, publishers of the *Medway Messenger*)

19. The castle at Deal, built during the reign of Henry VIII. As part of an attempt to acquire bombproof shelters for some of its residents, the borough of Deal made use of the stone cellars underneath the town castle.

20. A shelter beneath the St Martin's Terrace ARP post, Brighton, mid–September 1939. Brighton was just one of many south coast towns that was still building shelters on the outbreak of war. (Brighton Museum and Art Gallery)

21. Above Bar Street in Southampton, the city's main shopping centre. The introduction of rationing and restricting customers to designated shops for their food purchases (a scheme pioneered in Southampton by the Co-op) reduced the level of queuing during the Second World War.

22. During the first two days of September, many children from Chatham were evacuated by train to the supposedly safer areas of the south coast. (KM Group)

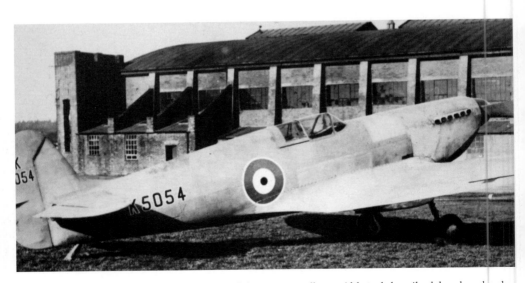

23. The Spitfire prototype (K5054), the super-fighter par excellence. Although heavily delayed, and only arriving at the front-line fighter stations of the south coast in early 1940, the Spitfire rapidly proved itself against German bombers.

24. A Gloucester Gladiator. If war had broken out at the time of the Munich crisis, in September/October 1938, the RAF along the south coast would have been entirely dependent for defence on biplane fighters such as this.

25. At Chatham dockyard, a major target in north Kent, only limited recognition was given to the predicted war, with this highly inflammable wooden storehouse (a former mast house) being given an outer cladding of asbestos.

26. Southampton during the 1930s. This aerial view demonstrates how the city would have appeared to German bombers intent on destroying the important commercial docks, while the tightly packed housing beyond would also suffer from collateral bomb damage.

27. A fort on the Isle of Grain, one of few that were retained after the First World War. This photograph was taken in the 1970s, twenty years after the fort was finally abandoned; it is about to be buried by many tons of soil.

28. This highly stylised contemporary illustration, which dates to 1937, shows HMS *Furious* being over-flown by a squadron of carrier-borne aircraft. Providing support for the RAF in the event of an invasion, the navy could provide additional aircraft through the positioning of aircraft carriers in the Channel.

29. The Chain Home radar station at Ventnor, partially extant. In the foreground is the base for one of the receiving masts; the original receiving block is also to be seen.

30. Old Needles Battery on the Isle of Wight, one of several batteries built during the 1860s as a result of a feared invasion by the French. It was constructed on unsteady ground and was subsequently replaced by the adjoining New Needles Battery.

area for evacuation purposes, in common with a number of other boroughs along the south coast, the Isle of Wight was not viewed as an area likely to be targeted by bombers. However, the government was ignoring both the existence of a large-scale military-industrial complex at Cowes and the proximity of the island to the even more certain targets of Southampton and Portsmouth. In the words of one recent commentator:

> It was, of course, entirely consistent with the official view on the Isle of Wight's vulnerability – or lack of it – that it should have been chosen as a reception area for evacuated schoolchildren, despite being a mere 4½ miles, just a 30-minute ferry trip, from the clearly 'unsafe' city of Portsmouth, the originating point for the majority of evacuee intake. The chances of the island remaining a safe haven in a modern air war were pretty remote – even if, for most of the time, enemy bombers were not going to be specifically aiming for it.[32]

It was the assumption on the part of the government that the Isle of Wight was safe from bombing that led to the various ARP authorities being frequently refused monetary support for any of their more financially demanding ARP schemes, including the building of public shelters. In addition, and up until August 1939 following an appeal by the Isle of Wight County Council, residents on the island were not permitted Anderson shelters.

For the south coast in general, a further exercise was held in July, in conjunction with a full-scale blackout. As well as testing the effectiveness of each coastal borough's blackout, a number of 'incidents' were staged to test the efficiency of the ARP response teams. In Herne Bay, for the purpose of the exercise, smoke bombs and fireworks were used to represent incendiaries and high-explosive bombs, with seventy occurrences arranged, including fires, injuries to people, roads contaminated by blister gas and damage to sewers.[33] In Deal, the *Kentish Express* reported the exercise:

> Those who saw any of the incidents staged at intervals during the evening must have been struck by their realistic effect. Especially was this so in the case of incendiary bombs and the promptness with which the fire engines and ambulances arrived on the scene but were but one instance of the high standard of training by all units of the ARP organisation, though, perhaps, some further collective training would be beneficial. During the exercise Deal was bombed and a large number of HE bombs strung across the town.[34]

In Rochester, the extensive blackout was used to test an unusual addition to the city police uniform by a member of the city constabulary situated at the Guildhall end of the bridge:

Controlling the cautious traffic stood a policeman in a uniform that had been treated with fluorescent dye. With the rays of a special lamp playing on him, motorists could see him as a ghostly bluish figure, but from above he was invisible.

In Chatham, whatever the success of the practice elsewhere, the need for improvements was certainly discovered. A mock air raid on the Army Technical School had resulted in thirty boys being trapped in a collapsed shelter. In a series of unacceptable delays, no rescue team was to arrive for thirty-five minutes: 'It took eight minutes for the message to reach the Control Room by telephone, and after a long wait, a reserve and first aid party numbering less than a dozen arrived to rescue the boys.'

To this, the local newspaper added: 'It would seem that the time taken for the squad to arrive on the scene was longer than was necessary, and moreover, the numbers sent were not sufficient to deal with a "major" incident.'[35]

One of the last practice exercises by a south coast town prior to the outbreak of war was held in Hastings during mid-August 1939. It was a full-scale alert and involved the staging of over a hundred separate incidents. As with all such exercises, the practice was considered a great success and reported as such by the media, ignoring the fact that the exercise had been cancelled for twenty-four hours due to poor weather. One assumes, on this basis, that an agreement had already been struck that Hastings would not be bombed on nights when it rained!

Of interest is that in subsequently explaining the purpose of the exercise, Hastings' chief ARP warden, Percy Le May, outlined the role undertaken by the volunteer wardens. Initially, and prior to any raid, they would embark on nightly patrols to ensure that all lights were screened, while on the sounding of an air-raid siren they would reinforce the alert through the blowing of whistles. Due to their knowledge of the area they patrolled, wardens were on hand to give assistance to those who needed guidance to the nearest public shelters. Following the raid, and if gas was present, the wardens were to sound rattles to prevent anyone entering a contaminated area. To all this, Le May added:

Wardens being quickly on the spot will often be able to deal with incendiary bombs with a stirrup pump, which is kept at all posts, and stop what might have been a serious fire.

If the bomb is a high explosive, there may be casualties, blocked roads, houses partly demolished and fires, and people driven into the streets, who will require shelter found for them.[36]

More exercises throughout the length of the south coast were, of course, planned for the latter part of the year, but with the declaration of war in September 1939, these practices were accompanied by the actual reality of war. As at the time of the Munich crisis, a degree of panic once again set in, with local ARP authorities scrabbling round to improve their overall Civil Defence schemes. Although they were greatly more advanced than in September 1938, most, if not all, were still sending out teams of their own employees, combined with volunteers, digging trenches, sandbagging public buildings and issuing gas masks.

## Notes

1. *Chatham News*, 30 September 1938.
2. Ibid.
3. *Kentish Express*, 23 September 1938.
4. Ibid.
5. Ibid.
6. *Worthing Gazette*, 12, 19 & 26 November 1938.
7. *East Kent Mercury*, 1 October 1938.
8. *Worthing Gazette*, 12, 19 & 26 November 1938.
9. Bernard Knowles, *Southampton: the English Gateway* (Hutchinson & Co., 1951), p. 114.
10. Ibid., p. 162.
11. Mass Observation Archive, Box 180.
12. *Brighton and Hove Gazette*, 8 October 1938.
13. *Chatham News*, 17 February 1939.
14. Brighton Museum, Photo Collections, Aug–Nov 1939.
15. *Brighton and Hove Gazette*, 15 October 1938.
16. Ibid.
17. Ibid., 1 October 1938.
18. *Southern Daily Echo*, 20 August 1939. Re-quoted in Bernard Knowles, op. cit., p. 94.
19. University of Sussex, Mass Observation file 66/16/D.
20. Ibid.
21. *The Protection of Your Home Against Air Raids* (Home Office, 1938), p. 10.
22. Ibid., p. 8.
23. G.T. Garratt, 'Air Raid Precautions', in *The Air Defence of Great Britain* (Penguin, 1938), p. 130.
24. Ibid., p. 125.
25. *Chatham News*, 11 March 1938.
26. *Herne Bay Press*, 1 October 1938.
27. Garratt, op. cit.
28. Ibid., pp. 138–9.
29. Women's Voluntary Service, Report of Ten Years' Work for the Nation, 1938–48 (WVS, 1949), pp. 9–10.
30. *London Times*, 31 March 1939.
31. *Isle of Wight Chronicle*, 9 & 16 March 1938.
32. Adrian Searle, *Isle of Wight at War* (Dovecote Press, 1989), p. 15.
33. *Herne Bay Press*, 15 July 1939.
34. *Kentish Express*, 15 July 1939.
35. *Chatham News*, 14 July 1939.
36. *Hastings and St Leonards Observer*, 19 August 1939.

# 6

# Hoses, Pumps & More Pumps

Nationally, a number of actions taken by the government through promptings by the Ministry of Home Security were to prove of significance for the overall Civil Defence programme. One exceptionally important area was that of fire fighting. Coming as an immense surprise to members of the House of Commons when debated was the fact that prior to 1938, no local authority outside of London was required to have a fire brigade.[1] As a result, a complete mishmash of facilities existed, with some authorities having highly efficient and dedicated fire-fighting teams, while others adopted the minimum possible standard. In Portsmouth, a south coast authority that must have automatically regarded itself as a wartime target, the city police were responsible for all fire fighting. It was this same body that also undertook ambulance-driving duties. Kenneth Hampton, a member of the Portsmouth constabulary from January 1939 onwards, offered this record of how he was first inducted into the skills of fire fighting:

Back then you had the opportunity of either becoming an apprentice fireman in the [Portsmouth] city police force or a shorthand typist in the Criminal Investigation Bureau. This meant that you were basically a civilian but you were working under the auspices of the force. At the end of our service as a city fire-man, we would be sworn in as a constable and that was at the age of twenty.

There was no question of us going away to training college, instead we went into local police classes for about ten or twelve weeks and we learnt police law and we did physical training. Incidentally, we also learnt fire fighting as well. We were expected to take on most of the duties with the possible exception of running the pumps on the fire engines, which we were never invited to do.

Apart from lectures, we had fire drills in the yard of one of the police stations and then we were taught how to roll out lines of hoses, how to deal with chimney fires and also how to deal with major conflagrations. The other thing we had to do was sheet jumps from the tower, hoping that the sheet was held firmly when we jumped into it.[2]

A general lack of government control meant that south coast authorities, even though they possessed a fire brigade, were not necessarily concerned with its overall ability to fight fires. At Lancing in Sussex, the council, during 1936, felt disinclined to replace an ageing Baco Ford fire engine – itself second hand – preferring to spend their money on the improved sartorial elegance of the men who manned the pumps. This report from the *London Evening Standard* was quoted in the House of Commons as an example of just why the government, with war clearly on the horizon, needed to become more involved in this issue:

> The twelve members of the Lancing Sussex Fire Brigade are worried about their engine and uniforms. Both are about 12 years old. The engine suffers from heart trouble and can no longer manage the Sussex hills, while the uniforms do not fit properly. The brigade applied for a new outfit and has been told that they could have new uniforms but not a new engine.[3]

Elsewhere, during the late 1930s and into the early years of the war, the Chichester brigade was still using an 1870s handcart, while both East Wittering and Selsey were reliant on volunteer brigades that were unsupported by their respective boroughs.

A first attempt by the government to ensure that existing fire brigades were both expanded and brought to a suitable level of efficiency for handling multiple air-raid attacks, came in the form of a detailed memorandum issued by the Home Office in 1937. In this, all local authorities were requested to devise schemes that would meet such an emergency. In particular, they were to consider the number of appliances and recruits available, water supplies, methods of communication and overall training. Later, in March 1938, the Home Office issued a set of regulations, setting out the minimum acceptable standards to which each submitted scheme was to adhere. Upon meeting these standards, and if the scheme was approved, government grants would be available to help implement the new arrangements. Finally, in July 1938, with the passing of new parliamentary legislation, all second-tier authorities, irrespective of size, were obliged to form effective fire brigades.[4]

To further ensure that local authority fire brigades would be both effective and of sufficient size to meet wartime needs, the government established a second fire-fighting force, the Auxiliary Fire Service (AFS). This was a self-contained organisation, initially made up of volunteers, who would be called into full-time service only on the outbreak of war. In the meantime they would receive training by the fire brigade authorities where they served, with a view to working with this same force if war broke out. John Leete explained the need for this enhanced force:

During air raids it would be necessary to have all commercial and private property under supervision and therefore fire crews would need to be of sufficient numbers to patrol the streets with mobile appliances to ensure that outbreaks were tackled immediately. Last but not least, heavy duty patrol apparatus would need to be maintained at stations throughout the boroughs and in readiness to respond not only to major emergencies in the area, but also for duties in other areas and other parts of the country if needed.[5]

To ensure that units of the AFS were quickly assembled and would be available in the event of war, all towns and boroughs on the south coast were encouraged to organise local recruiting drives. All recruits were to be medically examined and, ideally, were to be aged between 25 and 50. Once enrolled, each man was trained to handle fire appliances, enter burning buildings and carry an insensible person down a ladder. In Southampton, where sixty auxiliary firemen had been recruited by March 1937, both the headquarters and Woolston stations duly displayed the following poster:

RECRUITS WANTED

FOR AUXILIARY FIRE SERVICE

In response to an urgent communication from the Secretary of State from the Home Department, based on the highest advice in the national interest, the local authority proposes forthwith, to recruit and train auxiliary personnel for service in, or in connection with, the Fire Brigade in the event of an emergency consequent upon an air raid, and as a safeguard against the effects of incendiary attack from the air by hostile aircraft.

Much more effective than posters were displays put on by members of the AFS that would gain the attention of the public and so create a general interest in the work they were being trained to do. One such event took place in Southsea during the early summer of 1939:

Portsmouth Auxiliary Firemen staged on Southsea Common on the evening of 7 June, a large-scale display of fire fighting methods and the spectators (numbering over 2,000) were given an opportunity of seeing these volunteers put through their paces. It was also the first chance of seeing ARP fire fighting equipment in operation.[6]

At Brighton, in September 1937, a similar display was organised, to demonstrate how water could be taken from the sea and quickly conveyed through the town using specially constructed dams. On this occasion, water was pumped to a car park near the Black Rock Bathing Pool and then jetted into the air using fire-fighting pumps.

This exercise at Brighton highlighted a particular problem confronting the fire-fighting services: that of ensuring adequate water supplies. In Brighton, the problem had been partly eased through the construction of these dams, but much more had to be done. For most boroughs along the south coast it required the introduction of a greatly increased number of hydrants, use of mobile dam units and the training of crews in the difficult art of relaying water by means of a series of pumps and long hose lines. Indeed, a great many of the south coast towns had certainly not solved the problem by the time that bombing was at its height.

In Southampton, despite its claims to be one of the most advanced Civil Defence authorities, there were parts of the city where adequate water for the fighting of fires was simply not available. Instead, and as a result of a series of severe air raids during the winter of 1940/41, emergency 500-gallon static water tanks were installed in the lower part of the city. Replenished from time to time by water carts, these had to be borrowed from the army and other local authorities.

While all towns and boroughs in the south coast counties were keen to recruit men into their fire-fighting services, the crowded coastal resort towns and the industrial towns of Medway, Portsmouth and Southampton were particularly desperate to make up their numbers. Brighton, in particular, would face significant danger on the outbreak of any war. According to its chief fire officer, Charles Birch:

> Brighton is an old town. There are some very congested areas in the centre of the town with narrow streets and old buildings mainly constructed of wood. These old buildings constitute a grave risk, even in peacetime.
>
> We have also many large hotels, buildings rising to seven and eight storeys, buildings which offer no resistance to high explosive bombs and very little to incendiary missiles. Brighton is not a manufacturing town, but I would say that factories of a small nature and of great importance are numerous. We have a great number of nursing homes and institutions.[7]

Women were also recruited into the AFS, but their duties did not take them on to the front line. Instead, they worked alongside senior officers in the watch and control rooms that also had to be established. However, this fact appears to have been lost on the organisers of an AFS display in Hastings in April 1938, when a recruiting drive involved only women members of the service who showed themselves adept in the use of hooked ladders and escape drills – both of which were to be the wartime province of men.[8]

An important government initiative involved ordering the mass production of standardised equipment for use by the various brigades, including mobile trailer pumps (easily towed by any car or small lorry) and self-propelled heavy units (a utility model of the traditional red fire engine), while hose imports were arranged from Canada and the USA. Once assembled, these particular items of equipment were then quickly made available to the various authorities that would purchase according to their requirements. It was an essential move, ensuring that the expansion of the brigades was not hindered by a simple lack of such equipment. Perhaps, also, it was recognition on the part of the government that the national fire-fighting scheme, as now developed, had one serious fundamental flaw. As with the Civil Defence programme in general, it was horrendously splintered through being too heavily localised.

In all, the south coast area consisted of over seventy second-tier authorities, with each of them not only responsible for Civil Defence, but also now fire brigade authorities. While it might be realistic for ARP activities to have a very local edge, this was less sustainable when it came to fire fighting. The equipment required was much more expensive, and a more sophisticated level of training was needed. For this reason, it did not make sense for any one authority to be completely self-contained. The expense would be just too much. Instead, when a major fire broke out, it was logical to combine the brigades of more than one authority. In a wartime situation, with the possibility of major fires being a nightly occurrence, the need for co-operation would be paramount. However, without considerable overall co-ordination, such a process could not work. Apart from requiring equipment that was universal in design (such as hose coupling), it was also necessary that brigades trained together. While in some areas these factors were in place, there were other authorities that fought against such ideas. Of fundamental importance, particularly when air raids were under way, was the need for centralised decisions concerning the movement of units, ensuring that the effort made against an outbreak of fire in one area did not leave another vulnerable to fires from further raids.

Obviously, with the government taking responsibility for overseeing the mass production of new manufactured equipment, this partly tackled the issue of such items being universal in design. However, it did not solve the issue of training and overall co-ordination. As a result, the south coast entered the war in 1939 with a series of independent fire-fighting forces that had little experience of working together. Indeed, some boroughs, such as Shoreham-by-Sea and Arundel, managed to achieve the absurdity of possessing two separate brigades within their boundary, the former having distinct rural and town brigades, and the latter having a separate brigade for Arundel Castle. Of special concern to the inhabitants of Arundel, perhaps, was that the castle had its own brigade because the borough brigade was viewed as inefficient and unreliable.

The need for brigades to be able to co-operate was not only self-evident but soon a vital ingredient to neutralising the devastation caused by German bombers. When both Southampton and Portsmouth were subject to heavy raids in 1940, brigades from throughout Hampshire, Dorset and Sussex had to be deployed, with overall efficiency lost through a general lack of standardisation. Only with the decision taken in 1941 to form a National Fire Service (NFS) was this problem completely overcome. In one single administrative sweep of the pen, all local, works and factory brigades, together with all components of the AFS, were incorporated into one national body. As a result, pumps, trailers and heavy units could be moved when necessary to wherever they were most required. In 1944, with the south coast hosting the military forces poised to invade Europe, hundreds of fire-fighting units were moved into the area for purposes of safeguarding the army's communications and supplies from feared enemy retaliatory raids. To achieve this, less vulnerable areas of the country were called upon to give up part of their fire-fighting strength, with hundreds of pumps moved to the south coast. That this was undertaken smoothly and without undue delay was thanks to the creation of that national service. It was also on the south coast, at Saltdean near Brighton, that a national training school for fire fighting was established from 1942 onwards.

Returning to the pre-war AFS, it was officially mobilised on 1 September 1939, a Home Office 'standby' telegraph being sent to each town and district clerk:

> Emergency Fire Brigade Measure. Call out auxiliary fire service and proceed as in circular of 23 March 1938.

In other words, members of the AFS were to leave their regular jobs and immediately report to their area stations. In the meantime, schools, garages and other suitable buildings, which had been allocated to the AFS for wartime use, were now taken over. At the same time, numerous taxis and private cars were also acquired, to be used to tow the trailer pumps that had been obtained over the previous months and would soon be seeing the arrival of those now trained recruits. Fortunately, with air raids not beginning until the summer of 1940, members of the once part-time AFS had the opportunity to enhance their training by both working much more closely with the borough brigades and attending real fires as and when the possibility arose.

## Notes

1. Hansard, 10 May 1938.
2. Re-quoted from John Leete, *Under Fire* (Sutton Publishing, 2008), pp. 11–2.
3. Hansard, 10 May 1938. Speech given by Joseph Westwood, MP.
4. Fire Brigades Act, 1938.
5. Leete, op. cit., pp. 13–4.
6. V. Blanchard (ed.), *Records of the Corporation* (Portsmouth, nd), p. 111.
7. *Brighton and Hove Gazette*, 24 September 1938.
8. *Hastings and St Leonards Observer*, 12 April 1939.

# 7

# Evacuation

The wartime government was very positive about the success of the pre-war evacuation scheme that had taken many children away from vulnerable areas. And why shouldn't it be seen as one of the great wartime successes? On Friday and Saturday, 1 and 2 September 1939, the vast majority of those to be evacuated, nearly 2 million in number, were taken from various industrial and military towns to the safety of the countryside. Facilitating this move was the public transport system, which basically put its regular bus and train timetables on hold.

The printed medium did much to spread the government version of events. One national newspaper reported:

> The reception in various districts of the evacuated schoolchildren was carried out with the same efficiency that characterised the departures. Competent nurses and reception officers saw that each child got milk and food before being taken to the billeting centres, from where the children were conducted to their temporary homes.
>
> There was no confusion, the teachers who were in charge of the children paid close attention to the details of the arrangements that had been made beforehand.
>
> For all but a few, it was an enthralling but happy adventure, and homesickness and shyness quickly fled at the sight of new faces, new surroundings and new playmates … Some of them were soon eating high teas beyond their dreams and many went up later to bedrooms larger and airier than they had thought possible.[1]

The *Daily Mirror*, in its first wartime edition, also praised the scheme. In a message aimed at mothers whose children had now been evacuated, it suggested that there was absolutely nothing of concern:

> Just think how kind you would be to another woman's children, who were sent to you in the same circumstances.

That is how the mother, to whom your kiddies have gone, will feel about your children.[2]

Local newspapers took a similar line. In the Medway Towns, where over 9,000 children and nursing mothers had been taken to rural districts of east and south-east Kent, the *Chatham News* felt able to tell its readers:

> In each town of evacuation and reception the arrangements were carried through with efficiency, and characteristic of the scenes at the stations was the cheerfulness of the children. On arrival at their destination the children were marched to centres where they were allocated to their billets. From reports already received from the reception areas, the evacuees show that they are settling down in their homes and are happy and comfortable.[3]

The *Southampton Echo* also reported on the success of the scheme, telling of how on the first day of evacuation everything went without a hitch:

> There were no accidents and it was possible to adhere strictly to the arrangements. On arrival at their destination areas all the children wrote postcards to their parents informing them of their new addresses. Many teachers sent the Education Department reassuring telegrams.[4]

In the reception towns along the south coast, local newspapers adopted a similar line, only occasionally noting any difficulties. From the Isle of Wight, which was a reception area for a large number of evacuees from Portsmouth, the *Chronicle* reported:

> The excellent local arrangements for billeting evacuation children in the area ran smoothly and successfully during the chief two evacuation days – Friday and Saturday.[5]

In Deal, a reception area for London and the Medway Towns, the *East Kent Mercury* reported a further success story:

> The reception and billeting of the 2,400 evacuated mothers, schoolteachers and children from the congested areas of London and the Medway Towns into the safer haven of Deal during the weekend was expeditiously and sympathetically carried out. On the whole the children were remarkably bright and cheerful.[6]

Yet things did not go as smoothly as both the government and various newspapers would have the public believe. From beginning to end, the evacuation programme had been only one step from total disaster. To begin with, the take-up of those allowing their children to be evacuated fell far short of government expectations, being less than 40 per cent in the three south coast areas designated to be evacuated, namely Portsmouth, Southampton and the Medway. This led to a miscalculation of the number of trains required and accounts for why the transiting of evacuees was completed in such a short space of time. However, this did not prevent subsequent chaos, with school parties often being split and sent to completely different destinations. Often it took days for these parties to be reunited, by which time the original accommodation had been given over to others. As for the somewhat rosy view presented by the *Daily Mirror*, this again was far removed from reality. In billeting areas, some farmers selected the healthiest-looking lads as potential unpaid farm labour, while the pale, anaemic or less attractive children were hawked from door to door, with few prepared to house them.[7] In the words of Joan Widdett, an evacuee to the south coast: 'if you were a child with spots you were always left to the end'.[8]

Of the evacuees themselves, some were later to tell heart-rending stories of how they were received and treated, this often in total contrast to the make-believe world created by the *Daily Mirror*. Sheila Savage, who was evacuated from London to a convent on the Isle of Wight, remembers how the treatment she was given completely changed her whole character:

I suffered very badly from asthma, so I was sent to a convalescent home on the Isle of Wight. I was told I was going on holiday. The home was a convent, called St Catherine's, I think just outside Ventnor. I was there for about 18 months, and was very unhappy. I remember very little, but am sure corporal punishment was used for bed-wetting and other misdemeanours. I think I remember my Dad coming to tell me I was coming home. When I returned home, I had changed from a bonny looking child to a bundle of skin and bone.

The lack of an organised plan, whereby evacuating areas might have been informed which authority was to take care of their children and particularly where children were to be housed, led to another series of unnecessary problems. When families in transit were split and sent in different directions, it not only took many days for them to be reunited, but when they were brought together there was no available accommodation for them. As a result, older and younger members of the same family often spent part of the war living in different homes and going to different schools.

Again on the Isle of Wight, one former evacuee remembers that on first leaving the ferry at Ryde:

We were herded into trains, and when I say 'herded' I'm not exaggerating – it was absolutely chaotic. There seemed to be no organisation at all ... the police took charge and led us through, out on to the platform ... they took sixteen children away to fill up a train. I went to protest and tell them they couldn't do that – they were dividing a family of five children. That's as far as I got. For the first and only time in my life I was frogmarched by two policemen and pushed into the train behind those sixteen children. The door was locked behind me so that I could not get out.[9]

Another who suffered the fate of being split from a family member was 8-year-old Ron Watson, who should have been evacuated with his sister to Southbourne, in coastal West Sussex. Due to an illness, he was evacuated some days after his sister and was put off the train at Chichester. Here, with his family having no idea what had happened to him, a Mr and Mrs McColl of Melbourne Road took him in. Becoming very homesick, he showed many of the symptoms of a distressed child. Following the lapse of nine weeks, Ron was taken to Southbourne, but was not to be accommodated in the same house as his sister due to a lack of space. Instead, he was forced on to a second family, one that clearly had a dislike for evacuees, and who made life very difficult both for Ron and his parents when they were able to scrape together sufficient money for a visit.[10]

As to the wider well-being of evacuees, regarding health, recreation and the continuance of their education, this was only given consideration once the evacuees had arrived, with little attention having previously been given to the matter. The reception areas, for the most part, knew nothing of the background of the evacuees and were certainly not in a position to put school places aside or adequate medical facilities. All they were told, in various government circulars, was that each reception area should have facilities available for an unspecified number of schoolchildren, nursing mothers and the disabled. Beyond this, each authority was left to its own devices and, without knowing from which evacuating borough they might expect evacuees, they were not even in a position to make more specific arrangements.

The national evacuation scheme greatly affected all authorities along the south coast. Apart from the three military-industrial areas of Southampton, Portsmouth and Medway that were areas to be evacuated, much of the rest of the coastline, together with the Isle of Wight, were designated as reception areas. Not that there was a great deal of logic to all this. As already indicated, many of the south coast towns saw themselves as likely to be bombed. Instead of being evacuated to places of safety, many of the evacuees were being moved to the future front line and places of equal danger. In Southampton, a situation of near absurdity emerged, with children from some homes in the city being evacuated to Andover, while children from Portsmouth were moved into the homes of those recently evacuated. This resulted from the system of evacuating complete schools, irrespective of whether the affected children lived inside a specific borough or immediately outside. J. Sturgess of Bramshaw, in a written memorial of the evacuation period held at the City of Southampton Records Office, stated:

My memories are largely related to bureaucratic nonsense and incompetence. For example the western side of West End Road as far as Cutbush Lane was in the county Borough of Southampton. The eastern side was in Winchester Rural District. The western side, being urban, was issued with Anderson shelters and the children were evacuated; the eastern side, being rural [and officially designated a safe area] had no shelters and received children from Portsmouth. My cousin who lived at West End was evacuated to Andover and his bedroom allotted to Portsmouth evacuees.[11]

In simple terms, the various failings of the evacuation programme were a result of the government having adopted the management technique of 'muddling through'. Rather than draw up an overall scheme and place itself in a position to drive everything robustly forward, it chose to unload its own responsibilities, once again, on to the second-tier authorities. It was these authorities, in areas to be evacuated, that were expected to draw up plans for the departure of the evacuees. In turn, it was the second-tier authorities in the reception areas that were expected to make all the arrangements for receiving those same evacuees. Given that the reception areas were given neither indication of where their evacuees would originate from, nor information as to their likely ages or particular needs, little real preparation was possible. Instead, all they could do was to send out billeting officers to uncover sufficient accommodation for the expected arrivals.

It was the reception authorities that had the most difficult tasks, and often ones for which they were particularly ill suited. With several hundred children likely to descend on each second-tier authority throughout the three south coast counties, they were not only expected to provide sufficient accommodation, but also to put together a plan for their continued education and basic health requirements. Furthermore, any warning as to when, or even if, the evacuees would arrive was likely to be minimal, with the period of time over which they would remain being a further element of mystery. Of the three main tasks, education and health were not even in the normal remit of those authorities. Instead, they were tasks undertaken by the first-tier authorities, forcing the need for complicated negotiations that often saw children from certain schools straddling the boundaries of different authorities. A better-planned scheme might well have seen the county authorities taking full responsibility and entering into direct negotiations with the authorities that were sending out the evacuees. Without any prior knowledge as to who was going where, the authorities were forced into that same 'muddling through' process that characterised the entire programme. Schools, upon the arrival of the evacuees in September 1939, were suddenly inundated, forced to take on numbers for which they were never designed.

Typical of what took place in so many of the south coast districts was the experience of Chichester and its surrounding rural area. At the time, there was a clear urban and rural split in this part of West Sussex, signified by the existence of both urban and rural authorities covering an area that is now one single district. Within the rural authority, each village was selected to take anywhere between fifty and a hundred evacuees. Among the smaller parishes of this authority was Chidham, a farming parish with a population of no more than 600. Prior to the declaration of war, the village school had ninety-nine officially registered pupils. However, within just two weeks, the number had shot up to 139. The reason, quite simply, was that Chidham had become a designated evacuation centre, with children from Wimbledon's Ensham Central School having been settled into the village. Although a number had been taken into private houses, the largest single group were accommodated in the holiday camp at Nutbourne, this having been requisitioned on 31 August. Helping to settle the evacuated children on their arrival at Nutbourne station was the local Women's Institute, its members offering sustenance at the village hall before taking each child to their new wartime homes.

While those in Chidham seemed happy to support the new arrivals, there was a degree of bitterness as to the damage these children would cause to the long-term educational prospects of the local pupils. Olga Baldwin, for instance, who suffered through the arrival of the evacuees, later explained in her own published history of the village:

> Unfortunately the girls in the top class (including me) were taken out of school each morning to go to the village hall and prepare vegetables and help with the cooking and serving of dinner to the pupils. Our parents were not pleased about this because our education was being disrupted but not the evacuees'.[12]

To accommodate the new pupils at the school, several changes had to be made, with William Baldwin, the head teacher, entering into the school logbook:

> In order to meet the changed conditions, Miss Powell's class (Standard III and IV) are in the main room with the top class, Miss Crook (Standards I and II) has the small classroom and the visitors have been given the classroom from which Standards I and II came.[13]

The neighbouring Chichester urban authority took 4,800 evacuees, which immediately overwhelmed an area that had a total population only four times this number. Arriving on 2 September, they included 2,200 children and 2,600 adults. For their part, the adults (mostly mothers of very young children) were given overnight accommodation and communally fed in nearby halls. Unaccompanied children, on the other hand, were housed as family members in private homes while continuing their education in local schools. As with Chidham, the schools in Chichester had to operate a shift system, with evacuees using the school build-ing at different times of day to the local children. This did not mean a shorter day for either group, those not in school receiving additional lessons in a local hall. Even so, there was a severe lack of school accommodation, with the Bishop's Palace converted to school use for pupils from Streatham.

To get a real feel for how close the scheme came to disaster, or for a hint of future problems, it is necessary to return to some of the local newspapers and examine their comments with a little more depth. The *Southampton Echo* might have been fulsome in its praise of the scheme, but it did note that the city's evac-uation control officer was disappointed over the number of parents who had 'withdrawn from the scheme at the last moment'.[14] The *Isle of Wight Chronicle* made a similar point when reporting on evacuees arriving from Portsmouth:

> The accommodation in the Sandown-Shanklin area was not overburdened however as the numbers did not reach those expected. We understand that a contributing factor to this was the reluctance of some parents at the last moment to let their children go.[15]

In earlier issues of the *Isle of Wight Chronicle*, at least one further problem asso-ciated with the evacuation scheme had been noted, that of a lack of air-raid shelters in the schools to which the evacuees were being sent. This was a result of the complete lack of joined-up thinking that had accompanied the planning of the scheme. Although, unlike other coastal authorities, the Isle of Wight had been informed of where evacuees were to originate from, they were given little indication of their age groups – whether adults or children, and their precise educational needs. Consequently, when the Isle of Wight County Council began a long-delayed programme of placing air-raid shelters into schools, they were unable to take into account additional wartime expansion needs, so reducing the subsequent use of the actual school building.

In Deal, where the *East Kent Mercury* had described the housing of evacuees as 'expeditiously and sympathetically carried out', there was a hint that this, at the very least, was an exaggeration:

> There was some difficulty with the billeting of the evacuees, more particularly with the latest arrivals. For the most part the selection of the accommoda-tion was satisfactory, but there was what might be termed square pegs in round holes. These difficulties are gradually being overcome and a tribunal is being set up by the local authority to investigate [any complaints].[16]

And how could it have been otherwise? Deal, a town with a population of no more than 12,000, had suddenly seen the influx of 2,400 needy individuals. Over the course of one day, the borough of Deal had witnessed a 20 per cent popula-tion explosion in its numbers, with all of those new arrivals about to place a considerable strain on the education and medical services of the town. While the second-tier authority may have been warned of the likely arrival of 1,800 school-children, they were totally unprepared for the additional 628 pregnant women and nursing mothers who were also brought to the town. In preparing for the medical needs of the new arrivals, the original minor ailments clinic staffed by two nurses was simply not going to be adequate.

Evacuation, as an essential part of the nation's Civil Defence programme, had been discussed on numerous occasions after the First World War. Of particular significance was the establishment of a committee, under that reliable stalwart Sir John Anderson, that looked at the possibility of evacuating approximately 3.5 million citizens from certain parts of London. However, by the time this committee had presented its final report, some three years later, a number of other pressing ARP matters had emerged. Leastways, this appears to be the reason why no reference was made to evacuation in the Air Raid Precautions Act of 1937. Instead, the government chose to leave it to individuals to make their own arrangements. Where advice was given, it was simply to encourage civilians to remain within their own homes where, following a warning of imminent bombing, they could retreat into their ready prepared 'refuge rooms'. The widely distributed ARP booklet, *The Protection of Your Home Against Air Raids*, provides evidence of the government not even viewing evacuation as part of its remit: 'If you live in a large town, children, invalids, elderly members of the household, and pets, should be sent to relatives or friends in the country, if this is possible.'[17]

In fact, and possibly unwittingly, the government was creating a two-class ARP programme; those who could afford cars, second homes or who had country cousins with sizeable houses were able to get out of the threatened cities, while the working classes were left to bite the bullet by remaining in their less substantial, tightly packed terraced homes. Thousands of the more affluent would certainly have poured out of the cities at the first hint of bombs, many of them taking to the countryside irrespective of whether they had somewhere to go or not. The fictional 'future war' writers were clearly predicting this as a possibility, and the First World War bombing of London had witnessed a general mass exodus. In providing a realistic insight into what would result from a surprise air attack, Air Commodore Charlton suggested the following likely scenario:

> Outside London, the haunting dread of a raid would cause also a general exodus from the towns to the shelter of mine workings and colliery drifts in the Midlands and North; to the open fields at places like Hull; and to caves, subterranean passages and disused chalk pits in Kent and elsewhere on the South Eastern Coast where such facilities existed. The harassing effect on old and young alike of these nightly migrations is beyond computation.[18]

For the south coast, this would have been a disaster of immeasurable proportions. Apart from the snarling up of roads, the coastal boroughs would suddenly have found themselves besieged by thousands of squatters, placing extensive demands on food stocks, policing and accommodation. In turn, with the food supply chain disrupted by raids, it was likely that outbreaks of civil disturbance and food thefts would occur; the latter, it must be added, not through any inherent dishonesty on the part of an evacuee, but out of sheer desperation.

A mild hint that all of this could become a reality started with the Munich crisis. At that time, many hundreds of the more affluent citizens started to leave London, many of them making for the south coast. In Brighton, thousands of extra people descended on the town, with both hotels and guesthouses solidly booked. For the Civil Defence volunteers this appears to have caused considerable difficulty, the town having to provide everybody in residence with a gas mask. Unfortunately, with such an increase in the population, the number of respirators ordered quickly proved inadequate.[19]

At the outset of war in 1939, some property owners attempted to make capital out of the emergency, encouraging those with money to have nothing to do with the official scheme. The owners of Aldwick Estate in Bognor were among those who attempted to make a profit, widely advertising their very exclusive properties as 'a safe retreat' for those fleeing the bombs. To the working class, these pleasant middle-class houses set in a potentially quiet seaside resort were known as 'funk holes'.

The realisation that the working class, in particular, were going to be left to front out the bombers, while the middle class simply deserted the cities, led to the demand for the government to adopt a more realistic policy. Garratt, in a 1938 Penguin Special, was among those who were making such demands:

> If those who have the misfortune to live and work in danger zones are to be treated as refugees, and if safety in war depends, under present arrangements, on the possession of a motor car and of a house with a garden, then there is every possibility of Herr Hitler succeeding in that disruption of England, which will be the main purpose for sending a large number of his best pilots and machines upon a very dangerous journey.[20]

It was as a result of this outcry that in early 1938 Sir John Anderson was again asked to chair a committee on the subject, this time pursuing the issue with much greater vigour. With a remit to consider 'various aspects of the problem of transferring persons from areas which are likely to be exposed to continuous air attack' and to 'assist in the preparations of plans', the committee presented its findings to the government in July of that same year. Strongly in favour of the establishment of a government-led evacuation scheme, the committee, while recognising that such an arrangement would be fraught with difficulty, felt that bold action was required:

The transfer of large numbers of people from their homes and accustomed surroundings to other and often unfamiliar areas is not a task to be undertaken lightly. It raises problems of great complexity and difficulty at every stage, whether it be the collection and transportation of the refugees or their reception, accommodation and feeding at the other end. All the services, which are delicately adjusted to meet the needs of the community on the present distribution of the population, would have to be refashioned to deal with the new situation.[21]

Although the report did not clearly define which groups were to be evacuated, it certainly favoured the removal from threatened areas of children under 14 years and in school units. The report further advocated the billeting of those children in private houses and that the obligation to receive them should be compulsory. Finally, the committee concluded that the government 'should bear the entire cost of the evacuation and maintenance in safer districts of schoolchildren removed from vulnerable areas'.[22]

The report itself did not find its way into the public domain until October 1938. However, it appears that the government had already absorbed the main recommendations of the Anderson committee, as these are at the heart of a series of hasty instructions sent out by the Home Office at the time of the Munich crisis. Second-tier authorities in areas thought likely to be bombed were encouraged to consider moving children under 14, in school groups, to places of greater safety. No effort was made by the government to co-ordinate these arrangements, forcing a small number of second-tier authorities in high-risk areas to make contact with authorities in rural or coastal areas. In north Kent, the children from a number of schools were to be sent to the assumed safety of the coast, but their exact destination was never stated. The following circular was sent out at the end of September to parents of Gillingham schoolchildren:

> It will be impossible before the children leave home for the parents to be told where they are going, but arrangements will be made for the parents to be informed by post of their whereabouts within 24 hours. No expense on the part of parents either in respect of transport or maintenance will be involved, and as far as possible, children of the same family will be kept together, whether they attend the same school or not.[23]

Furthermore, the authority advised:

> Children will be required to take with them an overcoat or raincoat, a blanket and food for one whole day, light luggage including at least one change of underclothing, and stockings, soap, tooth brush and respirator. Children must be ready to assemble as soon as they receive instructions to do so.[24]

Similarly, the Southampton City Corporation made contact with second-tier rural authorities to the west of the city, who agreed to take a total of 60,000 evacuees. It was intended that the transfer would be undertaken by road, with the authority commandeering whole fleets of local buses. Those with cars, however, were urged to make their own evacuation arrangements. A much more ambitious scheme than the one carried out in September the following year, it included not only schoolchildren and nursing mothers, but all who were considered non-essential to the workings of the city under wartime conditions.[25]

Interestingly, when compared with the number of evacuees in September 1939, the response from parents at this time was quite favourable, the *Chatham News* indicating that 'replies received from parents indicate that the majority favour sending children to places of safety'.[26] As with Portsmouth and Southampton, the actual number of children evacuated during the following year fell far short of a majority, being nearer to a lowly 35 per cent.

Had the children of the Medway Towns been evacuated at this time, they would most likely have been directed to the south coast. This was certainly the intention of a number of London authorities. However, the Kent Education Committee was contemplating how best to protect children already in schools on the south coast, determining that the best course of action was for all schools to be immediately closed. In providing an explanation, the *Kentish Express* explained: 'During the Spanish war bombs have fallen on schools where children collected, and this experience has led authorities to believe there is greater safety if children are scattered.'[27]

With the immediate arrival of evacuees expected, many south coast authorities carried out a rapid survey of accommodation facilities that might be available. In the two separate areas of Brighton and Hove, with evacuees thought likely to be coming from south London, teams of local schoolteachers carried out house-to-house surveys. In both areas this work was carried out on Thursday 29 September, with schools closed to release teachers for this work. It was reported that in Hove a third of the borough was canvassed, with teachers calling on 5,000 homes in 92 streets.[28] The expectation was that thousands of evacuated schoolchildren were about to descend on the town and householders would be required to house them under compulsion, but would receive any out-of-pocket expenses. Incredibly, in an editorial appearing in the *Brighton and Hove Gazette*, the writer, using the pseudonym 'Gazetteer', was able to claim:

> Nothing could have been further removed from the traditional British practice of muddling through. The greatest credit is due to those at the head of the various departments and equally to those patriotic citizens who rallied to their support.[29]

This is ironic, since the whole evacuation scheme was an off-the-cuff arrangement that had been subject to absolutely no forward planning; the very epitome of a state managing its affairs through the process of 'muddling through'. That a few forward-looking authorities took the necessary steps to arrange accommodation is praiseworthy, but hardly permits the nature of Gazetteer's comments. After all, once the children had arrived, they would have to be fed, educated and entertained. No thought had been given to any of these aspects.

It was in January 1939 that the government began moving forward on a newly developed evacuation strategy. Providing a touch of decided originality was the naming of the Ministry of Health as the overall co-ordinating body, with local implementation through the local housing authorities – primarily the same second-tier authorities who already had the lead for most Civil Defence issues. Behind this lay a government assumption that evacuees required no other facilities than that of being billeted in private homes. As such, the second-tier authorities were expected to survey all accommodation within their areas with a view to finding householders who would accept evacuees on the basis of one person per room. Those refusing were to be notified that, if necessary, it would become a compulsory requirement that they receive evacuees. From the results of these initial borough-wide surveys, each area would subsequently be allocated an approximate number of evacuees.

Effectively, in placing evacuation into the hands of second-tier authorities, county councils, with responsibility for schools and hospitals, were pushed into the background. Indeed, the very issue that would eventually oblige first-tier authority involvement – that of whether individual evacuees were nursing mothers, disabled people or children in education – was not a matter to which the government gave thought. Instead, it was all viewed as a simple logistical arrangement, that of transporting a large number of individuals to a place of relative safety where they were to be housed. Get this right and it was assumed that all else would fall into place. Thus, the Ministry of Transport would oversee the movement of evacuees and second-tier housing authorities their accommodation.

Progress on the evacuation scheme throughout the months before the outbreak of war failed to move out of that basic logistical envelope. As such, a full-scale evacuation practice, held on Monday 28 August, could do no more than march huge numbers of children from their homes or schools to various railway stations. This certainly took place in Southampton, where the schools were open during the previous weekend for children to receive instructions on how the practice was to be conducted. In Chatham this involved some 1,300 children marching from their schools to the railway station, with each school preceded by a banner bearing its name and number. For the purpose of the Chatham rehearsal, the *Chatham News* reported:

> An imaginary timetable was set up with 'trains' leaving Chatham station every quarter of an hour from 11am to 12.30pm. The schools assembled at about 9am when inspections of kit were carried out by the teachers and each child

issued with a label with its name and school number and a card with the school number and the child's group number in the school.[30]

As for the reception authorities, they were even more hamstrung. In most cases they had no real knowledge as to the number of evacuees they would eventually receive or even an indication as to their age or particular needs. Despite this, Hastings did assemble a large body of children to test the borough's ability to receive evacuees. According to the *London Times*:

> A first aid station was ready, when the children arrived, and in 12 minutes 500 children were handed emergency rations lent by grocers. Communications with the schools, which would act as distributing centres, were then tested.[31]

On the principal days set aside for evacuation, the first thing that became clear was that the actual numbers of those to be evacuated, across the entire south of England, was considerably less than had been expected. Throughout the country as a whole, it has been variously estimated that less than 2 million of an expected 5 million actually turned up at the given assembly points from where they were to be evacuated. Many parents, on being asked during the early part of the summer, had simply refused to give permission for their children to be evacuated. Others, on previously giving permission, now withdrew it and merely did not appear at the assembly points. Some openly admitted it was because they were unwilling to be separated from their children, preferring to die together as one family. From Portsmouth, where a potential 39,900 children could have been taken out of the city, only 11,970 were evacuated. In Southampton, where 11,725 children out of a possible 30,200 left the city, the war report of the city medical officer was later to include a further illuminating comment that is suggestive of a series of ill-planned arrangements:

> The schedule was often upset by the last minute withdrawals of children who had been registered for evacuation; and by the last minute unexpected arrival at the station of hundreds of children who had not been registered.

Richard Padley, in an early study of evacuation, suggested that the numbers of children being evacuated might have increased had an incentive been provided to help break the 'dominant social habit of family solidarity'.[32] To do this would have required the government to put considerably more effort into the overall planning of the scheme, ensuring parents knew where their children were to be taken and even meeting future host families. Only through this greater awareness of where the children were going, and making a connection between the evacuation and reception areas, could this trend have been reversed. If the government had looked upon evacuation as a humanitarian rather than a logistical exercise, then the many failings within the scheme might have been considerably reduced.

Of additional significance, and a factor that should be considered, yet another major problem of the original scheme, was that the south coast had not been seriously considered a potential danger area, and instead was seen as a safe refuge point. Even without Germany being in possession of French airfields, few seemed to doubt the possibility of the south coast being bombed. The 'future war' novelists had invariably included this as a highly likely scenario, while some of the noted experts on the subject also considered raids on the south coast as a possibility. Indeed, if there was no such fear, then why were Margate, Dover and the other south coast municipalities intent upon the construction of deep and highly expensive shelters? In September 1938 Brighton's chief fire officer, Charles Birch, while speaking at a national conference, made it clear that south coast towns would certainly be bombed in the event of a future European war. Of Brighton, Birch stated:

> Brighton's position on the South Coast will not be so cheerful as in the last war, when it was considered a paradise of peace. Today, with aerial warfare at its climax and with Brighton's defence forces so deficient, it occurs to me that places similarly situated will be frequently attacked and in danger more so than inland towns.[33]

Of coastal towns in general, Birch went on to say that they would 'become the first target of approaching aircraft, and the last resort for the unloading of bombs after making an unsuccessful raid on inland objectives'.[34]

At the time, this was something of a controversial statement, and one with which the government clearly disagreed. Indeed, the town of Brighton had even seen the distribution of a circular issued by the local education office which contained the phrase: 'Brighton is regarded as a town of comparative safety.'

Residents of other south coast towns also questioned the wisdom of sending evacuees into these potential front-line areas. In Folkestone, during the crisis of September 1938, private schools in the area had been among the first to arrange the evacuation of their children to the perceived safer inland areas of Harrogate and North Wales, but in September 1939 over 4,000 London schoolchildren were brought to Folkestone. In Worthing, a town only slightly less threatened than Folkestone, a correspondent to the local newspaper pointed out a number of very obvious truths:

> This town is surrounded by military objectives – the aerodromes at Shoreham, Ford and Tangmere; it has an important railway running through it; and it is only about five minutes distance from Portsmouth by fast aeroplane. It is almost certain to be the scene of some aerial fighting in the event of war, and the

unfortunate refugees [evacuees from south London] would at best only be transferred from the fire to the frying pan.[35]

As to whether the government or its doubters were correct, one only has to consider the actual events of the war to see that the south coast became a major battle zone. In all, both Worthing and Folkestone received in excess of sixty raids, while Brighton was hit on fifty separate occasions between June and September 1940. As for the rest of the south coast, including the Isle of Wight, there was no town that completely escaped the bombing. Fortunately, by the time these raids had got under way, many thousands of evacuees brought to the south coast for their own safety had been re-evacuated to places much more distant. Similarly, many of the permanent residents of immediate coastal locations had also been evacuated, as their areas were possible objectives of Operation Sea Lion. In Hastings, to take just one example, the population of the town between June and September 1940 fell by some 40,000, suggesting this as a possible guide to the numbers who either voluntarily or forcibly left the south coast at this time.

## Notes

1. Re-quoted from Stuart Hylton, *Their Darkest Hour* (Sutton Publishing, 2001), p. 35.
2. *Daily Mirror*, 4 September 1939.
3. *Chatham News*, 8 September 1939.
4. *Southampton Echo*, 2 September 1939.
5. *Isle of Wight Chronicle*, 7 September 1939.
6. *East Kent Mercury*, 9 September 1939.
7. Hylton, op. cit., p. 35.
8. IWM, Joan Widdett interview.
9. Adrian Searle, *Isle of Wight at War* (Dovecote Press, 1989), p. 154.
10. Ron Watson. Interview with author.
11. Anthony Kemp, *Southampton at War* (Ensign Publications, 1989), p. 10.
12. Re-quoted from Olga M. Baldwin et al., *We Remember 1930 to 1960* (Chidham, 2002), p. 96.
13. WSAO, E47/12/3, 18 September 1939.
14. *Southampton Echo*, 1 September 1939.
15. *Isle of Wight Chronicle*, 7 September 1939.
16. *East Kent Mercury*, 9 September 1939.
17. *The Protection of Your Home Against Air Raids* (Home Office, 1938), p. 12.
18. Air Commodore L.E.O. Charlton, *War Over England* (Longmans, 1936), p. 19.
19. *Brighton and Hove Gazette*, 1 October 1938.
20. G.T. Garratt, 'Air Raid Precautions', in *The Air Defence of Great Britain* (Penguin, 1938), p. 158.
21. Report of Committee on Evacuation, 26 July 1938, Cmd 5837, p. 6.
22. Ibid., p. 25.
23. *Chatham News*, 30 September 1938.
24. Ibid.
25. *Southampton Echo*, 28 September 1938.
26. *Chatham News*, 30 September 1938.
27. *Kentish Express*, 30 September 1938.

28. *Brighton and Hove Gazette*, 1 October 1938.
29. Ibid.
30. *Chatham News*, 1 September 1939.
31. *London Times*, 8 August 1939.
32. Richard Padley & Margaret Cole, *Evacuation Survey* (George Routledge & Sons, 1940), p. 49.
33. *Brighton and Hove Gazette*, 3 September 1938.
34. Ibid.
35. *Worthing Gazette*, 19 October 1938.

# 8

# The Land Front

Throughout the interwar years there was an ongoing debate as to the extent to which agriculture should be prepared for a future war. The parameters of the debate had been set during the later years of the First World War, resulting from the extensive food shortages. As early as January 1917, Sir Joseph Compton Rickett, Paymaster General, commenting on the continued problem of the U-boat blockade, was reported as saying that on the war being brought to an end, 'we must be more than ever a food growing country'.

But in reality, once the war ended, such sentiments were forgotten and little was done to support the agricultural industry. In part, this was due to the nature of the debate. While the most obvious solution of moving the country towards a position of self-sufficiency in food might appear attractive, it could only be achieved at the expense of industrial output. And, as regards any future war, the size and nature of Britain's industrial capacity would prove crucial. It was, quite clearly, the nation's industrial capacity that ensured production of the extensive quantities of military weapons, ammunition, equipment and stores that would be necessary actually to fight the war. Furthermore, it was this same industrial structure that permitted the defence industry to survive and flourish. To put it another way, the money required to fund the munitions industry came not from savings on food imports, but from money earned in industrial exports.

Among those who clearly thought like this was resident of Hever Castle, 2nd Viscount Astor, a Conservative politician and businessman. Although keen to see agriculture more efficiently developed, he placed limits on the level to which it might expand. In a Pelican Special based on his September 1937 report on British agriculture, he, together with social reformer Seebohm Rowntree, concluded:

Naval power and a large overseas trade are the natural complements of one another. It might be argued that we might be safer in some respects, less vulnerable at least to the danger of starvation, if we were a small nation with a much smaller population, growing all our food at home. But that choice is not open to us. We depend on a large-scale flow of imports from overseas, and we cannot escape from this dependence however much we seek to mitigate it. It follows that our safety in time of war is dependent on naval power, on maintaining the command of the seas and keeping open our trade routes. For this purpose a large overseas trade in time of peace is an asset of utmost value. A country, which aspires to the command of the sea, is the last country which can afford to pursue a policy of self-sufficiency.[1]

To this, Astor and Rowntree further added:

It is, therefore, we believe, fundamentally false policy to look for security to a reduction of our food imports in time of peace. Our aim should rather be, while maintaining a high volume of imports during peacetime, to take such measures as will enable us to sustain without serious hardship a large curtailment of those imports in time of war.[2]

And that, fundamentally, was the attitude towards agriculture in the years leading up to the conflict with Nazi Germany and Fascist Italy. But it did not mean that the threat of war was ignored. Instead, it required British agriculture, including the many areas of farmland accounted as being part of the south coast, to be placed on a sound enough footing to ensure that it could be rapidly expanded in time of emergency. Again, it was based on the lessons of earlier wars, with land under cultivation at the beginning of the French Revolutionary Wars and the First World War being considerably less than that being cultivated at the end of these same wars. Furthermore, these wars had seen the dramatic mobilisation of additional labour both to work these new lands and replace those who had entered the military.

Such a policy, however, did not meet with everyone's approval. The mere fact that British agriculture was continuing to decline in the 1920s and '30s, with some 70 per cent of the monetary value of British food being imported, proved itself a strong argument for those unhappy with this policy.[3] Lloyd George, a former wartime prime minister, even went so far as to state in a speech to the House of Commons in 1936:

The government seems to ignore completely one of the most important elements in the defence of the realm, and that is the provision of food. We came nearer to defeat owing to food shortages than we did from anything else. I cannot understand why, when they are thinking of the whole problem of war, and possible dangers, that the greatest danger of all seems to be left out of account.[4]

Along the south coast there were a great many who supported the sentiments expressed by Lloyd George rather than the actions being pursued by the government. Novelist John Galsworthy, whose home at one time was Bury, near Pulborough, was a strong believer in more food being grown in Britain during this period. In an article he wrote for *Land*, a farming journal, he reinforced the idea of Britain's agricultural industry needing to be considerably expanded.[5] In 1936, Sir Merrick Burrall, who was later to chair the West Sussex War Agricultural Committee, stated: 'what we must have is an agricultural peace time policy which will produce on the day war breaks out, not two years later, the maximum quantities of wheat, beef and mutton.'[6]

It was a fine line that was being walked. While the military-industrial complex was given precedence, those either employed within the sector or making use of the weapons produced would still have to be fed. In simple and localised terms, the dockyard workers of Portsmouth and Chatham, together with the factory workers and dockers of Southampton, would have to be supplied with food, part of which would come from the farms that lay alongside that same coastline. If the latter were not up to the task, the former would be unable to perform their work. During the First World War, the industrial workers within those very towns became increasingly militant as a result of food concerns. Unless the problems of a sufficient food supply were completely solved, the war could be lost through an inability or unwillingness of those workers to manufacture the tools of war.

In pursuit of its somewhat dangerous policy of radically expanding agriculture only in the event of war, the government under Baldwin (1935–37) and later Chamberlain (1937–40) set about establishing the necessary infrastructure. A number of committees took responsibility for overseeing this work, of which the Food Supply in Wartime Subcommittee of the Committee for Imperial Defence (CID) was the most important. With the CID having responsibility for the overall preparation of the country for war, this subcommittee not only directly oversaw a number of actions designed to ease any wartime food shortages, but also co-ordinated the work of a number of more specialised committees established by other government departments. Among issues directly overseen by the Food Supply in Wartime Subcommittee were those of food control, measures for the distribution of food during periods of intense air raids and the control of pricing.[7]

At the heart of these particular measures was food control, through which both the means of distribution and pricing could be regulated. Locally, this involved the setting up of food control committees, with every local authority along the south coast directly approached for this purpose. The normal composition of these committees, which were to come into operation upon the outbreak of war, was that of a borough or town clerk taking the chair, with selected traders and members of the public being asked to join the committee. In Southampton, the Food Control Committee came into operation during the first week of war and was made up of eleven members, most of whom were elected councillors with knowledge of retailing. The role of these re-established Food Control Committees was to replicate the duties performed by the local food control apparatus that had operated during the First World War, and which had taken a number of essential acts to alleviate localised food shortages. Supporting these committees, and making it easier to relieve an area of shortage, was the establishment of a centralised purchasing system, whereby the government could step in and take possession of a product at source. In a more limited way this had also taken place during the First World War, but as often as not it was through local agreement between the borough food controller and a willing supplier. Now, the work was being carried out centrally, and the necessary emergency powers were instantly available for the taking of such an action. Hand in glove with these arrangements were plans for both the pooling and direction of publicly and privately owned transport for the conveyance of essential foods to wherever they might be urgently needed.[8]

Labour requirements were an important issue both for the CID and the Ministry of Agriculture and Fisheries; the former because it had to ensure high levels of wartime recruitment and the latter because it needed to retain high levels of production. To this end, the Committee for Imperial Defence Manpower Subcommittee agreed that immediately upon the outbreak of war, those over 21 and undertaking skilled farm work would be regarded as being in a reserved occupation. However, this would only be a temporary measure; those same skilled workers would eventually be allowed to enter the services through substitution on the farm by women or men unfit for service.

To facilitate the early recruitment of skilled farm labourers into the services, the Women's Land Army was reformed in June 1939.[9] During the First World War, this organisation had brought over 200 women on to the farms along the south coast, thereby playing an important role in maintaining levels of home food production. It was now intended that a cadre of trained women would be available to enter into farm work as soon as war might be declared. In this respect, East Sussex was to play a particularly significant role, as it was here that the administrative headquarters of the new organisation was established. Specifically, this was Balcombe Place, a large mansion situated near Hayward's Heath. This was the residence of Lady Gertrude Denman, appointed by the government as chairman of the new organisation in April 1938. It was her task to ensure that the new organisation would be fully operational when necessary.

Balcombe Place immediately became a hive of activity. While some of its 2,000 acres of mixed farm and woodland was used for training some of the new recruits, the emphasis was on the main house and the conversion of rooms into offices:

Imagine a baronial hall thus transformed. The red velvet curtains heavily in their place, the oak panelling makes a rich and sombre background but the splendid rooms filled with office desks and trestle tables, piled with card indexes and stationery, typewriters and telephones, pots of paste and stickphast.

These were the words applied to Balcombe Place by author and poet Vita Sackville-West, following the adaptation of the mansion to its new administrative role.

A team of female clerical workers was quickly put together, their initial duties centring upon contact with farmers who might be prepared to train the volunteers and establishing future hostels that could be used to accommodate the women once permanently attached to farms. For those employed in the offices of Balcombe Place, the experience was very different to that of a typical office environment. Caught between the 'upstairs' family of Lady Denman and the 'downstairs' staff who were still on hand to run the house, they had no obvious niche. A flavour of this is gleaned from the recollections of Maureen Strong, who joined the clerical team in 1941:

> On a dark chilly evening in February 1943 I first became acquainted with Balcombe Place, a large country mansion near Haywards Heath, West Sussex, the home of Lady Denman, founder of the Women's Land Army. I was accompanied by my Mother and we were met at Balcombe Station having travelled from Burgess Hill by train where we were living. The small van duly arrived at Balcombe Place where we were ushered in by Lady Denman's butler. My Mother remained in the large hall while I was interviewed before being offered the job of shorthand typist in the hostels department of the W.L.A. Headquarters. I received a letter from the Ministry of Agriculture offering employment and setting out the following Terms and Conditions. My starting salary would be £2.10.0 per week and the hours were 9.30 to 6pm on weekdays and from 9.30 to 12.30 or 9 to 12 on Saturdays. One and quarter hours for lunch to be brought with one, soup provided on Mondays, Wednesdays and Fridays at 2d a cup with a cup of tea and cake provided at 11am and 4pm. A van from Balcombe Place to meet the train arriving at Balcombe at 9.25 and return transport to the Station at night. Appointments are temporary, made upon a weekly basis and may be terminated by a week's notice on either side.[10]

Putting aside the internal social workings of the house-cum-administrative unit, the siting of Balcombe Place in the midst of rural East Sussex did rather cut it off from the rest of the world. It was a point raised in Parliament by the Conservative politician Lord Bingley of Bramham in January 1943:

> The Women's Land Army should have an Office, which is more accessible. At present they are based in an office, which is a long way from many parts of the country. It is extremely difficult for people in the Midlands or in the North to visit the head office in Sussex. It will be obvious, therefore, that very

often difficulties, which might be very small, have become very much greater. Personal consultation is of enormous value in cases of that kind. The Post Office seems to have found the office rather remote, judging by the difficulty which one has in getting replies to letters.[11]

A second important element in the workings of the Women's Land Army was the establishment of various county committees. As initially envisaged, the role of these committees was the seeking out of recruits and the overseeing of the general placement and well-being of volunteers. For the purpose of creating these committees, Lady Denman quickly sought out individuals to serve as chairmen. In most cases she chose those who emanated from the same social milieu as she did. In East Sussex, for instance, she appointed Countess de la Warr, whose ancestral home was at Withyan near Crowborough, while in Kent, the already mentioned Vita Sackville-West, of Sissinghurst Place, was much associated with the Women's Land Army.

Once established, these county committees set about the task of attracting an initial number of volunteers who could be given immediate training. In East Sussex, Countess de la Warr contacted a number of local newspapers, with this letter appearing in the *Eastbourne Herald* on 17 June 1939: 'in a future war, food production will be a work of vital importance – a work in which women will have to play an active part. At least 50,000 will be needed ... We want them to enrol in the Women's Land Army now.'[12]

Meetings, letters to the local press and general word of mouth eventually resulted in over 600 trained women being available for immediate employment on south coast farms on the outbreak of war.[13]

A further important subcommittee, set up in 1936 under the Ministry for Coordinating Defence, was that of Food Supply Rationing. It was recognised that rationing would be an early feature of any major war so as to prevent an artificial shortage through hoarding. A procedure was therefore put in place by the committee that would begin with forms being distributed to each household in which basic details as to the size and nature of the household were requested, together with the name of the retailer from whom they wished to receive their rationed items. Upon the return of these forms ration books would be issued, while arrangements were to be made to ensure that the selected retailer had the necessary supplies to fulfil expected demand.[14] It was this very scheme, introduced in Southampton by the Co-op in December 1917, that had gained that particular retailer a stern censure in the local police court. However, its universal adoption in the Second World War was proof that a system of registering with a named retailer was the real solution, rather than having hordes of individuals descending on any shop that had taken a recent delivery of a commodity in short supply.

The Ministry of Agriculture took primary responsibility for both a planned increase of wartime production and for the establishment of a reserve stock of both foods and essential farm materials. At the heart of the Ministry's thinking was the experience of the First World War and, in particular, the establishment of a much-increased level of output once a series of emergency measures had been put in place. The Ministry estimated that food imports would be curtailed by about 25 per cent and that this could only be made good by a considerable increase in land brought under the plough. To help ensure that this would become a reality, the Agricultural Development Act was pushed through Parliament during the winter of 1938/39. Its main purpose was to encourage farmers to make that conversion even before war had been declared. Through the offering of a grant of £2 per acre, it was hoped that farmers would begin ploughing up existing pastures or otherwise idle land with a view to clawing into the following year's harvest an additional 1.7 million acres.[15]

The Agricultural Development Act was also of significance in other respects. Apart from providing grants for drainage, it permitted the acquisition and storage for wartime release of farm machinery and fertilisers. Both were to have a considerable impact as they ensured the availability of products for farmers who were expanding their ploughed lands, as well as helping those seeking to increase efficiency through the replacement of horses by mechanised machinery. An important player here was the Dagenham-based Ford Company. Agreeing to increase the production of the Fordson tractor, they allowed the Ministry to purchase 3,000 at a discount of 27.5 per cent. These tractors would be stored at various dealers throughout the country, who 'would start the engines from time to time to make sure the Fordson tractors in their care were ready for action'.[16] Only if war were declared would these particular tractors be released, and 'if there was no war, the company guaranteed to buy the tractors back'.[17]

As stated, the Ministry of Agriculture started to develop an emergency stockpile of food, making a series of limited purchases in 1938 and 1939. Through this, a three-month supply was created of wheat, flour, oil seed, whale oil (for margarine), sugar, canned meat, milk and cheese. Adequate accommodation was provided by securing a number of warehouses on the outskirts of several major towns.[18] At Tenterden, for instance, one such storage facility was located in the grounds of the local railway station, with the contents on hand for easy conveyance to the towns of the south coast if this was required.

To oversee the required increase in levels of ploughed acreage, distribution of stored farm machinery and fertilisers, the Ministry of Agriculture and Fisheries also resurrected the wartime local agricultural committees that had been pioneered in the First World War. To act as the Ministry's 'agent in the field', they were to be organised at county level and be composed of those involved in farming or with a rural interest.[19] In addition, and operating immediately beneath the county committees, were a number of district committees. Among the duties performed by these district committees was the direct management of farms which were deemed to be failing to meet required levels of efficiency, as well as the provision of local advice on the supply of labour, machinery and fertilisers. The first element in creating these committees was put in place in December 1937, although they were not due to become operational until the outbreak of a war. This was when the Ministry approached those it thought suitable to become the committees' chairmen. The later chairman of the West Sussex War Agricultural Committee was approached through a letter, expressed in the following terms and signed by William Morrison, the Minister of Agriculture:

> I feel strongly that the pivotal position of chairman is one for which the selection should be made in time of peace, if only to ensure that the Committee may be brought into existence with the minimum of delay in the event of war. It is to invite you to accept the position of Chairman of the Committee for West Sussex that I am writing.

At that time, strict confidentiality was to be observed.

The County War Agricultural Executive Committees gained immediate authority upon the outbreak of war, with the East Sussex committee calling its first meeting on 8 September 1939. The county committees had very extensive powers, particularly over crops to be grown and areas to be ploughed. In their approach, however, the committees differed widely, with the one in Hampshire, responsible for the east Hampshire littoral, gaining a reputation for vindictiveness and dispossessing the land of some of the more progressive farmers because they were in conflict with the committees' views.[20] In contrast, the East Sussex committee was recognised for its willingness to work closely with local farmers, encouraging good practice. In a newspaper interview, the chairman recorded: 'Although we have wide and almost unlimited powers we have always sought the cooperation of the farmers and this cooperation had been given in a most willing spirit.'[21]

As part of their 'unlimited powers', the committee could assemble, as their First World War predecessor had done, large groups of mobile workers that could be transferred to farms at will. This not only included skilled farm workers and members of the Women's Land Army, but also prisoners of war. In Kent, a team of 400 'land girls' were organised each summer for bringing in the harvest, while a one-day school for the instruction of gang leaders was also held each summer. The one area in which the committee had very limited control was the use of land for military purposes. Efforts made by the committees were frequently undermined by sudden decisions on the part of the Air Ministry or War Office to obtain land for airfields or gun batteries, with no regard for its agricultural value. R.S. Hudson, the Minister of Agriculture, in a visit to the coastal areas of Kent and Sussex in June 1940, expressed his concern over the unnecessary damage to farmland at this time. Further damage was caused by training, with land around Stanmer House, near Brighton, being 'wantonly' destroyed in 1944.[22]

Although not everything had been set in place by September 1938, the Munich crisis of that month brought to the fore how the current structure might work in reality. At that time, the appointed chairmen of the Kent, Isle of Wight, Hampshire, West and East Sussex agricultural committees were alerted to the need to activate their respective committees, while action was taken to ensure that food stocks would be delivered to areas where evacuees were expected to arrive. Furthermore, and 'to discourage panic buying or a dramatic rise in food prices, newspapers informed the public that supplies of essential foodstuffs' was adequate.[23] One particular lesson that came out of the crisis was the effect of food hoarding, with some retail shops in Worthing, the Medway Towns and some coastal villages forced to close because of artificially high demand. To meet this it was realised that rationing would need to be introduced with the utmost priority, while a campaign was undertaken to encourage householders to buy their own reserves of non-perishable commodities but not stockpile at the last moment.[24]

## Notes

1. Viscount Astor & B. Seebohm Rowntree, *British Agriculture* (Pelican Special, Harmondsworth, 1939), p. 54.
2. Ibid., p. 55.
3. A.S. Milward, *War Economy and Society, 1939–45* (London, 1977), p. 246.
4. House of Commons, 10 March 1936.
5. *Land*, 1918.
6. Re-quoted from '"The Front Line of Freedom": state-led agricultural revolution in Britain, 1939–45', in Brian Short et al. (eds), *The Front Line of Freedom* (British Agricultural History Society, 2006), p. 4.
7. Alan F. Wilt, *Food for War* (OUP, 2001), pp. 39–42.
8. Ibid., pp. 81–3.
9. Ibid., pp. 115–6; Gill Clarke, 'The Women's Land Army and its Recruits', in Short et al., op. cit., pp. 101–3.
10. Maureen Strong, WW2 People's War: www.bbc.co.uk/ww2peopleswar/stories/95/a5825595.shtml.
11. Hansard, 26 January 1943.
12. *Eastbourne Herald*, 17 June 1939.
13. Vita Sackville-West, *The Women's Land Army* (London, 1944), p. 95.
14. Wilt, op. cit., pp. 62–3.
15. Ibid., p. 69.
16. Michael Williams, *Ford and Fordson Tractors* (Bounty Books, 2006), p. 74.
17. Ibid.
18. Wilt, op. cit., pp. 122–3.
19. Ibid., p. 69.
20. John Martin, 'The Structural Transformation of British Agriculture', in Short et al., op. cit., p. 31.
21. *Sussex Express and County Herald*, 6 December 1940.
22. Short et al., op. cit., p. 14.
23. Wilt, op. cit., p. 103.
24. Ibid.

# Part Three
## Preparing the Active Defences

# Introduction

In the predicted European war, the south coast would play a pivotal role in the defence of the nation. A likely route for bombers attempting to reach the metropolis, it was an entry point that needed to be sealed. Whether these aircraft came from captured airfields in France, direct from Germany or even from the new pro-Nazi territory of northern Spain, a south coast overflight was the most likely scenario.[1]

The south coast was also a likely target for aerial bombing in its own right, whether deliberately targeted or the victim of dropped bombs by aircraft unable to reach London. Its proximity to the Continent made its industrial and resort towns a primary goal and one easily reached. To this could be added the even more horrific possibility of invasion, the enemy's first footfall almost certainly on beaches somewhere between the Medway estuary and the east Hampshire littoral. In such an event, the coastline would be transformed into a bloody battleground from which few would emerge unscathed.

By 1935, Germany had clearly become the recognised enemy, with an air force that, while clearly breaking the terms set by the Treaty of Versailles, had reached parity with that of the Royal Air Force and would soon overtake it in size. Churchill, for one, was very open about the prospects that lay before the country at that time, and was more than aware that Germany would soon have command of the air. In November of the previous year, he had stated before Parliament his clear assertion that:

> Germany, at this moment, has a military air force – that is to say military squadrons with the necessary ground service, and the necessary reserves of trained personnel and materials – which only awaits an order to assemble in full open combination; and that this illegal air force is rapidly approaching equality with our own. Secondly, by this time next year, if Germany executes her existing programme without acceleration, and if we execute our existing programme

on the basis which now lies before us without slowing down, and carry out the increases announced in Parliament in July last, the German military air force will this time next year be in fact as least as strong as our own, and it may be even stronger.[2]

To confront this threat, the south coast would need sturdy and resilient defences. Or at least that would seem the most common-sense approach. But history and governments do not necessarily follow the course of common sense. For one thing, there were too many other factors at play. Not least of these was the great national fear of war – a fear that firmly held in check those who might have wished to increase levels of military expenditure. In the same year that Chamberlain announced his earth-shattering message that 'the bomber will always get through', defence expenditure certainly rocketed. But it rocketed downwards – not upwards. In that year, the defence estimates were set at £340,000 less than they had been the previous year.

From 1935 onwards, the pretence that war on the horizon did not require the use of additional government funding was finally overturned. Attention could now be given to purchasing the necessary weapons to defend the coastline of the south. But, once again, that is not what happened. A few improvements were made, and they looked adequate. Efforts were made to acquire aircraft of sufficient quality to match the Luftwaffe and several additional airfields began to be constructed in proximity to the south coast. But much of it was window dressing.

The airfields, for example, looked good, but were they capable of doing their job? Certainly they were built at a fantastic cost, but for this there was good reason. Instead of being designed for war, they were provided with landmark buildings of architectural splendour rather than military usefulness. Bereft of solid runways, bombproof hangars and underground workshops, the airfields were simply showcasing modern neo-classicism.

As for the vulnerable invasion beaches, they were not even given the courtesy of a series of expensive but militarily useless buildings. Where, during the First World War, numerous gun batteries, searchlights and observation posts had once stood firm, these were now abandoned, with no thought to their replacement or reconstruction. Guns, long removed, and ancient even by the time of their removal, were placed into storage, with no plan to restore them.

In common with the newly constructed airfields, the naval bases and dockyards of the south coast were also denied the advantage of underground workshops or bombproof, covered docks and slips. Similarly, the commercial ports, ordnance factories and aviation plants, assuming that they should have remained in the south, were denied bombproof facilities that would have allowed them to continue their important war-winning activities unimpaired by air raids or the damage that might be inflicted upon them.

To this extent, therefore, the south coast was much less prepared than it had been at the outset of previous wars. Prior to the outbreak of the First World War, when the biggest threat to the south coast had been that of invasion, gun batteries had defended vast stretches of the most vulnerable sections of the coastline. Around some of the industrial complexes were located inner rings of land forts, offering them additional protection. With many of the batteries and most of the land forts now abandoned, regarded as either unnecessary or obsolete, one might have expected them to be replaced by something more effective and in keeping with military developments. This, of course, was not so. Merely building a few more airfields and introducing additional squadrons to share these facilities was not comparable to the level of defences to which a previously prioritised south coast was accustomed. While the earlier anti-invasion gun batteries and forts had seen millions of pounds spent on them to ensure they were invulnerable to enemy action, the vital airfields of the south coast were not permitted a similar level of security, with only last-minute attention, at the time of the Munich crisis, given to even such basic ideas as camouflage.

A further element to both the defence of the south coast and to fighting the war in general was that of manpower. The First World War had certainly demonstrated the glaring problems of waiting for a war to be declared before recruitment really got under way. Apart from the need to implement a rapid training programme, it often left vital industries, such as agriculture and ordnance manufacturers, short of the skilled labour they required. Here, if only in part, one lesson of the First World War had been learnt. In those few vital years prior to the outbreak of that second European war, attention had been given to the needs of agriculture. More use was to be made of women through the Women's Land Army, thereby allowing farm workers who joined the army to be immediately replaced by those already trained in farm work. However, no similar scheme was to be developed, until the war had reached a very high level of intensity, for women to be trained and brought into industry.

In general terms, the British army in 1939 was both short of numbers and lacked the necessary equipment to fight a modern, fast-moving, mechanised war. Due to the background and age of many of its senior officers, the British army was still entrenched in the tactics of the Somme. At the heart of these shortcomings had been the 'Ten Year Rule'. Adopted in 1919, and based on a suggestion put forward by Winston Churchill, then Secretary of War, it deemed that no major war could possibly break out within the next ten years. Effectively stultifying military thinking and guaranteeing that the heavy post-war cuts could be retained, it continued in force until 1932.

The influential peace lobby, combined with a nation completely in fear of a future European war, held equal sway in this area. Such radical ideas as peacetime conscription or a general expansion of the voluntary army were seen as warmongering concepts that would make war ever more likely. Neither was recognised as being essential for the future well-being of the country. If implemented, one or both would have helped create a vast pool of trained individuals that could be called upon in the event of an emergency.

Instead, the nation had to fall back on a 'muddling through', last-ditch approach, with several innovations only seeing the light of day on the very eve of hostilities. Among them was that of re-establishing various branches of the military that had permitted the recruitment of women during the First World War. The earliest to be reformed, in September 1938, was a women's service for the support of the army, named the Auxiliary Territorial Service (ATS). This was followed by the Women's Royal Naval Service (WRNS), founded in April 1939, and the Women's Auxiliary Air Force (WAAF), founded in June 1939.

Of equal significance was an announcement in March 1939 that the Territorial Army was to be doubled in size, and the Compulsory Training Act was passed in May 1939. In the latter, men could be called up to the services for a period of six months' training before returning to their trades and professions. It was, in its purest form, a return to the old militia concept of the eighteenth century, which had helped firm up the south coast defences against the threatened French invasion. But no attempt, even at this stage, was made to engage one further element of the population – those of an age either too young or too old for military service or those in occupations that would, even if conscription was reintroduced under wartime conditions, have prevented their entry into one of the three services. A concept that had been used in both the French wars and the First World War, it was left uninitiated until the war was about eight months old. This, of course, was a further element of the earlier part-time militia service and subsequently redeveloped in the First World War as Volunteer Training Corps. In May 1940, following a call to arms by Anthony Eden, it was to be known briefly as the Local Defence Volunteers (LDV), before being renamed the Home Guard.

As much as anything, it was the early introduction of conscription that prevented the uneven flow of recruitment that had caused such chaos during the opening months of the First World War. In September 1939 it was announced that all men aged between 18 and 41 would be called into the armed services if required. At the same time, a previously published list of reserved occupations made it clear that certain groups would be exempt; this included dockworkers, farmers and utility workers. As for the last group, which included those employed by the water, gas and electricity supply companies, this was recognition of the importance attached to the repair of infrastructure damage in the event of bombing raids. To ensure the evenness of recruitment and so reduce the need for emergency training camps, and as belatedly introduced in early 1916, men were called into the services by age cohorts. Thus, in October 1939 only those aged between 20 and 23 were immediately required to register for one of the armed services. In turn, this early introduction of conscription cancelled out the need for, or even the possibility of, volunteer regiments being formed, with all those conscripted being directed through a centralised system that provided the limited choice of the already existing services and their attached units.

## Notes

1. In the late 1930s, and well before the unleashing of German mechanised forces into France, the well-publicised weaknesses of the French army permitted an assumption to be made that France might not withstand a crossing of her borders. As for direct flights from Germany, the south coast entry point made considerable sense if Germany wished to avoid flying over the neutral Low Countries.
2. Winston Churchill, 'The War Memories', in *Life* magazine, 19 April 1948, p. 114.

# 9

# Defeating the Bomber

For those who cared to dwell on the possibility of a future war, fear of the bomber would inevitably come to dominate their thoughts. Apart from the numerous fictional accounts, such as those already explored and which attempted to portray the devastation that could be inflicted, there were also the writings of a number of theorists who took a similar view. First among these was Giulio Douhet, whose influential *Command of the Air* was published in 1921. For him, air power had initiated the era of total war, where civilian populations would be subject to merciless bombardment. According to Douhet:

> The aeroplane has complete freedom of action and direction; it can fly to and from any point of the compass in the shortest time – in a straight line – by any route deemed expedient. Nothing man can do on the surface of the earth can interfere with a plane in flight, moving freely in the third dimension. All the influences, which have conditioned and characterised warfare from the beginning are powerless to affect aerial action.

To this Douhet added:

> There will be no distinction any longer between soldier and civilians. The defences on land and sea will no longer serve to protect the country behind them; nor can victory on land or sea protect the people from enemy aerial attacks unless that victory ensures the destruction, by actual occupation of the enemy's territory, of all that gives life to his aerial forces. [1]

In Britain, there were those who were prepared to agree with Douhet. Among them was Hugh Trenchard who, as Chief of Air Staff, a position he held from 1919 to 1930, had stated that 'fighter defence must be kept to the smallest possible number'. For Trenchard it was a long-held view, clearly expressed by him some seven years earlier when, as commander of the Royal Flying Corps in France, he had declared that the aeroplane was 'not a defence against the aeroplane'.[2]

So what did this particular viewpoint in tactical thinking mean for the south coast and the way it might be prepared for the war that eventually broke out in September 1939? Quite simply, it meant that the entire coastline area would be very much on the front line; the most likely entry point or gateway for the vast bomber armadas. In addition, because of their strategic, industrial and general economic value, the numerous towns of the south coast would suffer a high risk of devastating aerial bombardment.

All this applied whoever the future enemy might be. In the 1920s, France was reckoned to be the only potential, if somewhat unlikely, enemy. In this case, with parts of the south coast lying a mere 20 miles distant, the in-coming bombers would almost certainly pass over the south coast. From the mid-1930s onwards, it became increasingly clear that the enemy would be Germany and that war was a near certainty. Although, in the case of war with Germany, bombing raids might now be expected on cities of the industrial north, the south was still considered a likely target. An Air Staff paper of July 1934 viewed it as highly probable that Germany would make use of bases captured in Holland and Belgium. This would, therefore, make Germany 'quite as well placed to deliver effective attacks' on the south coast as there would be bombers based in France.[3]

In the event, of course, the situation was far worse than was being imagined at this time, Nazi Germany successfully taking possession of mainland Europe in its virtual entirety. Nevertheless, despite the awareness of this danger to the south coast it was, for much of the interwar period, left in a state of virtual defencelessness. Following the First World War, the south coast was entirely stripped or depleted of nearby airfields, coastal gun batteries and other functional fighting units.

The inability of the defences of the south coast to meet a concerted air strike was highlighted by a series of exercises that were carried out each summer. Invariably, a squadron or two of RAF bombers would attempt to reach London after first passing over the south coast. In turn, a squadron of fighters would be sent up from Tangmere, Biggin Hill or Hawkinge to intercept them. More often than not, these fighters would fail to intercept the bombers, with the latter successfully reaching their target. It was all done in a very sportsman-like way, a point highlighted by the aviation magazine *Flight* when reporting the summer exercise of 1927:

Thursday 28 July. The weather showed no improvement, and again was all in favour of the enemy, although it sometimes tried to equalise matters by obscuring the target from their view. The first raid of the day had to be abandoned on account of the weather. I am not sure whether this raid was made by No 11 or No 12 [Squadron]. One would imagine by No 11, as the clouds have been especially unkind to the squadron during the week. At any rate, No 11 sent up a flight, which crossed the coast near Worthing at 08.45 hrs. It reached Chelsea, but as clouds obscured the target the Horsleys did not release their bombs. There is still chivalry in war. A flight of No 17 Fighter Squadron was hunting these Horsleys, but failed to find them.[4]

Further highlighting their inability to prevent the bombers from reaching their target was the summer air exercise of 1933. On that occasion it had been adjudged that bombers flying in close formation and providing boxes of fire from their mounted Lewis guns had downed all the attacking fighters sent against them.

It was partly based on the evidence of those various summer exercises that Prime Minister Baldwin had become convinced of the supremacy of the bomber, leading to his 'the bomber will always get through' pronouncement. Baldwin's reasoning, as set out in that speech, was quite simple:

Imagine one hundred cubic miles covered with clouds and fog, and you can calculate how many aeroplanes you would have to throw into that to have any chance of catching odd aeroplanes as they fly through it. It cannot be done and there is no expert in Europe who will say that it can be done.

From this he drew only one horrific and frightening conclusion:

The only defence is offence, which means you have to kill more women and children more quickly than the enemy if you want to save yourselves. I mention that so that people may realise what is waiting for them when the next war comes.[5]

The debate over the primacy of the bomber had, at its core, the supposed greatly reduced value of the fighter. If the bomber would 'always get through', what was the point of acquiring fighter aircraft. Air Commodore Lionel Charlton, a Royal Air Force officer who entered the debate during the 1930s, explained the argument quite succinctly:

The abolition of the fighter aircraft is insisted upon. The contention is that they are useless to prevent a bombing raid, and that the cost of construction and upkeep, and the absorption of personnel, would again be at the expense of the offensive power of the nation's air arm.[6]

Instead of wasting money on fighters, everything should be directed towards the building of a massive force of bombers. In doing so, these bombers would act as a deterrent, frightening any one country from attacking another – a sort of 1930s version of Mutually Assured Destruction (MAD). Charlton, while appearing to accept the basic premise, also recognised the outcome as morally unacceptable. In

common with vast numbers of others, he looked towards the League of Nations
for a more rational solution, indicating his desire for an international air force
'with which to enforce the punitive sanctions ordained by a world tribunal'.[7]

While Trenchard, as Chief of Air Staff, might have held the view that the
bomber was supreme, others were prepared to question this assumption. Among
them was Hugh Dowding, head of RAF Fighter Command during the Battle of
Britain. He, together with a number of ministers attached to various departments
concerned with the defence of the country, regarded the primary role of the
RAF to be that of defending the country rather than directing its resources to an
all-out bombing policy.

A key factor for those who supported the concept of bombers being invincible
was the difficulty in detecting their approach. Baldwin had referred to bombers
becoming near invisible because of those 'one hundred cubic miles covered with
clouds and fog'. Charlton put it another way:

> If one were to go outside on any starlit night and gaze into the sky, the immensity of space becomes acutely realizable. It seems a sheer impossibility for defending aircraft, even aided by the guns and searchlights, to guard in three dimensions the approaches.[8]

To this was added a series of further arguments. First of these concerned the
nature of the fighter and whether such machines were even capable of overhauling the bomber if the latter was detectable. Apart from anything else, time would
be lost in the process of taking off and climbing to the appropriate height:

> Add now one more minute for manoeuvre to assume position for opening fire effectually and it will be found that fourteen minutes have elapsed between the first warning and the first machine gun burst. During this interval the bombers have been flying towards their goal at a speed of 250 miles an hour, and will have covered a further distance of sixty miles.[9]

Charlton, in this particular scenario, felt that actual interception would prove,
at the very least, 'enormously difficult'. However, he at least gave his imaginary
fighters a speed of 300mph, and so theoretically capable of catching the bomber.
In reality, the airfields that served the south coast at this time were equipped
with aircraft that had nothing like this speed. Instead, defence against the 255mph
Dornier bombers that Germany possessed was in the hands of the slower Gloster
Gladiator and Hawker Fury, neither with a speed much in excess of 250mph.

Finally, if one follows the argument completely through, there was a simple
belief that even if the fighter was able to seek out and approach a bomber formation, presumably by meeting it head on rather than attempt a futile chase, the
fighter would be unable to inflict upon the bomber any significant damage. The

bombers, through the tactic of flying in a box-like formation, would bring such overwhelming fire power on the small and lightly armed fighter as to ensure their continued security. According to Charlton:

> Bombing aircraft will normally fly by day in tightly packed formations, or groups of formations, varying in size from six to nine machines. They will be dual or multi-seaters. They will be capable of all round fire from both rigid and non-rigid gun mountings. They will be carefully designed for the avoidance of all blind spots, especially from underneath. They will be staggered and spaced in flight so as to afford each other the utmost mutual protection. They will on no account, unless they lose flying trim, break formation, for in that way lies disaster; they must form 'square' in the air as the British infantry once did on the ground. [10]

Fundamentally, it was developments along England's south coast that proved crucial in destroying not just one of these arguments, but each in turn. Most important was the establishment at various sites of a long-range warning system, which ensured that any approaching force of bombers would be detected well before they crossed the coastline. This, when used effectively, would provide fighter aircraft with enough warning to be in the air and at a sufficient height prior to the arrival of the approaching bombers. As for the fighters being in the right place at the right time, this was achieved through the development of a workable and efficient system of plotting, which allowed fighters to be directed to the best point of interception. Finally, through the creation of super-fast fighters, with much of the work on their development carried out at Southampton, these same bombers could now be intercepted on even terms and with the potential of destroying them prior to their reaching the target they sought.

The genesis underlying the system of detecting and tracking the progress of bombers as they passed over the south coast had its origins in the First World War. Along the coast were established a number of observation posts manned, originally, by either invalided soldiers or boy scouts. Having received little or no training, they consequently failed to correctly identify the aircraft they were observing. It was for this reason that a force of special constables eventually replaced them, whose sole duty it was to man these observation posts. Once aircraft were sighted, this information was passed to a central plotting room at Horse Guards in London, having first passed through a nearby sub-control room. Once received at Horse Guards, orders were sent out to the most appropriate airfield for a unit to 'scramble' and hopefully intercept the incoming raiders.

This system, however, was beset with problems; not least because of the impossibility of even attempting an intercept before raiding bombers were well inland. In fact, around London a series of defensive rings were created, with aircraft only permitted to patrol in a zone approximately 10 miles from the capital. Either side of this intercept zone were other relatively thin zones that were reserved exclusively for anti-aircraft guns and barrage balloons. While it ensured that the home defence fighters would not be subject to 'friendly' anti-aircraft fire, it also meant that areas in front of these zones, including the entirety of the south coast, were relatively open to attack.

At Biggin Hill, an airfield that was to become crucial to the defence of the south coast and which had first been established during the winter of 1916/17, a number of refinements were added to the overall scheme. In particular, through experimental work being undertaken in ground-to-air radio communication, machines already airborne could be given updated information as to where bombers might be heading. In his history of the airfield, Graham Wallace describes the system as developed there during the early months of 1918:

> Information on the enemy's movements was fed into an operation room in the North Camp from coastguard stations, observer posts, searchlight and gun sites, as well as patrolling aircraft. This data was sorted and coordinated so that the raiders' positions could be plotted with a fair degree of accuracy. The courses and altitudes that the pilots would have to fly to make an interception were computed and passed to [a] transmitter at Aperfield Court for relaying by wireless telephone to patrolling Bristol Fighters.[11]

However efficient those at Biggin Hill and other airfields might prove to be, there was a fundamental flaw that ensured the south coast remained totally unprotected. If the first notification of an incoming raid only occurred as the enemy passed over the coastline, fighters would not be able to intercept until reaching those pre-ordained fighter zones. If the target sought was actually on the coastline, then the bombers would be immune from any form of aerial countermeasure. Even during the 1920s this was the accepted situation, although by that time the zone of air combat had been pushed forward to include a wider stretch of Kent and part of the Thames estuary. Nevertheless, this still left a huge undefended area – a 50-mile-deep coastal belt – that would be permanently free of home defence fighters. Lying within this area, and totally at the mercy of these bombers, were such vital targets as Portsmouth and Sheerness dockyards, naval refuelling tanks on the Isle of Grain, a substantial part of the north Kent munitions industry, together with the port towns of Folkestone, Dover, Newhaven and Southampton. Furthermore, the summer air exercises clearly demonstrated that bombers entering the fighter zone were largely immune, it being unlikely that they could be successfully intercepted and destroyed.

To bring about a reversal to the bombers' winning hand, a system would need to be developed by which they could be detected long before their arrival over the south coast. If such a scheme could be introduced, then the fighter zone could be brought much nearer to the coastline and therefore provide a much longer time period in which to bring the enemy formation under attack. Indeed, there was an early belief that this might be achieved through the use of sound detection.

At Biggin Hill, ideally placed for such research because of its proximity to London and the War Office, an acoustics research team was established. Here it was determined that listening devices placed along the south coast might not only provide an early indication of approaching aircraft, but also their height, number and general direction. For the purpose of practical experiment, a 'sound mirror', so called because it focused and magnified sound waves, was cut into the cliff face near Kingsgate Castle. Its appearance was much like a giant bowl, being 15ft in diameter, and it collected distant sounds through the use of a trumpet (although a stethoscope could also be fitted) which were funnelled to a listening operator for analysis. Able to detect aircraft at more than 15 miles distant, the device was considered sufficiently successful to permit further experiments to be undertaken; this time on a larger 20ft concrete mirror constructed near Hythe.

All this was taking place during the 1920s, with the Hythe mirror in readiness for its first full test in September 1923. Using only the trumpet device, it was able to pick out aircraft at a distance of 18 miles, adding approximately eight minutes to the existing system of early warning. Although it was recognised that this amount of extra warning was not as significant as might have been wished, the simple lack of an alternative early-warning system encouraged further research. In particular, for the purpose of pinpointing the position of an approaching aeroplane, two 20ft mirrors were constructed either side of Hythe at Denge and Abbotscliffe. Later, and with the experiments showing continued progress, even larger 30ft-diameter mirrors replaced the Hythe and Denge mirrors. A further adaptation, built at Denge in 1930, was a 200ft curving strip mirror of reinforced concrete designed to pick out the lower pitched sounds that were detectable at a greater distance.

Given the lack of an alternative system, and the apparent success of the experiments, plans were conceived in 1933 for the introduction of mirrors that would guard both the Thames estuary and Portsmouth, with negotiations beginning for the purchase of suitable sites.[12] It was a decision based on desperation, the system being constantly weakened by the rapid increase in the speed of aircraft, thereby reducing any likely warning time that might be given. Furthermore, the use of acoustic location was flawed by interference from other sounds, including heavy rain, wind and passing motorbikes. In addition, the entire device could be jammed by the noise of nearby patrolling aircraft, preventing a fully workable and integrated defence system. This made it quite impossible for fighter aircraft to be used in the vicinity of the mirrors, as the sound of one type of aeroplane would overlay that of another. Nevertheless, none of this stopped the *Sunday Pictorial*, in June 1935, fully acclaiming the system:

I understand that the new system involves the use of a new invention by means of which sound is made visible. In other words it will be possible to see the approach of hostile aircraft long before they are in line of vision. An expert on acoustics has perfected the device, further details of which must not be revealed, and it will be subject to exhaustive tests in the neighbourhood of the Thames estuary before being adopted generally for coastal defence.[13]

Fortunately, given that acoustic sound detection could not possibly have provided the south coast with sufficient warning against speedy incoming bombers, the entire programme was dramatically abandoned shortly after the *Sunday Pictorial* had spoken. Instead, and unknown to the War Office that had partly funded the acoustic experiments, the Air Ministry had been working on an alternative project that involved the use of radio waves. These showed much greater promise, with a full stoppage suddenly placed on the sound mirror system.

Before turning to the development of radar, it is worth noting that Romney Marsh was involved in the development of another scheme associated with the detecting and plotting of aircraft. This was the creation of the Observer Corps (OC), a body specifically designed to identify and record enemy bombers as they passed over the coastline. While any detection system, be it sound location or radar, could indicate the approximate size and whereabouts of a force of bombers, neither could identify the aircraft type nor precise numbers. Furthermore, the Observer Corps could continue plotting aircraft once they had passed inland.

The Observer Corps was officially formed in October 1925 and, as with its wartime predecessor, was formed of special constables whose duty it was to observe potentially hostile aircraft. To ensure the effective working of the organisation and to refine its structure, a series of trials were undertaken on the Romney Marshes and in the Weald; and from this a rapid reporting system emerged. Subsequently, observation platforms, often no more than simple wooden structures, were established along the south coast with personnel duly assigned to each. Until the outbreak of war, those who had joined the Observer Corps were only called out for training during aerial exercises. Equipped with Royal Navy binoculars and a single armband marked 'OC', these individuals were to spend many a night ensconced in a freezing damp structure – reminiscent of a garden shed – that did little for their overall health.

Called out during the Munich crisis, the system demonstrated a number of serious shortcomings, not least of which was confused communication and the failure to man many of the posts. However, the breathing space created by that famous scrap of paper waved by Chamberlain on his return from Munich permitted further refinement of the system. Later to play an important role in the Battle of Britain, Hugh Dowding of RAF Fighter Command described the Observer Corps as the only means of plotting the course of enemy bombers once they crossed the coastline. Declaring 'their work quite invaluable', he went on to say that without it, 'inland interceptions would rarely have been made'.[14] As a result of their work in the Battle of Britain, the organisation was renamed the Royal Observer Corps (ROC) in April 1941.

As for radar, the detection system that was to be of such significance in beating the bomber, the role of the south coast was to ensure its efficiency in operation. With the development of the system, known as Chain Home (CH), most of this work was undertaken at Orfordness and Bawdsey Research Station, both in Suffolk. At these locations, under direct Air Ministry funding, Watson Watt, the creator of the system, was able to refine his invention into a truly workable long-range system of detection that far outshone that of acoustic detection. Known at that time as Radio Direction Finding (RDF), possibly its greatest weakness was its vulnerability to air attacks, being highly visible through its vast array of aerials and 360ft-high pylons that supported a cobweb of transmitter dipoles. It was Swingate, near Dover, that received the first of the south coast stations, this coming into operation during the early part of 1937. Others soon followed, and the south coast was completely covered over the next twelve months, with further Chain Home stations built at Ventnor (Isle of Wight), Dunkirk (Kent), Rye and Poling.

It was the Dover station that was primarily involved in the operational development of the system, partly because it was able to participate in a series of air exercises carried out shortly after it had been brought into service. One exercise of that year was proclaimed by Watson Watt as a particular success, the inventor declaring that 'most of the aircraft operating in the exercise area were reported by Radio Direction Finding with good accuracy at 80 miles'. However, in making this claim, he failed to detail some of the major problems that still had to be resolved. One of these was that no real assessment was possible as to the height and relative position of the aircraft to the coast. Indeed, on one occasion it even appeared that some aircraft, recorded as approaching the coastline, were, in fact, flying parallel to it.

Analysis of data proved a further problem, as did the failure of the system to detect aircraft flying at low altitude, the reflection from the ground swamping that of the aeroplane. Possibly the biggest dilemma was that of distinguishing between friendly and enemy aircraft. During the summer of 1937, the Dover station was able to record blips from aircraft taking off from airfields in Belgium, later identified as military sites. If these same aircraft had been bombers intent upon approaching the south coast, then their identity as enemy bombers would have been beyond dispute. In turn, similar blips from fighter interceptors rising from south coast airfields would have identified those as friendly aircraft. But once the two formations approached and intermingled, it was impossible to tell friend from foe.

With war very much on the horizon, there was simply no time to lose in overcoming each of these shortcomings. Indeed, if war had broken out in late 1938, the system of early warning would not have coped. Instead, it would have been completely overwhelmed, with enemy raiders able to slip through a whole series of invisible gaps or simply lost when they passed from the radar screens of one station to those of another. This is just one more reason why the time created by the Munich episode was of great value to the United Kingdom.

In many ways, the easiest of these shortcomings to be corrected was the means by which received information was recorded and analysed. Much of this hinged on improving ways of filtering, displaying and transmitting the information available, with a series of conferences held that led to a general refinement of the system. One particular improvement was that of more carefully selecting the huge amount of information being submitted from Observer Corps posts; since they reported on all aerial activity, this was inclined to clutter the plotting boards, thereby confusing the overall picture. Instead, only when they reported on raids already confirmed by the Chain Home system was information from the Observer Corps posts fully included.

For the identification of friendly aircraft from that of the enemy, a system of challenge and reply was attempted, by which pilots would be required to identify themselves through a response on a pre-arranged wireless frequency. On average, this took some fourteen minutes for the information to be returned to the radar stations, with bombers able to travel a possible 70 miles during this period of time. A much more immediate system was required, which came through the development of a radio transponder that transmitted a coded signal which would be visible on the radar screen. Known as IFF (Identification Friend or Foe), this essential adaptation to the operational functioning of the Chain Home system was only introduced on the very eve of war. Unfortunately, as it had not been completely refined and tested, several incidents occurred during the early months of the war whereby RAF fighters were directed to attack formations of other RAF aircraft.

The inability of the system to detect low-flying aircraft was overcome through a fortuitous coincidence. The War Office, which at that time had a separate research programme, was developing its own radar system that could be used by coastal batteries to detect ships approaching the shoreline. Through its use of a much lower frequency, it could more effectively isolate objects on the surface while also having the ability to detect aircraft at the very lowest of levels. On learning this and investigating the device, the Air Ministry realised that it was the answer to a prayer. With few changes, the new system, which had revolving antennae, was immediately added to the already built south coast Chain Home stations and was distinguished from the former through it being named Chain Home Low (CHL).

As for that major problem of the station being highly vulnerable to air attack, there was little that could be done other than to provide each station with upgraded anti-aircraft defences and buildings that were as secure as possible against a direct hit. In addition, each of the five coastal CH and CHL stations was provided with duplicate sets of the more vital pieces of equipment, these either buried below the ground or stored in buildings at a remote distance from the main site. Included within the reserve stock, and usually held underground, were the transmitter and receiver blocks, recoverable through entrance hatches set on steel rollers.

Bringing about the defeat of the bomber during the Battle of Britain would have been impossible without one further south coast development – the super-fast fighter. In June 1928 Reginald Joseph Mitchell, the man who designed the Spitfire, travelled to West Wittering on the West Sussex coastline, where he met with Henry Royce, one of the founders of Rolls Royce, the aero-engine manufacturer. It was a momentous occasion, leading to Royce agreeing to radi-cally adapt one of his engines for use on the S.6 Supermarine racing seaplane. The engine that emerged – the 37-litre 'R', producing 1,900hp – was far more advanced than any contemporary engine and, once fitted to the S.6, through a combination of power and design, produced an aeroplane that easily secured for Britain the much-coveted Schneider Trophy. Little of this story, and the subse-quent metamorphosing of the S.6 into the Spitfire, lies outside the south coast of England. Henry Royce, in designing the new engine, did so in his West Wittering workshop, although the engine itself was built in Derby. As for the S.6 aeroplane and its immediate successor, the even faster S.6B, both were designed and built at Woolston in Southampton. Furthermore, the two Schneider Trophy races into which these aircraft were entered, held off Calshot, saw hundreds of thousands lining the 50km course that stretched out to Southsea and beyond.

Few have disputed that the construction of both the 'R' engine and the Supermarine-racing seaplane was a major contribution to the subsequent emergence of the super-fast fighters that won the Battle of Britain. From the S.6 emerged the Merlin-engined Spitfire, a further Woolston product. Of equal importance to the Battle of Britain was the Hawker Hurricane. Although designed at some distance from the south coast, Sidney Camm, its designer, drew heavily on the Southampton experience of blending a high-powered Rolls Royce engine into the airframe of the sleek and fast S.6 monoplane. Of these two fighters, the Hurricane was the first to appear, test flown in November 1935 and soon demonstrating a speed in excess of 320mph; the Spitfire, first flown at Eastleigh some four months later, had a distinct edge by a further 28mph. Of the first flight of the Spitfire prototype (K5054), the *Southern Daily Echo* was pleased to record:

Keen observers in and around Southampton have recently been interested in the high-speed performance of a remarkable plane, which has made occasional flights from Eastleigh Airport.

This machine is the very latest type of single-seater fighter, designed and built for the R.A.F. by the Supermarine Aviation Works Ltd at their factory in Woolston.

Produced amid great secrecy, the plane is one of the fastest in its category in the world. Like all Supermarine aircraft, the new fighter was designed by Mr R.J. Mitchell, C.B.E., Director and Chief Designer of the firm, who designed every British winner of the Schneider Trophy since the war.

Even the uninitiated have realised when watching the streamlined mono-plane flash across the sky at five miles a minute and more, here is a plane out of the ordinary.[15]

The Spitfire and Hurricane between them could not only outfly and outper-form any bomber then known to exist, but could also dramatically outperform every RAF fighter then in service. In December 1938 *Flight* magazine confirmed the Spitfire as the super-fast fighter bar none, declaring that it was not only 'the RAF's fastest fighter', but also 'the world's fastest standard fighter'.

In the war against the bomber, the super-fast fighter had one further pos-sible ally: ground-positioned anti-aircraft guns. The Admiralty, prior to the First World War, had been the first to use ground-based anti-aircraft weaponry for the defence of its own facilities in north Kent. In August 1912 Chattenden and Lodge Hill, massive magazines sited near Chatham, were named as the first sites in Britain to be provided with land-based anti-aircraft protection, with two 3in 20cwt guns positioned at Lodge Hill by April 1913.[16] Among other sites along the south coast soon to be given similar levels of land-based anti-aircraft protection were the dockyards at Chatham, Portsmouth and Sheerness, and naval oil tanks located near the mouth of the River Medway at Port Victoria.

As with the home defence squadrons of the RAF, the number of anti-aircraft batteries available for the defence of the south coast was heavily depleted after the end of the First World War. Huge numbers of guns were put into cold stor-age, while recruitment into the regiment that would man them was brought to a virtual standstill. This remained the situation until the massive increase in the defence budget from the mid-1930s onwards. This created a situation whereby more guns were made available, together with attention being given to the mod-ernisation of equipment. Unfortunately, much of this came too late for the battle that was fought over the south coast during the summer of 1940.

Among such innovations that never quite made it was the linking of radar to anti-aircraft guns for the purpose of a more accurate direction of fire. Planning at an earlier stage might have ensured this valuable addition to the south coast defences at a time when it was desperately needed. Similarly, the guns themselves could have been both more advanced in design and of greater quantity. Orders for the powerful 4.5in calibre anti-aircraft gun were simply not being made suf-ficiently in advance to meet their early wartime need. As a result, a number of batteries planned for Southampton, Chatham, Portsmouth and Dover, which should have been up and running by September 1939, were unarmed and deserted. This did not mean that these towns were defenceless, only that the number of batteries that should have been available were down by about half the number planned. As for the rest of the coastline, there was nothing available other than lighter mobile guns that could have been brought to the coast if urgently required.

Of course, it was not until the summer of 1940 that all this could be put to the test. Indeed, it was a near-run thing, with all these components only finally assembled just before the skies of southern England became witness to mass bomber formations. If this jigsaw had failed to come together, then the bomber would have remained the premier weapon of the RAF. In turn, this would have meant that the battle fought over the skies of southern England would never have taken place. Instead, the Heinkels, Dorniers and Stuka dive-bombers would have been uncontested, opening up the possibility of the Wehrmacht invasion barges reaching those now even more vulnerable south coast beaches.

## Notes

1. Giulio Douhet, *Command of the Air* (Office of Air Force History, Washington, 1983), pp. 9–10.
2. Leo McKinstry, *Spitfire: Portrait of a Legend* (John Murray, 2007), p. 34.
3. TNA CAB13/18 Air Staff Memorandum, 30 July 1934.
4. *Flight* magazine, 4 August 1927, p. 549.
5. Hansard, 10 November 1932.
6. L.E.O. Charlton, *War From the Air* (London, 1935), p. 131.
7. Ibid., p. 183.
8. L.E.O. Charlton, 'The New Factor in Warfare', in *The Air Defence of Britain* (Penguin, 1938), p. 43.
9. Ibid., p. 54.
10. Ibid., p. 141.
11. Graham Wallace, *RAF Biggin Hill* (Putnam, 1957), p. 40.
12. TNA AVIA12/133.
13. *Sunday Pictorial*, 10 June 1935.
14. Vincent Orange, *Dowding of Fighter Command* (Grub Street, 2008), pp. 204–5.
15. *Southern Daily Echo*, 25 March 1936.
16. TNA ADM1/8269/55, 13 December 1912.

# 10

# Airfield Expansion

At the conclusion of the First World War, the Royal Air Force possessed nearly thirty useable airstrips in Kent, Sussex and east Hampshire, together with a number in more distant areas that could be used in the defence of the south coast. Admittedly, the nature of these varied considerably, incorporating emergency landing grounds, partly constructed training grounds, experimental stations and fully developed operational airfields. Following an extended period of retrenchment, the RAF found itself in possession of only three fully operational stations within reasonable proximity to the south coast, those of Biggin Hill, Hawkinge and Tangmere. To these should be added Eastchurch, Gosport, Lee-on-Solent and Manston, four stations primarily retained for training purposes. However, given the nature of the aeroplane and the distances that could be traversed, a few additional airfields in more distant areas could also be used to defend the south coast area in the event of invasion, aerial bombardment or hostile aircraft bound further inland. But regardless of the proximity of these airfields to the southern coastline, each had a few things in common. Their overall number had been severely slashed upon the silencing of the guns in 1918, and of those that remained none were held at their wartime strength, with each considerably reduced in terms of aircraft, personnel and available finance for upkeep.

It goes without saying that the lessons of the First World War had not been completely learnt. By stripping this vital zone of the necessary facilities to support an efficient air arm, it was paving the way for future aerial attack. Not only did the area of the south coast contain a number of potential targets in the form of factories, docks and naval facilities, it also served as a main gateway to London while also being the most obvious point of entry for a potential invader.

Of the three retained first-line airfields on the south coast or close by, Hawkinge was at one time the most significant, housing for a short period the only fighter defence squadron in the entire country. Established as an airfield in

1915, its function during the First World War had been to receive and dispatch aircraft to the Continent. At the end of the war, this function continued, but in reverse fashion. Instead of sending aircraft out to the war zone, it now received and stored aircraft that had once served on the front line. These machines were then kept at the airfield where they awaited final disposal.

The advantage of Hawkinge had originally been its proximity to the Continent, being less than 30 miles from France. As such, it acquired a sort of permanency that led to its post-war retention by a Royal Air Force that was attracted by the numerous residential blocks, sizeable hangars and workshops that had been built there. But this was no reason for subsequently giving the airfield a new peace-time role of housing front-line fighter squadrons for the defence of southern England. While proximity to the coast might have been of value for the transiting of aircraft to the Continent, it was a distinct disadvantage for scrambling fighters to meet bombers that had already passed inland. Furthermore, the closeness of the airfield to the Continent made it highly vulnerable, a problem highlighted in 1940. Visible from France on a clear day, it was subject to frequent attacks throughout the summer of that year.

Biggin Hill, much more sensibly located, was destined for great things. Established during the winter of 1916/17 on an 80-acre plateau site on the North Downs, it was particularly suited to the defence of London, being suffi-ciently far forward to have aircraft in the air and ready to meet enemy bombers before they reached the city. Furthermore, Biggin Hill's height above sea level gave it that extra advantage of being free from low-lying mists. At the time of its establishment it had only one task: to provide a working area for engineers of the Wireless Experimental Establishment (WEE), who were engaged on the development of air-to-ground and air-to-air radio communication. The work of the WEE was to prove of inestimable value during the Battle of Britain, with radio controllers being especially effective in directing squadrons of Spitfires and Hurricanes to where they could best intercept the enemy. Despite the important contribution made by Biggin Hill in communications, the airfield is far more famous for its front-line role. This was a task first assigned to it during the early part of 1918, when fighters based at the airfield were able to con-front night-raiding Gothas. Specifically, this was 141 Squadron and the aircraft they used was the Bristol Fighter, an aeroplane that has been described as 'the Hurricane of the first World War'.[1]

The wartime activities of 141 Squadron at Biggin Hill are worth exploring a little further, as in taking on the Gotha raiders of the German air force, they made use of the advances being made by the Wireless Experimental Establishment. Instead of just taking to the air at night and setting off in the general direction of where the raiders had last been seen, the Bristol Fighters of 141 Squadron were in constant wireless communication with an ad hoc plotting room established at Biggin Hill. From information received from coastguard stations, observer posts, searchlights and gun units, the approximate direction of a raiding force could be calculated and relayed to the Bristol Fighters while in the air. This, indeed, was the forerunner of the later plotting rooms that were to be established at various airfields some twenty years later, although by that time the whole system had been greatly refined through the creation of a specialised Observer Corps and the introduction of radar.

Upon the outbreak of peace in 1918, Biggin Hill was returned in its entirety to the scientists of the WEE, with the airfield seeing little squadron activity until the early 1930s. As for the scientists and engineers based at the airfield, they continued to make a number of important forward strides, while also reaching a few dead ends. Among the latter was a rather bizarre attempt to use magnified sound as an aid to navigation. By enhancing the scream of a klaxon, it was hoped that this high-pitched noise could be used as a homing beacon for pilots seeking out the airfield at night or in bad weather. Unfortunately, the only definite recorded outcomes were a number of broken windows and stampeding cattle. As for the device itself, a concrete structure topped by an outsize horn, this had to be demolished after several aircraft had flown into it during foggy weather.

Tangmere, the only Sussex airfield to be retained by the RAF in the immediate post-war period, had been first acquired in 1917 as a landing ground. While levelling and clearing of the 200-acre site was still under way, the airfield was formerly transferred to the United States Army Air Service for use as a training ground. Given an impressive range of facilities that included sizeable hangars and a large landing area, this was the prime factor in the decision to retain Tangmere. Although non-operational for a number of years, it was kept on the books before reopening as a storage facility for the future RAF Coastal Command in June 1925. During the late 1920s, Tangmere saw even greater utilisation with two Home Defence units based there, these being equipped with Gamecock and Siskin fighters.

The RAF in the immediate coastal area of southern England retained air stations at Gosport, Lee-on-Solent, Manston, Calshot and Eastchurch. During the interwar period they were primarily given a training role. However, their existence was to prove of value in the subsequent war, with each quickly converted to a wartime role and able to accommodate operational squadrons that were to be eventually moved into the area as the war intensified. Manston, which had the same drawback as Hawkinge in that it was situated immediately adjacent to the coast, had originally been established as a night fighter landing ground in 1915. From this relatively small beginning, it was expanded into a significant training ground that housed a number of operational squadrons during the war. Entering the immediate post-war period with a range of sizeable hangars and accommodation buildings still under construction, the airfield was selected for retention in order to avoid wastage of these new facilities, becoming a centre for the training of aircraft fitters and riggers. In addition, from May 1921 onwards, it became the home of No 6 Flying Training School, which specialised in refresher courses for pilots posted to overseas units.

Eastchurch, which had begun life in 1910 as a civilian airfield, had been acquired by the Admiralty both for the training of pilots and for the defence of the north Kent naval establishments. Subsequently merged into the RAF, its first post-war use was by squadrons in the process of disbanding. From October 1923 until November 1929, No 207 Squadron, flying DH9As and, latterly, Fairey IIIFs, were the main occupants of the airfield, although a Coastal Defence Cooperation Flight was also based at Eastchurch from 1924–32. Primarily, however, the airfield was devoted to gunnery training, with numerous squadrons temporarily sent there for the purpose of enhancing their skills on the nearby firing range at Leysdown. For this purpose, in April 1922, the airfield became the home of the Armament Gunnery School, which took responsibility for the training of pilots in the use of aerial weapons.

Lee-on-Solent and Gosport, because of their proximity to Portsmouth, were most strongly associated with the needs of the navy. Both could trace their origins to the First World War, having been first established for use by the Royal Naval Air Service. Although falling into the hands of the RAF on its formation in April 1918, the association of the two airfields with the navy remained strong. With both acquiring a post-war training role, their respective duties continued to be directed towards the needs of the navy, with Gosport responsible for training pilots to handle torpedo-carrying aircraft and Lee becoming a seaplane training base. In addition, Lee-on-Solent housed the School of Naval Cooperation.

RAF Calshot, a seaplane and flying boat station, housed both a School of Naval Cooperation and Aerial Navigation. Primarily concerned with the training of aircrew for flying boats and other marine aircraft, Calshot took on a secondary role, that of developing RAF Marine Craft. Its association with the Schneider Trophy competition also cannot be ignored; the RAF High Speed Flight was based at Calshot during its run up to the competition in 1927 and 1931.

The only conceivable enemy that could threaten Britain during this period was France. While it was accepted that war with France was extremely unlikely, it was nevertheless the only country with an air force capable of reaching England and inflicting damage on key industrial targets. As such, the main axes of defence were centred upon the south coast, it being believed that any attacking force would naturally come from this direction. However, the reduced state of the RAF in this area would have meant that any such attack would almost certainly have been carried off without any undue interference from the home defence force.

With Hitler's assumption of power in 1933, attention turned towards Germany as a likely future enemy. In having achieved absolute authority in Germany, Hitler not only hinted at his future aggressive intentions towards the rest of Europe, but gave immediate orders to Hermann Goering to construct an air force that would 'exceed and dominate all others'.[2] From England, in the following year, came an equally dramatic response, with the government deciding on a massive expansion of the RAF that began with the Air Ministry being allowed £20 million in 1935, rising from £17.5 million the previous year. Yet this was a mere starting point, with the Air Estimates having risen to £166.6 million by 1939.

For the south coast this change of attitude towards air defence meant that attention could now be given to expanding and increasing the number of air-fields. From 1934 onwards, most of the existing stations were given enlarged facilities which enhanced the functions that they already performed. In addi-tion, new stations were established and a few previously abandoned brought back into use. Of the existing front-line stations, both Hawkinge and Biggin Hill were already undergoing extensive rebuilding programmes, with Biggin Hill effectively completed in 1932 and Hawkinge in 1933. This allowed both to house additional squadrons, with Biggin Hill now home to three fighter squadrons and Hawkinge a fighter squadron and an army co-operation squadron.

In 1938 Biggin Hill was to see further expansion with an increase in the number of accommodation blocks. At Tangmere, the construction of further hangars, workshops and extensive accommodation units, together with an increased runway length, were all under way from 1937 onwards, thereby per-mitting an additional fighter squadron to be attached to this airfield. Manston, one of the four training establishments, was similarly expanded, its facilities put to greater use through the construction of an enlarged accommodation area. In contrast, Eastchurch, although increasingly visited by squadrons, saw no real development of its training facilities. Both Gosport and Lee-on-Solent were expanded, the former with extra hangars that were subsequently used to house a particularly effective torpedo bomber, the Bristol Blenheim. Lee was returned to the Admiralty in early 1939, being seen as more appropriate to the needs of the navy. This followed on from the Royal Navy's reacquisition of a separate air service (the Fleet Air Arm). Under firm Admiralty supervision, a considerable building programme was implemented, allowing the airfield to be adapted to the role of housing carrier aircraft when these machines were not actually at sea.

Much more significant was the construction of a new airfield at West Thorney and the decision to reopen the previously abandoned airfields of Ford and Detling. Thorney makes an interesting case study as to how a new airfield was acquired during this peacetime period, when the activities of the Air Ministry were unsupported by the strictures of a wartime Defence of the Realm Act. It also demonstrates how airfields constructed at this time, on the eve of a war that was now seen as inevitable, were not properly built for the dangers of war. For this reason, it is of interest to delve into the building history of this only completely new airfield built on the south coast during the wartime preparation period.

The Royal Air Force first came into contact with West Thorney on 26 September 1933 when a Tangmere-based Hawker Fury of No 1 Squadron crashed into a field close to St Nicholas' church. Representatives from the RAF who came to investigate the crash observed the unique suitability of the adjoining land as an airfield and their recommendation resulted in the building of this aerodrome. As for the acquisition of the 1,249-acre site, this had to be achieved through the purchase of Thorney Manor Estate. Valued at approximately £50,000, the area purchased not only included some of the best farmland in the country, but also a sizeable manor house and a village of 300 inhabitants. In normal circumstances, these might have proved a valuable asset, with numerous examples of other communities living in close proximity to military airfields. In the case of Thorney, however, this simply was not possible. The village of West Thorney, due to its location on the east side of Thorney Island, would be completely entrapped by the airfield runways. Furthermore, some of the outlying buildings of the village occupied areas that were now required for the construction of hangars and other airfield structures. In fact, with but few exceptions, only the medieval parish church of St Nicholas was retained.

Surprisingly, there was little real outcry against this draconian measure of destroying an entire English village. In part, this might have been due to the relatively easy means by which it had been purchased; all of the land, together with the houses of the village, had only one owner. According to the *Weekly Advertiser*, whose photographer visited Thorney at the beginning of 1936, the lack of opposition resulted from its general ordinariness when compared to other locations that had spawned successful campaigns to counter similar military interest:

> When the Royal Air Force picked on the famous swannery at Abbotsford, and again when they closed Holy Island as a suitable site for a bombing range, plenty of voices were quickly raised in protest. But now they have chosen the little village at Thorney Island, near Chichester, as a site for a Royal Air Force station, no one, except the villagers of Thorney has much to say about it.
>
> And there is no very special reason they should. Thorney is just another ordinary English village – the type of English village of which we destroy dozens every year in order to build arterial roads, or add more endless suburbs on to the already endless suburbs of our latest cities.[3]

At the time that this particular report appeared in the *Weekly Advertiser*, contractors were already at work on the airfield, with several large hangars beginning to appear above the skyline. Earlier, towards the end of 1935, they had been engaged in ground-levelling and the laying on of various services, including water supply, drainage and the provision of electricity. In particular, the creation of a grass runway was very specialised and relied on a process known as 'hunterizing'. Using the specialist firm of James Hunt Ltd, it involved the replacement of existing soil along the length of the planned runway with a high-density soil that would more easily shed water. Once this had been achieved, the area would be contoured to encourage more rapid drainage and the surface brought to a high level of smoothness to prevent puddling. The final part of this process was the laying of a dwarf turf that required only infrequent mowing.

As a sign of the rapid progress being made at Thorney on the new airfield, the *Portsmouth Evening News*, in December 1935, reported on the arrival of a large number of steel girders that were to form the main structural support for the hangars; these were first brought by rail to Emsworth and then transferred on to heavy lorries for the final part of the journey. They were part of a new design that had recently been developed. Known as Type C Aeroplane Sheds, the steel-supporting framework, once in place, would be given an outer cladding of brick together with a roof covering of timber boarding and asbestos slates. Large glazed panels would be fitted to the sides of the hangar, as well as to the rear and front sliding doors, allowing for maximum use of natural light. Internally, the hangars provided a large unencumbered working space with a width of 150ft, a length of 300ft and an internal clearance height of 35ft. Lifting facilities would be provided by four overhead runways, two at the centre, each capable of supporting a weight of 6 tons, and one at each end, capable of lifting 1.5 tons.

A peculiar difficulty for the airfield was that of permitting access to the church and the few remaining houses that made up the village of West Thorney, the only approach road crossing two of the three runways. This resulted in a flying control officer having to be stationed, using a caravan, at a point close to where these two runways intersected. His task was to keep an eye on those using the road, warning individuals through a loud hailer if they were about to stray on to a runway that was about to see a movement of aircraft. Additionally, through the use of a phone, he had contact with the control tower.

In later times, this particular layout attracted a large amount of criticism, not least from Wing Commander 'Dizzy' Allen, who described the difficulties of Thorney in a published account of his time in the RAF. Noted for his rather abrasive manner, he simply declared of Thorney airfield: 'Some half-wit had sited it so that it was necessary to cross the main runway to get to it from the entrance to the station, and this demanded traffic lights and a lot of prudence.'[4]

Thorney was actually built to an off-the-shelf design. In common with the Type C hangars, none of the buildings constructed during this period were specifically designed for that airfield. Instead, a series of generic buildings had been drawn up by the Works Agency which could be slightly modified to meet any local situation. A whole series of designs for various buildings was available, encompassing the complete range of technical and domestic buildings that would be required by any airfield wherever it was being built. Among the former were workshops, stores and the control tower, together with operational buildings,

while the latter included sergeants' and officers' messes, dining rooms, gymnasi-
ums and sick quarters.

An airman, on being transferred from one airfield of this period to another,
would have had little difficulty in navigating around the new posting. Buildings
for particular purposes not only looked alike, but, through the decision to adopt
a circular design that encompassed three runways laid out in a triangular pattern, were often similarly positioned. In part, this was due to the need to create
obstruction-free flight ways, buildings always being positioned to one side of
an airfield. In the case of Thorney, this was to the west. Hangars, by their very
nature, were located close to the centre of the airfield and, as a result of the
overall adoption of the circular design, were laid out in a curved pattern. At
Thorney, immediately fronting the airfield, were three hangars reserved for
second-line servicing (minor engine repairs and general aircraft maintenance),
while a further group of three hangars stood further back and were used for
major repairs. Alongside each of the hangars were a series of lean-to structures
that housed workshops, stores and flight offices. In addition, the forward hangars had a room set aside for operational aircrews, this area dispensing endless
amounts of NAAFI tea and coffee. Further forward of the hangars was the
airfield apron, which was used for first-line servicing, refuelling, tyre checks and
pre-flight procedures.

Beyond the hangars, and stretching out to the west, were the various domestic buildings of the airfield. The nearest of these to the centre of the airfield was
a barrack block for other ranks. This was a long building with a central barrack
room sleeping area and a series of single rooms for those promoted to the rank
of corporal. Nearby was a separate building that served as a mess for those
housed in the other ranks' barrack block. Further back from the centre was the
sergeants' mess (where sergeants and warrant officers were accommodated) and
the much more imposing officers' mess. The latter, which was midway between
a country house and a large hotel, provided the officers with individual bed-
rooms, sitting rooms and anterooms. A large dining room was a further feature
of the building, since it was a requirement on most evenings for all officers to
dine in the mess, wearing an adapted uniform that was a civilian version of full
evening dress.

Little urgency underlay the building of these airfields of the expansion period,
with attention also given to their aesthetic appeal. To this end, the original building designs were the product of the noted architect Sir Edward Lutyens, with
ultimate approval given by the Royal Fine Arts Commission. In addition, and
prior to the laying down of any buildings, their exact positioning was examined
by the Society for the Protection of Rural England, who advised on how any
detrimental effect on the local environment might be best mitigated. Given the
ultimate height of the hangars and the extensive area of the airfield, the society
could offer little that could realistically reduce its impact, the area surrounding

Thorney being flat and featureless. The addition of trees and other vegetation were the only suggestions that the society was able to make.

In general, the Campaign to Protect Rural England (CPRE) seemed quite satisfied with the initial layout of the airfield. In their monthly report for July 1938, it was stated: 'The air station on Thorney Island has been built with due regard to the amenities of the place and the aeroplanes have not so far disturbed the birds ...'[5]

In future years, of course, it seems unlikely that the CPRE or any other conservation body would be in a position to repeat such a claim, with later aircraft at Thorney being considerably larger and noisier than the two squadrons of Avro Ansons assigned to the airfield. However, during that summer of 1938, the CPRE did have one particular concern. This was the decision by the Air Ministry to develop a yachting centre of 'between 20 and 30 acres of land' on the east side of the island. Involving the construction of a large clubhouse, bungalows and a jetty, it was, according to the CPRE, to be located on 'a bird sanctuary, known to ornithologists all over England'. In their report, it was further added:

> The site selected is also the home of many rare species of wild plants. It is also suggested that it will entail interference with fishermen, cockle gatherers and the rights of the general public and that the buildings may spoil one of the few remaining unspoilt parts of Chichester Harbour, where there are already seven yacht clubs established.[6]

Although similar comments could have been directed to any one of a number of airfields, due to the universality of their general design, it was the one constructed at Thorney that drew the interest of the *London Times*. In a news item reporting on a visit by King George VI to the new airfield, the writer praised its overall design, seeing it as the physical evidence of the RAF's 'aspirations towards artistic expression'. In noting a number of 'attractive brick buildings', he wrote of the officers' mess that it was 'conventional in style' and set most peacefully 'among old elms'. A further structure that clearly impressed the writer was the station's water tower, this also constructed to a standard design and which he likened to the bell tower of Chichester cathedral. Finally, towards the evening, the glimpse of a heron flying 'to its fishing grounds' seemed to confirm that the station was at one with its surrounding environment.[7]

And this says it all: an airfield of 'artistic expression' in a peaceful setting 'among old elms'. Did the Air Ministry not realise there was a war on the horizon? Thorney was a front-line airfield that was almost certain to come under attack. In building an airfield in such a lavish way, with above-ground hangars of considerable height and easily recognisable as such, it was as good as building aerial road signs to show the enemy the way. Instead of the attractive brick buildings, constructed at no small cost, much should have been placed underground. Indeed, at the time of its construction, Thorney was not given a single underground air-raid shelter, much less bombproof workshops or subterranean hangars.

Officially opened on 3 February 1938, Royal Air Force Station Thorney Island was placed under the authority of Coastal Command. Not until the following month did the first aircraft arrive, Vickers Wildebeest torpedo bombers that belonged to Nos 22 and 42 Squadrons; these were the island's first permanent units. Shortly afterwards, on 4 April, a further unit was formed at the station, a School of General Reconnaissance. By that time, the strength of the station stood at 87 officers and 285 airmen. It was to be some years before the station was brought up to full size, it having been designed to accommodate five operational squadrons and one training unit.

King George VI visited the station on 9 May, a further landmark date for the site. Accompanied by a *Times* reporter, whose view of the station has already been recorded, the king took a short tour of the torpedo section, the School of Navigation and a number of the domestic buildings. Several aircraft were brought together for his inspection, including not only the Wildebeest of the attached squadrons, but also single examples of other Coastal Command machines, such as the Anson, Walrus, Swordfish, Shark, Osprey and Nimrod. The station diary records that tea was taken in the officers' mess and that, on conclusion of his visit, the king sent the following message to the Secretary of State for Air:

> I have spent an interesting and enjoyable day with the Royal Air Force and would like them to know how impressed I am with all I have seen. I congratulate them on the determined and successful way in which they are meeting the heavy demands made upon them by the expansion of their service and I send them my best wishes.

Thorney Island by that stage was firmly on the map, its duties over the next three years being primarily concerned with training, but were eventually to involve pilots being stationed there to familiarise themselves with new types of aircraft. In particular, the Wildebeest, a biplane that had more in common with the First World War than any future war, was soon to be replaced by a much faster monoplane, the Bristol Blenheim. As for the station's standing upon the outbreak of the Second World War in September 1939, only one squadron was based there at this time: No 48 Squadron. In keeping with the particular duties assigned to Thorney, this was a further squadron that specialised in shipping strikes, equipped with the torpedo-carrying Bristol Beaufort, a variant of the Blenheim.[8] A final pre-war transfer took place on 31 August when a detachment of the 7th Battalion of the Hampshire Regiment was moved to the island, their purpose being to defend the station if brought under enemy attack. By that time, the strength of the station stood at 100 officers and 759 airmen.[9] As regards that fateful morning, 3 September 1939, the station diary entry, made at 11.15 hrs, simply records: 'Great Britain declared war on the Nazi Regime in Germany, in accordance with her pledge to Poland – that Poland's frontiers should not be violated.'[10]

Although previously used during the First World War, both Ford and Detling had to be completely rebuilt and re-equipped upon reacquisition in the late 1930s. Ford, which had originally been designated as a training station when first acquired in 1917, had at that time been given over to the United States Air Service for use by aircrews preparing to fly heavy bombers on night raids into Germany. As with Tangmere, which at this stage was undertaking a similar role, a number of sizeable hangars were built at Ford to accommodate the giant Handley Page 0/400 bombers that were to be using the airfield. In the event, aircraft destined for Ford had not arrived by the time that the First World War had ended, bringing an immediate end to these plans. Although Ford was temporarily retained, with a number of squadrons disbanded from this airfield, the station itself was finally deserted in 1920.

The existence of the hangars gave the site a certain attraction, with the Ford Motor Company taking up a lease in the early 1930s, attracted by the publicity value of its name. Within the hangars, maintenance work was conducted on Ford Trimotor civilian passenger airliners that were at that time being sold in the United Kingdom. Following the departure of the Ford Company, the airfield was used by Sir Alan Cobham's flight refuelling company for the development of tanker aircraft.

The RAF returned to Ford in 1936, and it was used by army co-operation squadrons in that year's summer air exercises. Prompting the Air Ministry to reconsider the value of Ford as an airfield, it was decided to reacquire it, with £109,000 placed into the Air Estimates for construction of new hangars and accommodation; all of which were in the same style as Thorney and clearly visible from the air by those intent on bringing it harm. Designated for use as a training ground for Coastal Command, Ford was officially reopened on 1 December 1937. In the following year, Ford housed a number of squadrons for the annual air exercises, while serving as the home station for No 17 Training Group. In 1939 the airfield was transferred to the Admiralty and commissioned as HMS *Peregrine*. It continued, however, in the training role, becoming the Royal Navy Observer School.

Detling, the second of these reacquired airfields, had been used in the First World War in the defence of London, adopted by the Royal Naval Air Service in 1915. At the end of the war the airfield was abandoned and returned to its original use as farmland. With the expansion of the RAF during the 1930s, attention was often given to those sites that had been deserted at the end of the First World War, with Detling reacquired and sanctioned for development in 1937. Throughout the early part of 1938, work proceeded on the highly visible hangars and other conspicuous buildings. Additionally, an area of 1,300yd in length was established for a north-east/south-west oriented runway. Officially opened on 14 September 1938 as part of Bomber Command, it was very quickly turned over to Coastal Command. From inception the airfield was home to 500 Squadron, this being initially equipped with single-engined Hawker Hind light bombers before replacement in March 1939 by Avro Ansons. The latter, although obsolete by the outbreak of war, were more suited than Hinds to the maritime reconnaissance role.

To the various airfields so far described might be added Worthy Down and Odiham, both in north Hampshire and at a much greater distance from the southern coastline. Their significance and reason for inclusion here is that in the event of the south coast being invaded, they were in the first line of airfields that were far enough back to provide essential landing facilities for both conventional and torpedo bombers engaged in attacking either the enemy invasion barges while at sea or at the beachheads, if established. Both airfields will be returned to later. However, Odiham's particular value was in being the nearest military airfield to the south coast with a concrete runway. This was constructed in early 1939 and was to permit Odiham to handle much heavier aircraft than its more southerly neighbours. In particular, Odiham was home to a number of Army Cooperation squadrons, with the twin-engined Blenheim light bomber a mainstay of the airfield at the time war was declared.

It was the Munich crisis that first put these various airfields in southern England on a wartime footing. At each of the airfields, aircraft and buildings were hastily daubed with camouflage, trenches were dug, gun posts sited and bomb and ammunition dumps established. But none of this hasty work could conceal a series of shortcomings that made the airfields of south-east England most unfit for a future intense war against the world's most sophisticated air force. Apart from the poor location of certain airfields, such as those of Manston and Hawkinge, the airfields of south-east England, in their entirety, lacked adequate protection for the aircraft they accommodated and were only suited to summer-time operations due to none having solid runways.

Manston, in 1918, might have served as a model of how an airfield could have been built. It was due to receive underground hangars; perhaps also, given that it was to house some of the heaviest aircraft of the age, concrete runways. However, the end of the war brought an end to all such plans. It was also Manston that seems to have attracted the particular interest of the Luftwaffe a few weeks before the outbreak of the Second World War. On 12 August a 40-seat German passenger airliner, flying from Berlin to Croydon, deliberately over-flew the aerodrome, having been ordered to do so by those in the Luftwaffe charged with assembling aerial photos of RAF airfields on the south coast. The over-flight was completely illegal, Manston being well inside a prohibited area. The British government could do nothing other than extract a formal apology and hear an excuse that the pilot had made an unfortunate navigational error. But it was proof, if proof were needed, that Germany was preparing a very definite war strategy that required knowledge of those south coast airfields and the aircraft with which they were equipped.[11]

Permanent runways, hard stands, perimeter tracks and concrete anti-blast walls for the protection of aircraft were all of fundamental importance on a front-line airfield, and all were missing from the south coast airfields during the 1930s. Indeed, only Gosport had such a facility, but this was a training field. Furthermore, the solid tarmac runway was actually removed before the outbreak of war. Robin Brooks, in his book on Hampshire airfields, provides an explanation:

> The reason that Gosport had tarmac runways in the beginning was that a solid surface was essential for carrier borne aircraft to practise hard landings for flying and landing on carrier flight decks. With the outbreak of war, most of the aircraft would be embarked on the ships and therefore tarmac landing facilities were not so important.[12]

The failure to have ready-prepared solid runways meant that heavier two-seater fighters would not be able to operate in the south – a further serious shortcoming. It was for this reason that No 25 Squadron, normally based at Hawkinge, had to be removed to Northolt, and informed that by being re-equipped with twin-engined Blenheims, they could no longer use the slippery grass runway at Hawkinge. As a result of this peacetime oversight, considerable time and effort had to be put into creating such runways once war had actually broken out. For this purpose, various organisations were involved, with Wimpey, a road construction company, undertaking the laying of solid runways at Tangmere in 1941.

At both Thorney and Ford, where runways were also laid in 1941, West Sussex County Council Highway and Bridges Department undertook this work. A body not usually associated with airfield work, their involvement made a great deal of sense. In the first place, they had a significant amount of experience in the laying of roads. Much more important, however, was the machinery they possessed, this being otherwise unused due to the cancellation of all road-building projects. Obviously, it was necessary to recruit a number of new labourers (previously employed young labourers were now called up for military service), with this shortfall being met by recruitment from neutral Ireland.

Another of the essential features that the airfields of the south coast lacked was that of adequate air-raid shelters. Prior to the Czech crisis, if shelters existed at all, they were nothing more than slit trenches dug into the ground. Open to all weathers, they were invariably flooded in winter and early spring. Towards the end of 1938, a lot more slit shelters had been added, with a number of these roofed over and given drainage during the following year. In reality, the situation should have been very different. Quite simply, all new accommodation buildings should have been constructed with deep cellars that also possessed emergency exits. Indeed, it seems quite incredible that airfields such as Thorney, Detling and Ford, all planned from inception during the 1930s, were not provided with such from the very outset. Instead, much greater thought was given to aesthetics rather than the safety of those who might soon be subjected to air raids of devastating proportions.

It was not just the airfields that lacked the ability to withstand a sudden declaration of war. The aircraft based on these airfields were not up to the task either. Upon the outbreak of the Czech crisis, not a single monoplane fighter was to be seen at Biggin Hill, Tangmere or Hawkinge. Instead, the most modern fighter available was the Gloster Gladiator, an aeroplane equipped with four machine guns and with a maximum speed of 253mph. This compared most unfavourably with the contemporary Messerschmitt Bf109E that carried greater firepower of both cannon and machine guns and was capable of speeds in excess of 350mph.

Fortunately, the Munich crisis did not result in the actual outbreak of war, giving the RAF an important chance to rearm with both Spitfires and Hurricanes. Even before Chamberlain had left for Munich, Hurricanes were re-equipping the front-line fighter squadrons of the south, allowing old and obsolete biplane fighters to be consigned to the scrapheap. The end of 1938 saw the completion of this task, although the pilots who flew them still had to adjust to the demands of a monoplane.

With war declared in September 1939, there were still too few squadrons in the south and far too few aircraft coming off the production line. On the day war was declared, the number of modern fighters available for the defence of the south coast amounted to a mere seventy or eighty serviceable Hurricanes. This was far short of the number required to stave off a determined attack by the Luftwaffe, equipped, as it was, with over 3,000 bombers. As for the Spitfire, this was so far behind planned production levels that no single squadron in the south had yet received the aeroplane, with the first squadrons not receiving it until May 1940 – this being Nos 242 and 610 Squadrons, both based at Biggin Hill.

## Notes

1. Graham Wallace, *RAF Biggin Hill* (London, 1975), p. 39.
2. Cato, *Guilty Men* (Victor Gollancz, 1940), p. 29.
3. *Weekly Advertiser*, March 1936.
4. Wing Commander H.R. Allen, *Fighter Station Supreme: RAF Tangmere* (London, 1985), p. 112.
5. CPRE, Monthly Report, July 1938 (Vol. XI, 3), pp. 22–3.
6. Ibid.
7. *London Times*, 10 May 1938.
8. For a more detailed operational history of Thorney Island, see Robin J. Brooks, *Sussex Airfields in the Second World War* (Countryside Books, 1993); David J. Smith, *Britain's Military Airfields, 1939–45* (Patrick Stephens Ltd, 1989); Chris Ashworth, *Action Stations 9: Military Airfields of the Central South and South-East* (Patrick

Stephens Ltd, 1989); Ken Delve, *The Military Airfields of Britain: Southern England* (Crowood, 2005).

9.  TNA AIR28/838, Operations Record Book, 31 August 1939.
10. Ibid., 3 September 1939.
11. Suspicion also existed that a flight along the south coast, made by the *Graf Zeppelin* in 1938, was for the purpose of photographing beaches and their defences.
12. Robin J. Brooks, *Hampshire Airfields in the Second World War* (Countryside Books, 2005), p. 69.

# 11

# Coastline Defence

Since so much emphasis was placed on the bomber and how best to protect the south coast from the effects of an air raid, relatively little attention was given to the means by which the beaches and immediate inland areas of the south could be defended in the event of invasion. Despite this, the possibility of invasion was not entirely forgotten. A number of reports were issued that attempted to examine the threat, but these had relatively little impact. Among them were a number issued by the War Office through a specialist committee on coastal defence requirements, these placing an emphasis on the introduction around the coastline of quick-firing guns, a recommendation that was fundamentally ignored.[1] Instead, the sophisticated network of anti-invasion defences that had emerged during the First World War and earlier were either removed or totally abandoned. Even the larger fixed defences, those that would be required to provide the backbone and a secure area of retreat, had been considerably reduced. In many cases a number of these larger fortifications were disregarded and their ordnance either put in store or scrapped. In theory, some thought might have been given to the replacement of this ordnance, as the guns being removed and scrapped were often more than thirty years old. Even if retained, they would have been of questionable value by 1940. Instead, the opportunity might have been taken of implementing the main recommendation of the War Office Coastal Defence Committee and replacing them with smaller quick-firing guns, which would certainly have been a valuable addition to coastal anti-invasion defences.

During those two interwar decades, the government was happy with the notion that should an invasion threaten, there would be plenty of time to return the defences of the south coast to a state of absolute readiness. It was assumed that any potential enemy set upon such a course would require an extensive amount of time to assemble both the necessary troops and transport ships to complete the task. And a manoeuvre such as this could not be carried out in secrecy, thereby providing enough time for the rebuilding of sound coastal defences. In reality, of course, within less than a year of the war against Nazi Germany being declared, the country was under very definite threat of invasion. More particularly, it was clear that this invasion would have as its target the open beaches that lay along the southern boundaries of Kent, Sussex and Hampshire. These were the traditional invasion beaches that had been used by the Romans, Saxons and Normans. Napoleon, too, had threatened to land on this same area, as would Kaiser Wilhelm II in 1915 or 1916 had the French Channel ports fallen into his hands. Quite naturally, this entire coastal stretch is littered with past defence structures that had been designed to keep out those who threatened the peace and prosperity of England.

Undermining the strategy behind a minimal interwar defence plan for the south coast beaches was the speed with which Operation Sea Lion was actioned. The fall of France, in June 1940, was incredibly swift and unexpected. Between the initial German entry into France and their complete acquisition of the country, a mere six weeks elapsed. From relative security, the south coast of England had suddenly become extremely vulnerable. Furthermore, in having gained possession of a whole string of French ports from which to mount an invasion, the Germans set about rapidly assembling the necessary ships and barges. Nobody could doubt the intentions, with Hitler having issued a directive that an invasion be undertaken in mid-September. So, within six weeks, the entire notion of time being available to rebuild the south coast defences in time of need was totally destroyed. Instead of a leisurely build-up of defences, as had been seemingly envisaged, the nation had only a few months to bring into absolute readiness a 200-mile stretch of coastline (the area covered by this book) and upon which at any point a landing might take place.

Specifically, the planned invasion of England, Operation Sea Lion, as conceived by Hitler during the early summer of 1940, would have been a broad-front invasion that stretched from Ramsgate in the east to a point west of the Isle of Wight. However, the need to provide adequate protection for an invasion fleet so widely dispersed resulted in a general scaling down of the original plan. By the end of August a much reduced front had been agreed, to include landings at four defined areas named as Folkestone to Dungeness, Dungeness to Bexhill, Bexhill to Beachy Head and Brighton to Selsey Bill. Paratroopers would also land near Brighton and Dover to help secure these areas. Initially, each of these landings would have concentrated on the acquisition of a series of beachheads before pushing north to Gloucester and the encirclement of London. At the same time, and to ensure the future arrival of heavy artillery and other essential supplies, an established port would have to be secured, with Folkestone or Newhaven the best suited to fulfil this role.

Traditionally, it was the Royal Navy that acted as the nation's first line of defence. When Napoleon threatened invasion, the Royal Navy blockaded the ports of the French and Spanish fleets, preventing the sailing of these vessels in support of troop-carrying barges. In addition, a squadron of warships raided Boulogne, the main assembly point for troops and transport vessels. During the First World War, despite the fear that an invasion of the south coast might be mounted, this was never likely to have come about, through the simple fact of the Royal Navy having complete control of the waters through which a highly vulnerable invasion fleet would need to pass. The more recent emergence of the heavy bomber as the ultimate weapon of war led many to conclude that the aeroplane had supplanted the navy as the nation's first line of defence. It was a view shared by neither the German naval staff nor the British Admiralty. For his part, Admiral Räder, commander-in-chief of the German navy since 1928, had observed during the summer of 1940, in a general memorandum sent to the general headquarters staff, that:

> The invasion of Britain is an exceptionally daring undertaking, because even if the way is short, this is not just a river crossing, but also the crossing of a sea, which is dominated by the enemy. This is not the case of a single crossing operation as in Norway; operational surprise cannot be expected; a defensively prepared and utterly determined enemy faces us and dominates the sea area, which we must use.[2]

As regards the south coast defences that were 'prepared and utterly determined', he spoke not of coastal batteries or even of the RAF, but of the Royal Navy. Furthermore, and to underline the significance of sea power in the conducting of such an invasion, Räder added that it could not 'be assumed that the Luftwaffe alone will succeed in keeping the enemy naval forces clear of our shipping'.

Given, then, that naval commanders were absolutely convinced that sea power was crucial to a cross-Channel invasion, the German navy was simply in no position to secure success. Although its fleet was composed of some very modern ships, for the most part launched within the previous ten years, they were simply overwhelmed by the much greater number of warships available to the Royal Navy. In terms of destroyers, one of the most valuable ships for both supporting and attacking an invasion fleet, the German navy had a mere eight available during the summer of 1940, while the Royal Navy had thirteen destroyers already positioned in close proximity to the south coast.

Portsmouth, Chatham, Sheerness and Dover served as the home bases for these thirteen destroyers and, as such, were of crucial importance to the anti-invasion defences of southern England. Although each in turn was susceptible to air attack, these fleet bases ensured that naval warships were within easy striking distance of any invasion fleet approaching the south coast from the likely embarkation ports of Boulogne and Le Havre. However, in common with the fixed coastal defences and military airfields of southern England, each of these naval ports had suffered considerable neglect since the end of the First World War. In particular, the royal

dockyards of Portsmouth, Chatham and Sheerness, vital facilities for the maintenance of a seagoing fleet, had all seen a massive reduction in the size of their
skilled workforce.

In addition, none of these yards were engaged in the production of anything
more than a token range of newly built ships, ensuring that while the Royal
Navy had the advantage of size, it had few of the modern types of ship that
would be available to the German navy. Instead, the Royal Navy, on the outbreak of war in September 1939, was primarily composed of numerous ageing
and unmodernised vessels. While ships that might be involved in defending the
south coast against invasion were not necessarily built in the royal dockyards of
southern England, or even in the private shipbuilding yards of the south coast, the
cutbacks witnessed at Portsmouth, Chatham and Sheerness were symptomatic of
what was happening throughout the United Kingdom. At Chatham, where the
situation had been particularly bad, a dockyard that might at one time have been
constructing several cruisers and possibly a battleship instead saw the launch of
only four submarines and a cruiser during that first post-war decade. Portsmouth,
an even larger dockyard, saw construction of only four cruisers during this same
period. Not until the 1930s, with the realisation that war had become inevitable,
was an attempt made to speed up warship production.

At these essential naval complexes more might have been done to reduce
their vulnerability to attack. With each of these facilities within easy reach of
Continental airfields, none were given an ample number of underground air-
raid shelters or, of equal importance, underground workshops. Instead, some of
the older buildings in these yards, those most susceptible to destruction through
fire, were simply given an outer cladding of asbestos. This did little in the way
of providing real protection. Even new buildings, those constructed at a time
when aerial attack should have been uppermost in the thoughts of those responsible for designing the yards, were no less vulnerable than buildings dating to the
early nineteenth century or earlier. At Portsmouth, for instance, of new buildings
constructed during the interwar period, all seemed to be designed specifically
to help the zealous bomber in its cause. A coppersmith's shop, built in 1929, was
given huge glass windows and a glass roof that would ensure any bomb exploding nearby would send shards of broken glass cascading upon the workforce.
Similarly, the No 4 Boathouse, completed in 1939 when fear of the bomber was
at its height, was a tall and easily visible building that offered protection to neither
items held in store nor the workforce employed within. As it happens, both buildings did survive the war, but more from good luck than a well-structured plan for
the defence of the yard.

Dover, in one sense, might be considered the exception. Not, however, the
port complex, which had been given little more than a few requisite air-raid
shelters and certainly lacked any underground workshops for the repair of
small coastal craft and naval warships that were likely to operate from the port.

Instead, it was Dover's other important naval role: that of the headquarters staff charged with overseeing naval operations in the Channel. In 1938 it was determined that with this being the particular role of Dover, those charged with pursuing this duty would need to be protected from the dangers of bombing and shellfire. To this end, galleries cut into the chalk face beneath Dover Castle would be converted to this use. Originally dug out during the French wars of the early nineteenth century, they ended at an embrasure in the cliff face. Here, a number of offices were created together with a larger conference room. The latter had been built out of an area that once housed an auxiliary electrical plant and was consequently known as the 'Dynamo Room'. A point of interest, the name of this room has gone down in history, the evacuation of Dunkirk, which was planned in that conference room, being given the code name Operation Dynamo.

The role of the Royal Navy, on the outbreak of any war, was that of keeping open vital trade routes, denying free movement of the oceans to the enemy and transporting or convoying armed forces and supplies to selected areas of operation. To these has to be added the prevention or defeat, in conjunction with the army and air force, of any attempted invasion of the United Kingdom. While the first three appear unconnected with the defence of the south coast, this was far from so. Without the safe arrival of convoys, there would be no food imports to help sustain those living on the south coast; no oil and petrol would be available and additional weapons from the USA would be unobtainable.

It was particularly important that the south coast ports were able to receive these essential supplies. Southampton had a potentially vital role, being a major centre of commercial shipping, handling, on average, over 1 million tons of cargo during the years immediately before the outbreak of war. This it might have continued to do if the port itself had not been so vulnerable to air attack. As with the south coast naval ports, little had been done to ensure that the port of Southampton could continue to operate under wartime conditions.

Apart from having an ARP service that was separate from the town, and the addition of a few air-raid shelters, the port lacked any real security. The warehouses, unloading machinery and docks were not only highly visible from the air, but were unprotected by blast walls or bombproof shelters. Thus, the ability of such a large port, and one that had been essential in the years prior to the war, was now reduced to a shadow of its former self, with tonnage passing through having fallen by the third year of the war to less than a quarter of what it had been in those pre-war days. It was for this same reason that the navy, which might have made considerable use of ship repair facilities in Southampton, chose not to do so, recognising that their vessels would be equally as vulnerable as that of the merchant cargo ships.

As regards the role of the navy and its ability to offer a defence of the south coast in the event of invasion, the most useful of the vessels with which it was equipped were the smaller inshore vessels and destroyers that operated out of the Medway, Dover and Portsmouth. In addition, and providing aircraft specifically designed for maritime operations, the Royal Navy had several aircraft carriers that could be used to reinforce the defences of the south coast. However, other large warships, including cruisers and battleships, would only be used in the Channel as a final, desperate resort, as they were vulnerable to air attack and were better suited to the open waters of the Atlantic.

Another factor that would have worked to the benefit of the Royal Navy while attempting to counter an invasion of the south coast was ship-borne radar. Unlike the systems produced for the air force and for use by artillery, this had a clear south coast genesis through a number of experimental centres established in and around Portsmouth. Its particular importance in the countering of an invasion was that by June 1940 it had already been installed on to a number of destroyers, giving them even greater value in their efforts to break up the invasion fleet. Furthermore, the system being installed was significantly better than the one available to the German navy, giving the Royal Navy a decided superiority.

The origins of radar, as developed by the Royal Navy, date from 1936 and the erection of a single hut on the grounds of Fort Eastney, near Southsea. Admittedly, the project grew out of work being undertaken by the Air Ministry, but the Admiralty's requirements were quite different. They were not looking for shore-based equipment that could be developed irrespective of size and weight. Instead, the navy needed much lighter and smaller equipment that could be installed on ships while also having the important requirement of not interfering with essential radio equipment also being carried on board. Initially, this meant that the navy had to examine radar that used a much lower frequency; one not dissimilar to that being used by the War Office and which permitted the use of more compact aerials.

Despite very limited resources, the experimental centre at Eastney was soon demonstrating equipment that was suitable for shipboard use and which could detect the existence of vessels at a distance in excess of 5 miles. Initially, the aerial equipment was quite substantial and was only being fitted to the larger ships of the fleet. To permit the experimental section to expand, two additional sites were acquired during the late 1930s at Southsea Castle and Nutbourne. The castle site was used to develop radar using a second frequency, while at Nutbourne, which lies between Chichester and Emsworth, work was undertaken on designing and producing aerials. Indeed, it was at the latter site that a particularly important breakthrough was made – that of designing aerials that were sufficiently compact to fit destroyers. This was a task achieved during the summer of 1940, at a time when it was realised that smaller vessels would be much more significant in defeating an invasion than the larger ships based at Scapa Flow.

Moving to the inland anti-invasion defences, a number of emplacements were built at various times to fend off potential invaders. A useful starting point, geographically, is that of the Thames and Medway estuaries. While this estuarine area might not have been an identified target in the planning of Operation Sea Lion, it was nevertheless a vulnerable point, and its protection would ensure the continued movement of ships to both London and the naval dockyards and naval supply facilities of Chatham and Sheerness. In addition, the Medway was an important naval anchorage and served as the home base for a number of destroyers and light craft that could be used to inflict considerable damage on an invasion fleet undertaking a Channel crossing.

At the beginning of the century, this entire area had included a number of powerful gun batteries, with large forts at Cliffe, Garrison Point (Sheerness) and on the Isle of Grain. Following the Treaty of Versailles, and with the exception of Garrison Point Fort, all were completely stripped of their heavy guns. In the case of the numerous gun batteries, not only were they divested of guns, most were completely abandoned. Where rearmament did take place, this involved the substitution of coastal defence weaponry with that of anti-aircraft guns, further evidence of military thinking outside of the navy being overwhelmed by the notion that it was the bomber that was to be feared rather than attack from the sea.

The demobilisation and neglect of the defensive positions of the Thames and Medway was nothing unusual. Along the entire length of the south coast, fortifications built specifically to defend against invasion were, for the purpose of financial saving, discarded in the years that followed the First World War. Dover, which had once possessed a number of surrounding coast defence batteries, had been reduced to two: Langdon and Citadel. The former, which overlooked Langdon Bay, had four 9.2in guns, with two of these installed as recently as 1920. Citadel Battery, on the west side of the Western Heights, was armed with similar 9.2in guns, but these had been installed in 1902. To ensure a limited amount of protection for the harbour area, a number of lighter guns that had been added to the pier and breakwater during the First World War were retained, making them immediately available on the outset of war in 1939.

Between Dover and Portsmouth, a length of coastline more than a hundred miles in length, only two batteries had been retained, both at Newhaven. Consisting of four 6in heavy guns and two 12-pounders, both batteries and their guns dated to the first decade of the century. Even on the outbreak of war in September 1939, the batteries at Newhaven were not immediately mobilised, having been given a C classification, meaning that they were not to be manned even during periods of mobilisation.

At Portsmouth, together with nearby Gosport, previously the most heavily defended military-industrial complex in the entire country, the years following the First World War had seen the abandonment of a number of the more ageing forts and batteries, including the massive ring of land forts built on the crest of Portsdown Hill. In fact, only Horse Sands and Spitbank Forts, both lying in the

Solent, were retained, together with additional guns mounted in Southsea Castle. Of the two forts in the Solent, both had seen the removal of deteriorating and obsolete 12in guns and their replacement with relatively new 6in guns in 1920. As for Southsea Castle, this retained a number of larger guns that had been added to the fort some time around 1900.

Although highly vulnerable to air attack, Southampton did have a degree of coastal protection due to a number of batteries and forts on the Isle of Wight being retained. Many of these either stood guard over the Solent or protected the two relatively narrow entry points into this stretch of water. Only by entering the Solent was it possible to gain access to Southampton water, at the head of which lay both the port and city of Southampton. Although Hurst and Calshot castles – the two most obvious defensive points – had been stripped of any armament by the late 1920s, a string of retained batteries along the north-west coast of the Isle of Wight more than made up for this loss. Once again, the available ordnance mostly dated back to the beginning of the century but, given the narrowness of the channel, would certainly have given a good account of themselves should an enemy have chosen to mount an operation in these waters. Among the batteries retained on the west side of the island, and close to Yarmouth, were Bouldner and Cliff End, equipped with sets of 6in breech-loading guns, and the more southerly situated Fort Warden, with 9.2in breech-loading guns. To make up for the slowness of these particular guns – although they did provide a more powerful punch – two additional batteries, sited at Freshwater and Golden Hill, were equipped with lighter quick-firing guns. On the east side of the island, between Ryde and Sandown, a total of five functional batteries existed, these variously equipped with heavier breech loaders and a number of small quick-firing guns.

Responsible for manning these coastal batteries were units of the newly established Territorial Army. This was the successor of the earlier Territorial Force, a body disbanded at the end of the First World War. As with the earlier force, those who joined the Territorial Army were only to be called upon (apart from periods of training) during times of emergency and were not required to serve abroad. As such, they were ideally suited to coastal defence work, as these batteries did not require the constant presence of a full complement of soldiers. Yet, through local recruitment, these part-time territorial soldiers were always on hand to service the guns if the need arose.

As with the body that had preceded it, the various units of the Territorial Army had strong local associations, carrying this with the name of their regiment. Manning the coastal batteries of north Kent, for instance, was 516 (Thames and Medway) Coast Regiment, while further south, manning the batteries of Dover and Newhaven, were 520 and 521 (Kent and Sussex) Coast Regiments. Given a very special local affinity were those who manned the coastal batteries of the Isle of Wight; this regiment was allowed to retain the name of the original volunteer rifle company from which it could trace its provenance: 530 (Hampshire) Coast Regiment (Princess Beatrice Isle of Wight Rifles). Finally, recruited from among volunteers in the east Hampshire littoral, there was a further Hampshire-based coast regiment, supplying men both for the Isle of Wight and those batteries retained in the Portsmouth area. In all cases, volunteers in these regiments had been called forward to man the coast batteries in September 1938, as a result of the Munich crisis, and once again from 25 August 1939.

Airfields would also have an important role in the event of an invasion, with the fighters already allocated to southern England being responsible for maintaining air superiority. Other types of aircraft would also take on a role of increased importance, among them the medium and heavy bombers of Bomber Command, the reconnaissance and torpedo bombers of Coastal Command, and the communication and ground support aircraft of Army Cooperation units.

For the most part, the airfields of Bomber Command lay outside the immediate south coast area. In the event of invasion, the role of these aircraft would be that of attacking the invasion fleet as it approached the south coast. In turn, if landings proved successful, these same bombers could be used to pulverise the enemy both on the beaches and while advancing on objectives further inland. This would only be possible, however, if fighter squadrons within reach of the south coast were able to offer protection from the German fighters providing air cover for the landings.

The inability of the Luftwaffe to gain air superiority during the summer of 1940 was a factor, together with the overwhelming strength of the Royal Navy, in the German failure to launch Operation Sea Lion. One airfield from which bombers would certainly have been operating was that of Odiham in Hampshire. An airfield that, in such a situation, would have acquired a multiplicity of roles, the main bomber type based here in the months immediately prior to the outbreak of war was the Fairey Battle. First arriving at Odiham in 1938, it was a monoplane design that had replaced Hawker Hart and Hind biplanes that were fundamentally little different from aircraft that had fought on the Western Front. However, the Battle failed to meet its early promise. As a light bomber it was acutely underpowered and had little defensive capability. When sent into combat during the German attack on the Low Countries, it was completely outclassed and suffered horrendous losses. Used in any desperate bid to stem the advance of an enemy invading southern England, it would have suffered similar high losses.

Particularly crucial for preventing landings on the south coast would have been airfields allocated to Coastal Command. Within the three south coast counties, these airfields were Thorney, Detling and Worthy Down. Ideally situated for opposing the initial landings, they may well have been quickly overwhelmed if the strikeout from the beaches had proved successful. Again, while retaining their operational status, they would have seen a great number of aircraft types using them. Prior to the outbreak of war, the aircraft most frequently seen at these airfields were Avro Ansons. At the time, they formed the backbone of Coastal Command but were already obsolete by September 1939. But during the first months of war, they were still being used in a front-line role for purposes of reconnaissance and that of depth charging enemy submarines. At all three Coastal Command airfields the Bristol Beaufort, a torpedo bomber that combined speed and agility with a powerful defensive punch, was replacing it. This was an aircraft that those on board ships of any approaching invasion fleet would have learnt to fear. Its speed during low-level attacks and accuracy in placing its underbelly torpedoes would have wreaked havoc upon larger ships caught in the Channel.

In addition to its Coastal Command role, Worthy Down, from 1938 onwards, was home to a Fleet Air Arm squadron equipped with Blackburn Skuas and Rocs. The former was a dive-bomber, the first British aircraft to take on that role, while the latter was a fighter equipped with a rear gun turret. Both were obsolete by the outbreak of war and would have been overwhelmed by the German fighters of that period.

From this brief résumé of the anti-invasion defence arrangements in the period prior to the outbreak of war, it is clear that the south coast was hopelessly ill prepared. But it should not have been. If Germany was to be fought, then the battleground would be mainland Europe. In such a situation, it could not necessarily be expected that a stalemate would occur on the eastern fringes of France, with the Germans never getting beyond the Maginot Line. Such might be the object of any overseas expedition from Britain – but the outcome could not be guaranteed. Should the Germans, therefore, make such a breakthrough, they might also (as in fact they did) capture a range of seaports that would place them in a position to mount the invasion that they had been unable to attempt during the First World War.[3] Therefore, greater attention, as required by the Coastal Defence requirements committee, should have been given to how the nation would fend off a south coast invasion.

While such an invasion did not take place, it was a near-run thing. Muddled thinking on the part of the German High Command ultimately saved the country. With the Luftwaffe switching its attention in September 1940 from the destruction of airfields and dockyards in southern England to that of bombing inland cities, both Fighter Command and the Royal Navy were able to maintain themselves as a continuing threat to any invasion attempt. The securing of the south coast through more adequate ordnance, better protected dockyards and airfields, including underground shelters and workshops, would have ensured that had the Luftwaffe not switched tactics, Operation Sea Lion would still have been a non-starter.

# Notes

1. TNA WO33/1201.
2. Duncan Grinnell-Milne, *The Silent Victory* (London, 1958), p. 53.
3. Churchill was one of those who felt that such an eventuality was possible. In June 1940, prior to the Germans having introduced plans for an invasion, Churchill indicated that he had an inkling of their intentions. See Grinnell-Milne, op. cit., pp. 89–90.

# Conclusion

*And consequently this country is at war with Germany.*

Shortly after 11 a.m. on Sunday 3 September 1939, Prime Minister Neville Chamberlain uttered these words, which brings this book to its ultimate conclusion. The war, predicted by so many, had finally come about. And yet, as demonstrated, the nation, including the south coast, was hopelessly ill prepared. To meet the expected onslaught of bombers, the long-delayed super-fighter – the Spitfire – had not even reached front-line squadrons, while the Hurricane had only just entered service. As for the airfields from which these fighter aircraft would operate, they were neither concealed from aerial attack nor especially well protected. To help the enemy, some of them were positioned so close to the coastline as to encourage fast hit-and-run raids that stood only the slightest chance of interception. Had the war more rapidly devolved into a lightning strike against France followed by a hastily attempted invasion, few coastal batteries would have existed, leaving the south coast totally dependent upon the navy for its defence.

Ultimately, what saved the south coast from complete devastation were two interconnected time periods that created an extended delay: the 'phoney peace' and the 'phoney war'. The first of these, the 'phoney peace', was the period between October 1938 and September 1939 and which was to merge seamlessly into the 'phoney war'. The first allowed for a dramatic improvement in the passive and active defences of the south coast, shocking into action those with a responsibility for such matters. The subsequent 'phoney war', the period between September 1939 and the summer of 1940, created an even greater level of desperation, resulting in a ten-fold improvement on what had gone before. While the period of the 'phoney peace' had established the real foundations of a nation about to enter into a war, the 'phoney war' permitted these foundations to be extended into something more solid.

It was the 'phoney war' in particular that allowed both the passive and active defences to be brought to a reasonable stage of readiness. Of numbers involved in Civil Defence, this grew quite considerably, with both those who were longer serving and those newly recruited into ARP work permitted an extended period of training. For the Auxiliary Fire Service, it meant that former part-time fire fighters were now undergoing full-time training, working with the regular fire fighters and called out to actual fires. As for the active defences, the 'phoney war' saw completion of the Chain Home radar stations around the south coast, the arrival of the first Spitfire squadrons and the rearming and building of new coastal batteries.

Without the 'phoney peace' created by the Munich agreement, and the eight months of the 'phoney war', the south coast would have found itself in a position from which it was impossible to survive the coming war. The air raids would certainly have taken a greater toll of life, even catching the newly evacuated. As for the threatened invasion, if this had also come at an earlier stage, pitted against such weakened defences, it would probably have been quite impossible to prevent.

To put it bluntly, it was not government planning that ensured the survival of the south coast, the gateway to London and the rest of the country, but a massive slice of good fortune.

# Bibliography

Allen, Wing Commander H.R., *Fighter Station Supreme: RAF Tangmere* (London, 1985)

Anon, *Air Raid Precaution Handbook No 1: Personal Protection against Gas* (HMSO, 1938)

Anon, *The Protection of Your Home Against Air Raids* (Home Office, 1938)

Ashworth, Chris, *Action Stations 9: Military Airfields of the Central South and South-East* (Patrick Stephens Ltd, 1989)

Astor, Viscount & Rowntree, B. Seebohm, *British Agriculture* (Pelican Special, Harmondsworth, 1939)

Baldwin, Olga M. et al., *We Remember 1930 to 1960* (Chidham, 2002)

Blanchard, V. (ed.), *Records of the Corporation* (Portsmouth, nd)

Brooks, Robin J., *Sussex Airfields in the Second World War* (Countryside Books, 1993)

Callaghan, John T., *The Labour Party and Foreign Policy: A History* (London, 2007)

Cato, *Guilty Men* (Victor Gollancz, 1944)

Charlton, Air Commodore L.E.O., *War Over England* (Longmans, 1936)

——, *War From the Air* (London, 1935)

Curtis, Edward E., *The Organization of the British Army in the American Revolution* (Humphrey Milford, London, 1926)

Delve, Ken, *The Military Airfields of Britain: Southern England* (Crowood, 2005)

Douhet, Giulio, *Command of the Air* (Office of Air Force History, Washington, 1983)

Forester, C.S., *The General* (Penguin, 1936)

George, Michael, *Dover and Folkestone During the Great War* (Pen & Sword reprint, 2007)

Grieves, Keith (ed.), *Sussex in the First World War* (Sussex Record Society, 2000)

Grinnell-Milne, Duncan, *The Silent Victory* (London, 1958)

Hylton, Stuart, *Their Darkest Hour* (Sutton Publishing, 2001)

Jasper, Ronald, *George Bell Bishop of Chichester* (Oxford, 1967)

Kemp, Anthony, *Southampton at War* (Ensign Publications, 1989)

Knowles, Bernard, *Southampton: the English Gateway* (Hutchinson & Co., 1951)

Leete, John, *Under Fire* (Sutton Publishing, 2008)

Livingstone, Adelaide, *The Peace Ballot* (London, 1935)

Milward, A.S., *War Economy and Society, 1939–45* (London, 1977)

MacDougall, Philip, *The Story of Chatham Dockyard* (Meresborough Books, 1982)

McIlraith, Frank & Connolly, Roy, *Invasion From the Air* (London, 1934)

McKinstry, Leo, *Spitfire: Portrait of a Legend* (John Murray, 2007)

Morrison, Sybil, *I Renounce War* (London, 1962)

Nicolson, Juliet, *The Great Silence* (John Murray, 2009)

Orange, Vincent, *Dowding of Fighter Command* (Grub Street, 2008)
Padley, Richard & Cole, Margaret, *Evacuation Survey* (George Routledge & Sons, 1940)
Patterson, Ian, *Guernica and Total War* (London, 2007)
Playne, Caroline, *Britain Holds On* (Unwin, 1933)
Sackville-West, Vita, *The Women's Land Army* (London, 1944)
Saunders, Andrew, *Fortress Britain: Artillery Fortifications in the British Isles and Ireland* (Oxbow Books, 1995)
Searle, Adrian, *Isle of Wight at War* (Dovecote Press, 1989)
Shepherd, H.R.L., *The Impatience of a Parson* (London, 1927)
Short, Brian et al. (eds), *The Front Line of Freedom* (British Agricultural History Society, 2006)
Shute, Neville, *Slide Rule* (Pan Books, 1983)
Smith, David J., *Britain's Military Airfields, 1939–45* (Patrick Stephens Ltd, 1989)
Walbrook, H.M., *Hove and the Great War* (The Cliftonville Press, 1920)
Wallace, Graham, *RAF Biggin Hill* (Putnam, 1957)
Wenyon, Lieutenant-Colonel H.J. & Brown, Major H.S. (eds), *The History of the Eighth Battalion, the Queen's Own Royal West Kent Regiment* (London, 1921)
Westerman, Percy F., *Winged Might* (Blackie & Sons Ltd, 1937)
Williams, Michael, *Ford and Fordson Tractors* (Bounty Books, 2006)
Wilt, Alan F., *Food for War* (OUP, 2001)

## Journal Articles
Charlton, L.E.O., 'The New Factor in Warfare', in *The Air Defence of Britain* (Penguin, 1938)
Cookson, John, 'What if Napoleon had Landed', in *History Today*, Vol. 53 (September 2003)
Garratt, G.T., 'Air Raid Precautions', in *The Air Defence of Great Britain* (Penguin, 1938)
Grieves, Keith, 'Rural parish churches and the bereaved in Sussex after the First World War', in *Sussex Archaeological Collections* (2001)
Elliott, Walter, 'Medicine and the State', in *British Medical Journal* (29 December 1945)
Hurst, S.V., 'The Volunteer Movement in Kent', in *Bygone Kent*, 17:12, 722 (1996)

## Newspapers
*Bexley and District Times, Brighton Advertiser, Chatham News, Chichester Observer, Daily Mirror, Eastbourne Herald, East Kent Mercury, Faversham and North East Kent News, Hastings and St Leonards Observer, Herne Bay Press, Isle of Wight Chronicle, Kentish Express, London Times, Southampton Times, Southern Daily Echo, Sussex Express and County Herald, Weekly Advertiser, Worthing Gazette*

## The National Archives (Kew)
AIR 28, RAF Operational Record Books
HO50/88-311, Correspondence of the Sussex Militia
PC2/156, 431, Privy Council Records

## University of Sussex
Mass Observation Archive, Box 180
Mass Observation file 66/16/D

# Index

## Index of Places

*(Hampshire, Kent, Sussex and Isle of Wight only, including airfields and military bases)*